CONTEMPORARY CONSUMPTION, CONSUMERS AND MARKETING

Contemporary Consumption, Consumers and Marketing: Cases from Generations Y and Z explores current consumer, consumption and marketing cases and issues, posing questions that complement, extend and challenge established marketing theory while keeping in mind megatrends such as climate crisis, economic inequality and digital connectivity. It also considers how such major changes affect consumer societies, cultures and individuals, especially those from Generations Y and Z.

Each chapter is built around a theme that encapsulates current theoretical and professional debates around consumption, consumers and marketing. Examples and up-to-date case studies throughout the book explore how brands are adapting to current circumstances across Generations X, Y and Z and investigate the state of marketing at a time of flux.

This book is essential reading for undergraduates, postgraduates and practitioners interested in marketing and consumer behaviour.

Brendan Canavan is Senior Lecturer in Marketing at University of Huddersfield, UK.

CONTEMPORARY CONSUMPTION, CONSUMERS AND MARKETING

Cases from Generations Y and Z

Brendan Canavan

LONDON AND NEW YORK

First published 2021
by Routledge
2 Park Square, Milton Park, Abingdon, Oxon OX14 4RN

and by Routledge
52 Vanderbilt Avenue, New York, NY 10017

Routledge is an imprint of the Taylor & Francis Group, an informa business

© 2021 Brendan Canavan

The right of Brendan Canavan to be identified as author of this work has been asserted by him in accordance with sections 77 and 78 of the Copyright, Designs and Patents Act 1988.

All rights reserved. No part of this book may be reprinted or reproduced or utilised in any form or by any electronic, mechanical, or other means, now known or hereafter invented, including photocopying and recording, or in any information storage or retrieval system, without permission in writing from the publishers.

Trademark notice: Product or corporate names may be trademarks or registered trademarks, and are used only for identification and explanation without intent to infringe.

British Library Cataloguing-in-Publication Data
A catalogue record for this book is available from the British Library

Library of Congress Cataloging-in-Publication Data
Names: Canavan, Brendan, author.
Title: Contemporary consumption, consumers and marketing : cases from generations Y and Z / Brendan Canavan.
Description: 1 Edition. | New York : Routledge, 2021. | Includes bibliographical references and index.
Identifiers: LCCN 2020035193 (print) | LCCN 2020035194 (ebook) | ISBN 9780367820923 (hardback) | ISBN 9780367820947 (paperback) | ISBN 9781003013532 (ebook)
Subjects: LCSH: Consumption (Economics) | Consumers' preferences. | Branding (Marketing) | Generation Y—Attitudes. | Generation Z—Attitudes.
Classification: LCC HB801 .C316 2021 (print) | LCC HB801 (ebook) | DDC 339.4/7—dc23
LC record available at https://lccn.loc.gov/2020035193
LC ebook record available at https://lccn.loc.gov/2020035194

ISBN: 978-0-367-82092-3 (hbk)
ISBN: 978-0-367-82094-7 (pbk)
ISBN: 978-1-003-01353-2 (ebk)

Typeset in Bembo
by codeMantra

CONTENTS

Illustrations vii
Preface ix

1 Relevance: connecting with consumers – generations Y and Z inspired by K-pop 1

2 Reconstruction: ideological consumer engagement – vegan extremism and BrewDog revolution 22

3 Reassurance: consumer nostalgia and never growing up – Otaku, Pokémon, Lego and Hikikomori 36

4 Reinvention: evolving consumer identities – observing RuPaul's drag race fans and reading Taylor Swift's lyrics 54

5 Reputation: building and breaking brands offline and online – Halo Top, Angelababy and Fan Bingbing 68

6 Refraction: alternative realities and marketing fairy tales – myths around dropshipping, meerkats and backpackers 83

7 Renown: consumers at the centre of attention – tourists as celebrities and narcissism normalisation 99

8 Rebalancing: producing as well as consuming – the success of home-made spread versus the failure of Juicero 113

9 Re-evaluating: marketing amidst shit life syndrome – Oxycontin and iron challenges 128

10 Reviving: bringing marketing back – inspired by sex toys, slave-free sugar and Marks & Spencer 142

Index 157

ILLUSTRATIONS

Figures

1.1	The brand lifecycle	6
2.1	Consumer temperature-brand exposure index	30
2.2	Ideological perceptual map	32
3.1	Degrees of consumer reassurance	37
3.2	Nostalgia brand matrix	46
4.1	Overview of consumer outcomes, actions and context	55
4.2	Consumer habits and loyalties	60
5.1	Sources of brand reputation	69
6.1	Reality refraction	89
7.1	Evolution of the tourist gaze	103
9.1	Inverting Maslow	133
9.2	The four fundamentals of marketing	139

Table

7.1	The NPI-15	107

PREFACE

Contemporary consumption, consumers and marketing are going through a period of flux. The 21st century so far has been characterised by on-going instability and rapid change. Technological innovations have transformed ways of buying and owning goods. They have even altered the ways consumers interpret reality. Social and cultural shifts have liberated some, but left others behind. Consumers are now more able to explore and express their identities; yet they may struggle to fulfil basic quality of life requirements. Ecological issues meanwhile are becoming an ever more urgent concern. It is no longer possible to consume carelessly. Instead, more responsible and ethical forms of consumption are committed to and occasionally clashed over.

Old assumptions around consumption, consumers and marketing have been upended. This can be seen in the rapid decline of traditional consumer spaces, such as shopping malls and high streets, and the rise of others, such as fandoms, often digitally based. Patterns and roles of consumption have also shifted. Social status, personal identity and group belonging may now come as much from making as from consuming items. Marketing content and communications are increasingly caught up in ideological debates that have the potential to make people feel seen, but not always in a positive way.

These shifts have impacted younger consumers in particular. When it comes to consumption, the attitudes, behaviours and lifestyles of generations Y and Z are highly distinctive. Generation Y consumers are frequently contradictory. Ambitious and outgoing, they are simultaneously juvenile and seek reassurance. Sometimes confused and exhausted, signs are of this age group withdrawing into comforting forms of consumerism. Meanwhile, generation Z consumers are particularly combative. This cohort is assertive in its ideological views and determined to make changes both through and to consumer culture.

Identifying and accommodating these idiosyncrasies are vital to making connections with these increasingly influential consumer cohorts. Likewise there is a need to understand the surrounding influences that have and continue to shape consumer behaviour. Themes of global economic, political, ecological and socio-cultural change are the focus of this book. Megatrends such as climate crisis, economic inequality and digital connectivity are in the background throughout. Consideration is of how such major changes affect consumer societies, cultures and individuals, especially those from generations Y and Z.

In turn, the imperative for marketers to be aware of and analyse such issues is stressed. The volatility of the contemporary world poses significant challenges, but also opens new opportunities for marketing. Impetus is to do marketing differently in order to remain relevant to changing consumer needs and desires. Throughout, examples and case studies are used to explore how brands are adapting to current circumstances. Companies such as Taylor Swift have understood and led consumer youth culture expertly. Insight and inspiration can be taken from their success. However, companies such as Juicero have failed to connect with their consumers. Their missteps help to illustrate how marketing can be done better.

This book is divided into ten chapters, each built around a theme that encapsulates current theoretical and professional debates around consumption, consumers and marketing.

- Chapter 1 highlights the importance of relevance to marketing success. This means understanding individual and collective consumers in their surroundings. Breaking through into culture means complementing prevalent routines and aspirations. Doing so greatly increases the likelihood of making meaningful connections with consumers.
- Chapter 2 looks at reconstruction and the trend for more ideological consumption that is committed to making changes in line with beliefs and causes supported.
- Chapter 3 explores reassurance and the ways that consumers may be more introverted, as manifest through trends towards social withdrawal and into obsessive interests.
- Chapter 4 reviews reinvention, referring to the role consumption can play in individual or collective identity building and sharing. Explored are ways that identity may be played with by consumers and brands.
- Chapter 5 considers reputation. This covers consumers and brands as increasingly conscious of being under surveillance and having to manage their public image accordingly.
- Chapter 6 outlines refraction, and the various ways that consumers and marketers can manipulate reality towards their particular self-interests.
- Chapter 7 looks at consumers seeking renown. These assume and solicit attention and appreciation through their consumption.
- Chapter 8, rebalancing, looks at consumers as becoming more involved in producing as well as consuming. In doing so, they challenge longstanding assumptions of the role of consumption in individual and collective lives.
- Chapter 9, re-evaluating, challenges readers to think about the potentially out of date or darker sides of consumerism and marketing. Consideration is of how these issues can be addressed.
- Chapter 10, reviving, then explores how marketing can become more of a force for positive cultural change.

Themes covered and examples used throughout this book are eclectic. These attempt to do some justice to the globalised marketplace consumers and marketers now find themselves in. In addition, the book will help frame the surrounding influences on and expressions of generation Y and Z consumers. Connections made, broken or reinvented now, between marketers and young adults are likely to be long-lasting. Consideration is of the world in which generation Y and Z consumers have grown up within, influenced by, and which they are now stepping out into and shaping.

Overall, this book hopes to share an interesting and informative exploration of consumption and the ways it is altering, influenced by current circumstances. Likewise, the book discusses contemporary consumers, the pressures they are under and their expectations from consumption. In turn, intention is to stimulate analysis and perhaps rethink marketing as a professional and academic practice uniquely placed to contribute to cultural conversations.

1
RELEVANCE

Connecting with consumers – generations Y and Z inspired by K-pop

Introducing consumption

Consumption is the act of acquiring, using, owning and displaying items. Humans have needs that push them to consume things, such as food, needed to maintain life. They also have desires, which encourage them to consume items, like entertainment, wanted because they make life better. All humans are consumers. Consumption is a part of day-to-day life, meeting routine needs. It is also a part of longer term living, helping to imagine and reach towards future aspirations. For these, almost anything can be consumed, but the terms products, services and experiences are usually used to summarise:

- *Products* are physical items. They are objects that can be interacted with through the five senses. A bar of chocolate looks, smells, feels and tastes tantalising, and even the sound of unwrapping can whet appetites. A product is tangible in that it can be possessed by the owner, perhaps for a lifetime, albeit many products have a shelf life.
- *Services* are provided by humans (or increasingly human programmed AI and robotics). Services take the physical, emotional or intellectual abilities of people, and make available for others to consume. For example, stand-up comedy is a service provided by people who share their skills at making others laugh. Entertainment, transport, physical labour, accounting, education, ideas, caring, security and other such things that draw upon people to provide are services.
- *Experiences* are situations and moments that stimulate feelings. These are place and time specific events or activities that trigger a physical, emotional or cognitive reaction. A music festival for instance might lead to experiencing feelings of connectedness with others in the audience, and through them a sense of being in touch with oneself. Such things as travel, festivals, gatherings or challenges can be experiences.

Whilst consumption occurs in all societies, it can manifest quite differently depending on the particular society it occurs within. Influences such as politics can shape the type of consumption permitted. Economic factors can affect the accessibility of consumption. Cultural surroundings might orientate the style of consumption which is considered desirable. These and many other surrounding influences shape the behaviours and attitudes of individual consumers.

Marketing is one of these influences, and it is a powerful one, whose goal is to facilitate consumption. For example, marketing can develop new sales outlets that are more convenient for shoppers. Marketing can also be used to encourage particular types of consumption, by nudging consumers in a particular direction. To illustrate, store layout can affect the browsing habits of customers. If consumption is about understanding what, how and why people acquire, use, own and display items, then marketing is about facilitating and sometimes modifying these items.

Introducing marketing

Marketing is used to initiate and manage exchange relationships between diverse stakeholders. Accordingly, marketing is an academic discipline that tries to understand these three components. The hope is that such understanding will assist in identifying what could be mutually rewarding exchange relationships. In addition, marketing is a professional practice that seeks to use this understanding to facilitate these relationships. Marketers use their knowledge to begin, look after and deepen on behalf of particular stakeholders.

- *Exchange* refers to the swapping of things such as products, services or experiences between two or more parties. In capitalist societies this swap is usually for money, but goodwill, consent, time, ideas and other resources might be exchanged. Exchanges should be mutual and fair, in the sense that all parties involved get what they want out of the swap, and feel they are treated appropriately. A focus of marketing is on facilitating exchanges, for example making it easier to transfer payments, setting out a clear price or introducing complementary parties to each other.
- *Relationships* go beyond a single exchange to create a deeper and more enduring interaction between parties. Initiating a single exchange is relatively expensive, as it takes time and effort to introduce different parties and negotiate a mutual and fair swap. By working together, a single exchange can be built into a series of regular and long-lasting exchanges. This has advantages of being reliable, in the sense that parties can depend on each other to exchange resources each needs. Marketing is used to develop and support relationships between parties. This involves building mutual trust, respect and loyalty over time.
- *Stakeholders* are all of the parties involved in an exchange relationship. Customers are the most well known of these. Organisations depend on their customers to generate income, awareness, enthusiasm or other sustaining resources, in exchange for the products, services or experiences they assemble. Various other stakeholders are also important to successful relationships however. For example, service staff deal with customers and set the tone for exchanges, whilst influencers shape relationship expectations. Marketing is therefore used to monitor and manage diverse stakeholders.

This broad nature of marketing means that it is difficult to neatly define. Different academics and industry professionals adapt and interpret marketing to suit their knowledge and purposes. As a social construct moreover, meaning that marketing is interpreted in line with prevailing social surroundings, how marketing is understood evolves over time. This is recognised by the American Marketing Association, which has a panel of experts update its definitions of marketing every three years (see ama.org for the latest and other various useful resources).

Ultimately there is no neat definition of marketing. Instead, as illustrated by Shaw and Jones (2005), there are various schools of thought on what is marketing. Shaw and Jones outline ten schools of thought, historically arising, and each concentrating on certain questions about what marketing should address and with different focuses of analysis. Highlighted is that marketing is a dynamic discipline, with broad agreements that it thinks about exchange relationships between stakeholders, but many disagreements over what this thinking should emphasise. It is this variety that makes marketing such an interesting and inclusive subject. There is a lot of space to seek inspiration for, interpret and apply marketing.

Relevance: breaking through to consumers using marketing

Relevance is about being required and wanted. In relation to consumption, and the marketing that facilitates consumption, this means being required and wanted by people as they go about buying, using, owning and disposing of items. People in this role are consumers. Something that fits into consumers' routines, and that comes to be seen as essential to these, is relevant. Likewise, something that becomes a sought-after and anticipated addition, helping consumers to reach for and fulfil aspirations, is relevant.

There are two ways this being relevant can happen. Relevance as pertinent means being useful to consumers' individual needs and desires. This might involve slotting into and facilitating their established habits. Meanwhile, relevance, in the sense of being current, means being up to date with why consumers' needs and desires arise, and how they are expressed in a contemporary setting.

Therefore, relevance implies getting to know the consumer individually and in their surroundings. Consumers are individuals with their own unique personal routines and aspirations. At the same time, individuals exist within specific surroundings, which have an influence over routines and aspirations as well. Being pertinent means being aware of individuals' unique characteristics and their surrounding circumstances.

Consumers, their surroundings and their consumption, are all constantly changing. Individuals' requirements and routines can shift. So too their aspirations and cravings evolve. For example, someone starting a family is likely to have different lifestyle priorities than from before they had children. As change happens, things that were once relevant may become less so. Opening is for new needs and desires to be met via alternative sources. Being current means keeping up to date with changes in individuals' characteristics and their surroundings.

Issues of relevance are especially marked when it comes to younger age groups. These tend to be particularly flexible as individuals. Their habits and aspirations are yet to become more crystallised. Because of this, their routines and aspirations are likely to respond to new ideas, norms and technologies faster and more markedly than older people. What is pertinent to and current for young consumers is likely to be distinctive.

In addressing consumer relevance, marketing involves a series of tools, techniques and thinking used to find out what contemporary issues are affecting consumers individually and collectively. Through this it is possible to better respond to consumer changes, to keep up with their evolving routines and aspirations and to stay or become pertinent and current to these. Doing so is important to organisations looking to initiate, maintain and develop relationships with consumers.

Gaining and loosing relevance

For marketers, relevance is an aspiration. Referring to significance, necessity and being indispensable, relevance underpins successful exchange relationships. Where stakeholders feel that such relationships are important, they are more likely to become invested in these. Irrelevant products, services, experiences and their brands by contrast, no matter how well respected or powerful, fail to seem essential.

Aaker (2012) explains that brand relevance means developing appealing 'must haves'. These can include characteristics such as personality, self-expressive benefits or community benefits. If these can be developed they provide a significant competitor advantage in that these help to make a brand seem indispensable.

Blackberry for instance was at one point a highly regarded phone brand with must have features that made it highly relevant to young professionals. The brand's products complemented business people's work requirements and sense of style. Because colleagues owned a Blackberry, others wanted to emulate and purchase likewise. Ownership helped to fit in and look good.

However, Blackberry had a short lived boom before rapidly falling from favour. This experience demonstrates that relevance can come and go in a relatively short space of time. A combination of factors may explain this. Blackberry faded from significance because of changes in wider cultural trends. The exclusivity of digital communications rapidly shifted as phones became cheaper and more accessible. Blackberry also lost its unique selling point as competitors moved aggressively into the same market.

Explaining the importance of cultural relevance to brands, Holt (2016) articulates that these succeed when they break through in culture. Indeed, Holt describes branding as a set of techniques designed to generate cultural relevance. This summary highlights the importance for brand managers of reading and responding to cultural shifts if their clients are to become or stay integral to customer's lifestyles.

Blackberry did not manage to become a more enduring lifestyle component in the way that the iPhone did. The brand's cultural cachet was not particularly substantial. It did not become so integral to business people's routines that ownership was necessary to perform at work. Unlike Microsoft, whose software employees depend upon to function, Blackberry was more of an optional extra. Neither did Blackberry become an essential symbol of business person ambitions. Its devices were appreciated more for their functionality. When others became available, switching came easy.

The brand lifecycle

Illustrating the importance of connecting with young consumers is the notion of the brand lifecycle. This concept treats a brand as a living entity. It is given life by the people involved with it such as managers, employees and customers. As with any living thing, a brand ages over time. The brand lifecycle involves different stages of youth, middle and old age, and in many cases, eventual death.

The brand ageing process follows a general pattern. This is associated with the concurrent ageing of the customers involved with the brand. As customers age, so too do the brands that depend upon them. This is because a connection between a brand and a core customer group is made when a brand is able to break through into their culture. Hereby, a brand becomes seen as pertinent or current to their lifestyles or aspirations. Relationships may be initiated as a result. Banks for example often target young adults becoming financially independent for the first time, with attractive deals.

Exchange relationships will persist only as long as a brand is able to stay relevant. Where an individual's circumstances change, such as their becoming more economically privileged, their consumer tastes may change likewise. If they become wealthier, bank customers may expect better quality customer service.

In order to stay relevant to their customers therefore, brands must evolve alongside them. This evolution of brands alongside their customers slowly changes them. As customers age, so their lifestyles adjust, opinions re-orientate, ambitions shift. Brands will update accordingly to keep in step with them.

These changes might be necessary to stay relevant to core customers. However, by remaining relevant for one group of customers, a brand may isolate itself from others. In tailoring towards the specific needs and identities of a certain group, relevance for other groups may be lost. The fancier customer service provided by a bank for some of its long-term customers might be lost on others who just want a basic and efficient service.

So, over time, brands become ever more closely associated with their core customers for whom they stay relevant. They may begin to struggle to recruit new ones for whom they become less relevant. They then become even more closely associated with their core customers. It is a vicious circle that can lead to a brands' ageing alongside its core customer base.

Modelling the brand lifecycle

Knowing the stages and signs of the brand lifecycle is important to guiding appropriate marketing management at each of these. In order to assist this, the brand lifecycle model (Figure 1.1) breaks brands into five categories. These are categorised according to two criteria. First, their stages of cultural relevance. *Cultural breakthrough* is when a brand first makes it into public consciousness, routines and lifestyles. *Cultural establishment* is when a brand has become an integral part of these. Second, used to judge brands is their gaining of new customers or not. A *growing market* points towards brands recruiting new customers. A *declining market* suggests those which are shrinking to focus on core customers only.

According to these two axes brands pass through stages from maturing to rejuvenating. This occurs as they become more or less culturally established, gain or lose market share. Thus, brands can be classified as representing youth, adulthood, middle and old age. Not all brands age at the same rate, and not all brands age past a particular stage at all. For example, many youth brands never mature as they struggle for market share and eventually close down. This model represents a simplified overview of the likely stages which brands go through, as summarised below.

- *Brand birth:* All brands are brought into the world by their creators. At the nascent stage they are vulnerable, needing to connect with stakeholders. Initiating and then maintaining relationships with these is vital. Brands which can cut through into popular culture may have greater chance of success.
- *Brand maturing:* As brands become more well known they expand. Mature brands are those which manage to grow market share. Appealing to wider audiences they become

6 Connecting with consumers

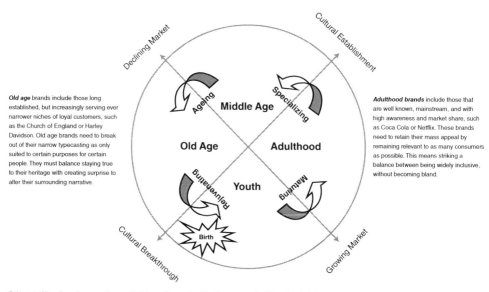

FIGURE 1.1 The brand lifecycle.

a part of consumers' lifestyles and routines. Part of the cultural furniture, people are well aware of and use these brands as standard.

- *Brand specialisation:* As they mature, brands often become more closely associated with a particular set of activities they do particularly well. These brands focus on refining their particular specialism and serving the needs of loyal customers better than the competition.
- *Brand ageing:* As brands become ever more focused on a niche specialism, they may retrench into a particular corner of the market. Sales tend to shrink down to core customers who value that specialism. Other customers with less similarly specialised requirements move on from or avoid such brands, which can come to be seen as dated and unappealing.
- *Brand rejuvenation:* Brands are not condemned to reach the old age stage, or to remain in it. They can gain a second lease of life by breaking back into current cultural conversations. Careful management can help brands to connect with a new group of consumers.

The death of Yardley

Ideally a brand does not leave it to the old age stage before attempting to rejuvenate. The more culturally irrelevant a brand's offering is to the majority, the harder it is to reclaim. Furthermore, the narrower a customer base gets, the harder it is to change in order to recruit new customers, whilst still satisfying existing loyal ones. Evidence of this can be seen with Yardley. Established in 1770, the cosmetic brand became known for its signature lavender scent. Very popular in Victorian England, the brand slowly aged. It and the very smell of lavender became associated with older consumers. Trendy, fashion conscious, young consumers, did not want to associate with. Attempts to revitalise Yardley in the 1990s with adverts featuring the model Linda Evangelista failed to connect with new customers. They even isolated existing customers unused to the edgy imagery of the new campaign. In 1998 the brand went into receivership after failing to update its old-fashioned image. Death is a potential outcome of brand ageing, and many brands do indeed close down once their lifecycle is spent.

Brand longevity

The brand lifecycle suggests that brands are fated to move through various age-related stages, often in line with their core customers, from birth to eventual death. Lehu (2004) argues that this process is not inevitable, albeit without careful management it is likely. There is no simple managerial solution. Rather Lehu suggests that rejuvenation comes from deep analysis of the brand itself and evaluation of as many alternative solutions as possible.

Defying ageing means keeping up to date with cultural changes, staying relevant to young consumers and being able to adapt to accommodate their unique needs. At the same time, brands are under pressure to stay true to the heritage that made them successful in the first place. Kapferer (2012) recognises the tension between brands needing to have a strong and predictable identity to be easily understood by consumers, whilst simultaneously needing to be flexible and adaptable to stay interesting, inclusive and relevant. As the brand lifecycle shows, this tension is difficult to resolve.

Nevertheless, strategies can be applied to extend the brand lifecycle and improve the longevity of brands. Kolbl, Ruzzier and Kolar (2015) point towards retro branding for example, as a way to revitalise a brand. This approach involves a resurrection of attributes from the brands past, which are then adapted to a more modern marketplace and the current aspirations of consumers. Car manufacturers, such as Fiat with the 500 city car, often tap into their heritage when combining throwback styling with latest technology. Doing so helps to resolve the tension between staying true to brand legacy whilst also adapting to latest consumer trends.

More broadly, Kapferer suggests a number of initiatives brands can take to stay relevant. These include line extensions to capture short-term trends, distribution extensions to make more available, altered market positioning regards customers and competitors, and innovation regards USP and differentiation.

The coffee brand Nescafé for example stays fresh through such things as launching new sub-brands. Its Nespresso pods are more upmarket and experiential for example, and may appeal to a different type of consumer than the parent brand. Through such constant tweaks Nescafé marketers keep the brand relevant to a wide spectrum of older and younger consumers.

With such careful management it may be possible to rejuvenate and sustain brands over long time periods. Indeed, some of the world's oldest brands, such as Tate & Lyle, a British sugar label, are well over 100 years old, and remain successful. If a brand is to be prosperous long-term, it needs to recruit new customers. This means reaching across generational divides to appeal to young and new consumers entering the marketplace.

Generational cohorts

Marketers often look to cluster groups of people together, because although every individual is unique they are also shaped by their surroundings. People tend to share broad similarities with other people in similar surroundings. In turn, these likenesses may shape their consumer attitudes and behaviours in a common direction. Knowing such characteristic information helps to inform marketers when attempting to initiate, build and maintain relationships.

Economically for example people in similar financial circumstances might have in common a certain level of disposable income and particular tendencies in terms of their spending of this. Postcode and occupation are instances of classic dimensions that marketers use to try and establish which economic group someone belongs to. Accordingly, if people are living in the same neighbourhood, then this might suggest they have similar incomes as properties are likely similarly priced.

It is useful to group individuals together because doing so is efficient. Sweeping generalisations can be made that inform marketing strategy. A trendy bar targeting hipsters for instance might have a more promising outlook opening in an urban centre. Here we expect such people to live, work and play. In a suburb by contrast, inhabitants might likely be different and have alternative interests. Such broad generalisations can help speed up strategic decision making.

One way of characterising large groups of people is according to age-based generations. Generational cohorts are a means of collating groups of people together based on the idea that people born within rough timeframes of each other will share the same formative influences growing up. This is because particular time periods tend to have specific conditions for things such as economic make-up, education style or social attitudes. People who grow up in these conditions are shaped by them together in ways that make them reasonably cohesive.

For example, growing up at a time of economic uncertainty, children might learn from their parents the importance of saving money. Whereas growing up during an economic boom, spending to have fun might seem more normal. Picked up during childhood and early adulthood, these formative spending habits persist later in life.

The generational approach therefore looks to categorise individuals based on their membership of distinctive cohorts that are defined according to age group. The idea is that people who are born within a certain time period will share similar patterns of behaviour with regard to work, leisure and consumption. Generational cohorts henceforth provide an interesting perspective for considering the formative influences in consumers' pasts. In turn, these help to make sense of and characterise consumers today.

Generational theory

Inspired by the work of the German sociologist Karl Mannheim, who published his essay 'The Problem of Generations' in 1928, generational theory is an area of academic research that seeks to understand and characterise cohorts of people according to their membership of a generation. The idea of doing this is that common patterns across generation groups are revealed.

Mannheim refers to three core principles for studying generational behaviour:

1. *Location* refers to the span of time for the birth years of a cohort of individuals.
2. *Units* relates to sub-cohorts within the broader generational segment. Various sub-cohorts may be readily observed within such a broad classification.

3   *Actuality* relates to the manner in which a generation responds to social changes and how these responses form the persona of the generation. The sharing of these particular events, especially those experienced during formative ages, shapes a collective identity.

Using these three principles it is possible to identify different generational cohorts. As per Mannheim, these are assigned based on age span, often broken down into sub-cohorts, and described in terms of their personality. Today there are seven living generations, five of whom represent major consumer groups.

Each of these generations is said to have been shaped by particular formative influences. These are major political, economic, sociocultural or technological events, issues and movements occurring during their youth. In turn, these formative influences are said to have informed distinctive characteristics of each generational cohort. They think, behave and live in certain ways as a result.

It must be noted that the birth spans (years each cohort was born between) used in this chapter are rough estimates. Birth spans are much adjusted according to different sources and people born on the cusp of divergent generations may identify more with one or the other. This is intended as a loose guide only therefore. Dates for demarcating generations in this book are taken from the Pew Research Center (Parker & Igielnik, 2020).

It also needs to be noted that various labels can be applied to describe the same or broadly similar age cohorts. 'Millennials' is a term often used to describe all or only part of the youth cohort of 20 and 30-something's. The 'i-generation' label can be used to refer to people in their twenties, teenagers or younger. This book uses the terms generation Y to refer to youngish people in their mid-twenties to late thirties, and generation Z to refer to those young people in their early teens to mid-twenties. The term millennials is used as a shorthand to describe all of these together.

The greatest generation: born 1901–1927

Few of the greatest generation are still alive today. Hence, these are a somewhat negligible consumer cohort. These were known as the greatest generation because this was a cohort who faced major obstacles during their formative years. The First World War, the Great Depression, and the Spanish Flu all occurred during the youth of this generation.

The silent generation: born 1928–1945

The silent generation are so called because their youth was heavily influenced by the Second World War and its aftermath. The young adulthood of the silent generation was made difficult by circumstances beyond their control. The silent generation are therefore shaped by hardship, supposedly leading to a modest outlook and strong sense of self-sufficiency.

Traumatised by the chaos and destruction of war, members of this generation sought solace in private lives that could be controlled. Often marrying young, the silent generation are characterised by couples who have lived their lives tightly together. Cohort members focussed on self-contained nuclear families and aspired towards suburban lifestyles that emphasised peace and stability.

Holding stable but not necessarily heartfelt jobs, post-war prosperity meant that many people were able to improve their economic standing. Medical advances extended their lifespans. The silent generation did not have the luxury of taking time to discover themselves when young, but they were often able to lead stable and comfortable adult lives.

The silent generation are nevertheless typified as careful with their money. This has remained the case even as they grow older and richer. Silent generation pensioners hold significant wealth in many societies. However, they are often relatively disinterested in spending it, as well as resistant to having it taken away by governments in taxes.

Consequently, these are a tough cohort to win over through marketing. Utility and value are often prioritised by consumers from this age group. Managing or coping with the effects of ageing is now a consumer priority in many cases. Japan, which has a particularly high proportion of elderly citizens, pioneers many products and services suited to silent generation needs.

The silent generation are often considered to be more socially conservative. However, that is not to say they are inflexible. The cohort has been able to adapt to a world which has changed dramatically during their lifetimes. In such situations older people have not only preserved many of their traditions, but as evidenced by things such as their enthusiasm for the internet have embraced radically new outlets and activities.

Baby boomers: born 1946–1964

Children of the silent generation are known as baby boomers because they were born en masse in the prosperous post-war period. They rebelled against parents considered to be conservative, small scale and unambitious. A quiet family life in the suburbs was for boomers a stifling rather than aspirational experience.

Thanks to the post-war economic uplift in North America and Europe, this generation grew up at a time of relative peace and prosperity. Circumstances gave boomers a comfortable upbringing, but also the space to experiment with identities. Boomers had the opportunity to pursue education. The rise of the automobile industry gave them the freedom of the road. Birth control gave them liberation in the bedroom.

The result was a confident generation keen to enjoy themselves and challenge those who would deny them their right to self-expression. Youth culture took off with the boomers. They came to the fore during the 1960s decade of sociocultural conflicts and changes. Free love, anti-war, pro-equality, the baby boomers became associated with radical music, fashion and counter culture, all of which eventually became mainstream pop culture.

To this day more individualistic, self-expressive and liberal lifestyles enjoyed by many draw inspiration from this era. The activism of the boomers helped push forward social democratic ideals in many parts of the world. This was an outgoing and ambitious generation who left their mark.

It is sometimes said that boomers never grew up past the age of 21. Coming of age at such an exciting time, they seem to have forever remained young adults in their heads and habits. This can be observed in relation to their consumption, which has remained somewhat stuck in the 1960s and 1970s. Boomers are still wearing denim, still listening to the Rolling Stones, still watching Woody Allen movies.

Often wealthy thanks to being born at such a fortuitous time, boomers frequently spend their considerable disposable income on toys. Boomers are the main purchasers of Harley Davidson motorbikes, Chevrolet Corvettes and Winnebago RV's. They own summer homes in Florida, France or Friesland. Initially suspicious of consumerism, this cohort has to large extent become self-indulgently spendthrift.

OK Boomer

'OK Boomer' is a meme that developed on TikTok, the online video-sharing platform that came to prominence in 2019, and is used almost exclusively by the under-25s. The tagline embodies the collective eye roll of this age group when they hear older people criticising them. OK Boomer is a catchy, t-shirt print friendly, response to the unsolicited opinions of older generations. Considered by generation Z to have had it easy growing up, and blamed for the problems of the planet being as it is, OK Boomer dismisses generation Z's elders in a way that baby boomers once dismissed theirs. This cultural shrug is an example of a youth cohort finding their voice, expressing it, and challenging the divergent opinions of those other cohorts where they do not share them.

Generation X: born 1966–1980

Generation X came of age in the 1980s. This was a decade of economic transformation. In many parts of the world old industries, such as mining, as well as the communities built alongside these, rapidly declined. Elsewhere, new flourishing service industries created pathways to wealth, but also inequality.

Some city centres boomed, hosting financial services and attracting young urban populations. These 'yuppies' were young and upwardly mobile. Motivated by money, they worked and partied hard. Other places suffered badly from economic malaise however, and the yuppies pursuit of bling was undercut by the fear of being left behind.

These formative surroundings can be linked to the competitive edge generation X often have. Often well educated, hardworking and ambitious, generation X have been successful in various careers. They may particularly prioritise the work side of the work-life balance. This group is now at the peak of their career in many instances, with the influence that goes along with this.

X is a desired demographic for marketers for a number of reasons. Not only are they often financially well off, but consumption is especially important to this age group. Purchases and ownership are a way for generation X to show off their success.

They are said to be a high spending and flashy group who like make ostentatious purchases. Expensive watches, designer labels, home extensions, showy purchases and brands are used by generation X to demonstrate that they have made it good.

What is more, generation X are seemingly far less cynical than the generations before or after them towards the limitations of consumerism as a source of personal development or existential meaning. They are more committed than most to consumption as a source of individual and social validation.

Generation Y: born 1981–1996

Generation Y grew up during a period when Western democratic capitalism seemed highly successful. The Iron Curtain came down. China joined the World Trade Organization and began its economic boom. Globalised trade, education and tourism brought diverse peoples together. From this background, three overlapping influences are considered to have informed the persona of generation Y.

The first of these, and most often used to describe and define generation Y, is their technological embedment. Generation Y are the first cohort to have grown up with ready access to and increasingly immersed in online worlds. Virtual connectivity provided this cohort with a space to develop their own unique cultural codes and identity. Today, their lives take place to a large extent in the digital realm. For generation Y friendships, dating, playing, shopping and working all increasingly take place online.

The second influence on generation Y is globalization. This refers to the increased connectedness on a world level of people and places that has been brought about by such things as communications technology and free trade. Generation Y are perhaps the first truly global generation in the sense that young people worldwide are connected as never before. This connectivity has been associated with a group which transcends things like geography or ethnicity. The result is an open-minded and flexible cohort who are exposed to diverse ideas and lifestyles from an early age. Generation Y tend to have relaxed attitudes towards social issues such as sexuality.

Third, the indulgent parenting of generation Y relates to these being much wanted, valued and protected by their parents. This nurturing upbringing has been linked to high levels of self-esteem, optimism and confidence. Cohort members hold a firm belief in being special. Brought up being told so by their parents, they have internalised these messages. As a result, this age group prioritises self-development. They look for spiritually fulfilling, not just utilitarian, work and leisure.

Generation Y have received plenty of marketing attention over the last decade as they have grown up and emerged in force as consumers. This group is finally transitioning into adulthood after long extended adolescences, some of them at least. Generation Y are now entering careers and gaining significant spending power. This explains their appeal to marketers keen to connect with a global cohort who are starting to earn and spend on a large scale.

However, as will be explored further, generation Y are a somewhat contradictory and confusing cohort. They exhibit bipolar qualities of being self-assured, yet craving peer approval. This may relate to the fractured influences on Y's upbringing. The stable and supportive surroundings of generation Y's childhood have been rapidly eroded, leaving members of the cohort somewhat confused by and ill-prepared for the new world in which they find themselves.

Generation Z: born 1997–2012

Generation Z overlap in many ways with their gen-Y forebears. However, they are an increasingly distinctive cohort of their own. In their teens and early twenties, the identity of generation Z is still forming. The influential events shaping generation Z may likewise still be unfolding. But these likely include the lingering aftermath of the 2008–2009 financial crisis and the fallout from the Covid-19 pandemic. Generation Z have also grown up with the pressures of climate change and cultural conflicts constantly in the background.

These influences mean that generation Z seem to be a resilient cohort. Aware that surroundings are uncertain and not easy, they appear ready to take action individually and collectively to address challenges. Cohort members are engaged, sincere and looking to make a difference to their world even at a young age.

This involvement is exemplified by the global climate strikes led by children and teenagers refusing to go to school in protest at older generations' neglect of the climate crisis. Where other generations are in denial, complacent or defeatist, generation Z are driven to do something. Captured by this movement is the ethos of a cohort which is well informed about current issues and causes, and willing to take actions to make the changes they want.

In addition, generation Z seem to have a strong sense of identity and purpose. Perhaps prompted by their unstable surroundings, they have often focused on finding and building fixed identities. Asserting individual and collective identity seems to be important to generation Z. Cohort members can be quite tribal in their affiliations to such things as like-minded groups, ideology or consumption.

Generation Z have apparently matured at a much earlier age than generation Y and their self-confidence seems far more complete. Where generation Y are torn between self-assurance and self-doubt, generation Z appear to have a more consistent sense of themselves. This personal sophistication may be exemplified by the pop star Billie Eilish, whose self-confident stage presence and analytical lyrics belie her young age.

Generation Z are emerging as distinctive consumers therefore. If this is to be an activist and assured generation, then marketers need to be alert. Young people will not accept things as they are. They expect meaningful changes in line with their worldview. Clarity of purpose and positioning will be important. This is a clued-up cohort which wants to be treated with respect.

Snowflakes

A put down of youth cohorts, 'snowflake' is the term used to deride members of these as overly sensitive and indulged. Snowflake stereotypes today's young people as easily provoked, but quick to avoid conflict. This is the idea that they are liable to respond to supposedly innocuous minor details. Simultaneously, snowflake critiques the superficiality of their indignation. This melts away easily when challenged, or does not endure over time, because this cohort is easily distracted and unable to commit to anything long-term. Snowflake might have some truth in it, but whether this is distinct from older generations is debateable.

The next generation

Today's children, those born after 2012, will grow up and become consumers rapidly. The oldest of the next generation will be able to vote from around 2028. Children's pester power means they are already indirectly influencing the consumption of their families. What will comprise major formative experiences, how these will shape their attitudes and behaviours and what sort of world they will step into and inherit are all forward gazing questions. It is already time to begin considering the answers to these however, if marketers are to be prepared to reach out and connect with in coming years.

Generations Y and Z: new and distinctive consumers

The interest youth cohorts hold for marketers is obvious. These represent the future consumers of the world. They are the people relationships that need to be established with if brands are to gain, maintain or regain their cultural relevance. Human lifecycles are short. If brands want to avoid being similarly time-framed, then they need to reach out beyond their core customers and recruit new younger ones.

Generations Y and Z are also becoming increasingly powerful consumers in terms of their growing spending power. As they enter the jobs market en masse and progress up career ladders, these cohorts are earning more money, have growing disposable incomes and have increasing consumer confidence. At the same time, as older generations approach retirement, and eventually as they die, their collective consumer power lessens.

Finally, generations Y and Z are extremely numerous. These age groups make up sizeable chunks of national populations. This is especially so in many parts of the world such as South America, Africa, the Middle East and Southeast Asia. There is therefore significant commercial potential and cultural clout associated with these youth generations.

The appeal of generation Y and Z consumers may be clear. However, acting upon this is less so. Recruiting young consumers is not simply a case of business as usual. When it comes to consumption, generations Y and Z have their own unique combinations of needs and desires. They likewise have attitudes and behaviours that mark them out from their predecessors.

Because of their distinct surrounding influences growing up, generations Y and Z have unique traits. In particular, these cohorts have come of age during a period of global uncertainty. Such things as 9/11, the global financial crash, climate crisis, terrorism, high school shootings and latterly Covid-19 have created an often tense and traumatic atmosphere to grow up within.

These uncertain surroundings have formed the outlook of these age cohorts, albeit they have done so in subtly different ways. Generation Y consumers are contradictory and need all-encompassing treatment by marketers, while generation Z consumers are more combative and require careful handling.

Generation Y: contradictory consumers

Generation Y are old enough to remember the decade before 9/11. They were children and teenagers during the largely stable 1990s. This tranquillity was disrupted by the uncertainty that has typified the 21st century so far. Generation Y entered job markets that had flat-lined due to global recession. They grew up in lazily liberal cultural surroundings that then turned angrily ideological. They embraced early social media as spaces for sharing and connecting with each other, which were taken over by outsiders. This split between happy childhood and then troubled young adulthood has seemingly left generation Y as bipolar. They are a frequently contradictory group, split simultaneously into such things as being confident yet anxious, ambitious whilst withdrawn, independent at the same time as needy.

For marketers, these contradictions make for a complex consumer cohort. On the one hand, this cohort can be demanding, even entitled, when it comes to consumption. A sense of consumer empowerment comes from access to plentiful information, connectedness with others, and a strong sense of being special. This has created bold consumers happy to experiment with their purchases, try new experiences, stand out and express themselves. On the other hand, members of this cohort are often unsure of themselves. Prone to anxiety, self-critique and defeatism, generation Y consumers can be needy. They seek reassurance through comforting consumption.

Evaluating one theme said to have particularly shaped generation Y, globalisation, demonstrates the contrariness of such an influence. Referring to the structures and systems that have shrunk our shared planet, awareness of global variety and opportunity means that young consumers are highly open-minded and keen to seek out new and varied experiences. Generation Y are confident exploring and experimenting with their identities and not afraid to express who they are.

Nevertheless, if globalisation has opened many opportunities to generations Y and Z, it may be linked to challenges experienced by these cohorts as well. The globalised world is a competitive one, where things like employment, education and housing are in short supply. In China for example, the term 'ant tribe' has been coined to describe recent graduates who live in subterranean apartments. All they can afford, they put up with poor quality living conditions in the hope that they will one day find the jobs for which they were trained in university. Such a situation is disempowering, anxiety inducing and undermines self-esteem.

This bipolarity has led to the emergence of consumers that are at times contradictory, often unpredictable and always complicated. Such things as high self-confidence and anxiety are present simultaneously. Thus when it comes to tourism consumption for example, generation Y may seek out adventurous travel that is physically and emotionally demanding. Enduring such extreme tourism is an opportunity for self-development. Yet at the same time, generation Y seem to need constant affirmation whilst travelling. Through social media they spend much of their travel time carefully editing and presenting flattering versions of themselves online in the hope of soliciting positive feedback from peers.

Accordingly, the challenge and opportunity for marketers lie in encompassing both sides of generation Y at once. This means providing goods, services and experiences that manage to meet the contradictory expectations of a cohort who simultaneously want to be challenged by their consumption, at the same time as they need to be reassured by it. Customisation for example may support such blending of different and somewhat at odds elements.

Customisation and consumer complexity

One means of dealing with Y consumer contradictions may be customisation. Customisation, which involves putting a unique spin on established goods, balances the desire to stand out individually with that to conform. Social media is an excellent example of customisation. This offers users a means of following a set template for self-expression. Different social media platforms provide standardised tools for uploading content and connecting with others. At the same time, social media also offers aspects of customisable self-display. Working from a basic profile page, users can adapt the content that share and create a tailored impression of themselves. This blend of standardisation and personalisation offers an excellent balance of fitting in with and standing out from peers. Contradictory motivations for Y and Z can be accommodated simultaneously through social media and its customisation potential.

Generation Z: combative consumers

Generation Y seem somewhat unsure of themselves and contradictory as a result. This is far less the case for generation Z. Members of this age group have come of age in surroundings that are more unipolar. That is to say, they have been more uniformly bleak. Generation Z do not know a world outside of the 21st century. Antagonism and uncertainty are what they have grown up knowing. Things such as politics, culture, climate change and social media are understood as frequently disagreed over. This is an age group who are wised up with regard to the often harsh realities of the wider world.

The downside of this is that generation Z have had to toughen up in the face of political, economic, sociocultural and ecological challenges. The upside is that this has left them motivated to engage with and drive change. Generation Z seem more driven, determined and prepared to push for changes on their terms. Such things as the Extinction Rebellion and Black Lives Matter movements have drawn considerable energy from generation Z members. This is an assertive and sometimes combative cohort.

Generation Z frequently prioritise ideology when consuming. For this age group consumption is recognised as a means to drive desired change. They link with organisations that share their values and support likeminded causes. It is important for consumers from this demographic that what and how they buy reflects their moral and ethical values. Those businesses and brands that can connect with these may be rewarded, whilst those that do not may be challenged. Increasingly activist consumers do not shy away from criticising, boycotting and attacking organisations and others they do not agree with.

Research by Deloitte (2018) finds that the core values of generation Z are reflected in their prioritising social activism more than previous generations. Generation Z no longer form opinions of a company solely based on the quality of their products or services, but also now on their ethics, practices and social impact. Not only must companies have strong ethics, they have to demonstrate they take action consistent with their ethics and values. This action must be front and centre of their brand for prospective generation Z buyers and employees to see.

Related to this, generation Z consumers may be especially tribal. This is in the sense that they like to group together with peers who share likeminded beliefs and who push for similarly desired changes. Conversely, they may feel isolated from and clash with others who do not share their same values. Such things as brands or consumers that diverge ideologically can be cancelled, switched off and turned away from. In turn, this can generate reactions from those who are targeted by generation Z's ire. Contemporary culture clashes are often marked by especially stark divides between younger and older age groups.

The challenge and opportunity for marketers therefore lie in connecting with generation Z through emphasising likeminded values and commitment to shared ethical issues or causes, without isolating consumers, often older, who may not prioritise or share such a stance. This means navigating ideological conversations as they unfold with sensitivity, and trying to include, or at least not exclude, target niches. Celebrating diversity may be a way of doing this.

Diversity and consumer plurality

Generation Z are said to be the most ethnically diverse generation ever (Parker & Igielnik, 2020). Their mixed backgrounds mean that Z are especially open minded and tolerant when it comes to issues of ethnicity and culture. Fusions of different backgrounds and cultural plurality are the norm for Z. Marketing can do more to recognise this. Simple efforts to better reflect the actual diversity of gen Z consumers in marketing content and communications will make feel more welcome. This does not have to be framed ideologically, perhaps avoiding the clashes that can come with doing so. Yet representing diversity is a positive way to signal to gen Z consumers that they are recognised, valued, and welcomed.

Consumer case: the K-pop phenomenon

As a way to better understand young consumers, it is useful to look at their cultural interests. Discussed throughout this book, surrounding culture both shapes and reflects the attitudes and behaviours of consumers. Prevailing cultural conversations, and how consumers engage with these, give useful insights into their routines and aspirations. The cultural activities of generations Y and Z are, as with any generation, often quite distinct. Evaluating the particular music, films, books, television, and other cultural products specifically consumed by these generations can therefore be a source of insight into their influences and interests.

One particular cultural phenomenon that might exemplify is K–pop. In the past decade, Korean pop music has gone global. After conquering the domestic South Korean market the genre has spread throughout East Asia and recently made inroads into places where Anglo-American pop has long dominated. This success is the result of more than just an extremely polished product. A breakthrough into wider cultural consciousness is based on the relevance of Korean pop songs to global listeners. K–pop is tapping into cultural themes that resonate with increasingly worldwide youth. It is reflecting their experiences, fears and ambitions back at them.

In terms of its product development, the Korean music industry has analysed and emulated older established Anglo-American and Japanese pop music. Manufactured 'icons', as different performers are often referred to, are produced by the industry akin to the Western pop model followed since the 1960s. With carefully choreographed public images and branded personalities, these icons are targeted towards pre-teen and teen audiences.

K–pop takes this well-established business model and turbocharges it. Pop videos are even more frenetic. Dance sequences are more elaborate. Bands comprise dozens of customisable members rather than a handful. The public presentations of icons are closely studied, inter-group dynamics carefully choreographed and interactions between singers and audiences carefully managed. Little is left to chance or spontaneity in what is a slick corporate machine. Thus, Shin (2009) distinguishes the Korean pop music industry from Western counterparts by its all-encompassing nature; not just the music production, but live concerts, and the stars themselves, are micromanaged together for maximum profitability.

Thanks to its slick production values Korean wave music has become wildly popular. The K–pop fandom is passionate to the point of obsessive. Devoted followers are willing to give a lot to their preferred stars, and they demand a lot in return. Cyber-battles between followers of different icons are pitched. These clashes highlight the close identification fans have with pop brands and how seriously these consumption relationships are taken.

Underpinning this passion is a connection between K–pop and young people. K–pop seems to strike a nerve with generations Y and Z as global cohorts who are used to a wide variety of cultural influences. The genre may also appeal to the combative side of these age groups, who are able to gather into rival fan tribes and play out rivalries online. K–pop additionally resonates with cohorts' contradictory characteristics. Outgoing and withdrawn, confident yet group dependent, ambitious but anxious, such themes appear in K–pop songs and leak out through the carefully stage managed lives of performers.

The Korean dream

To an outsider, K–pop videos are initially both relatable and confusing. The combination of accustomed and bizarre references makes for a compelling experience. For insiders, K–pop can become a way of life. The K–pop fandom is often passionate to the point of obsessive. Particularly active online, fans invest their resources in following favourite icons.

K-pop makes a powerful connection because of how the contents and presentations of songs, and their singers, resonate with the lives of listeners. K-pop places greater emphasis on collective emotions than its Western counterparts. Hereby, song lyrics explore social status. A break up for example might be less about how it affects the individual's feelings, and more about how it affects their public image. Themes of belonging, fitting in and being loved by peers are heavily referenced in K-pop.

As such, K-pop may be selling a Korean dream. This may be more group conscious than the individualistic American dream. Where American pop stars sing about their individual experiences, Korean ones spend more time on reading and fitting in with social surroundings. Loneliness in a US pop song might be because of one's own mistakes. In a Korean pop song loneliness might be a result of misunderstanding peer's social cues. In turn, loneliness might, respectively, be portrayed as personally devastating or socially losing face.

These differences in emphasis are relatively small, but potentially significant. Where the American dream measures success through individual accumulation of prestige, the Korean dream places more emphasis on contributing to the prestige of a social group. Extending these orientations from pop culture into consumer culture, it may be that consumers are likewise altering their attitudes and behaviours.

The American dream places emphasis on a specific style and role of consumption. Emphasised in myriad cultural products, such as films, novels, plays and music, is an idealised American dream identity to be aspired towards. Hereby, individuality is achieved partly through buying and owning products, services and experiences. These help to develop identity through expressing certain values, linking with specific groups, and living in a particular way. The American sitcom family lifestyle can be replicated off-screen by making similar consumption choices.

Such consumption style and role may evolve however, as individual identities are subject to different cultural influences. As the world becomes increasingly interconnected, and as places such as East Asia grow in influence, new ways of thinking and being are emerging. America is less dominant culturally, economically and politically than it was in the 20th century. American values are aspired towards less than they once were. As a globalized, connected and socially conscious cohort, generations Y and Z may find K-pop references complement their cultural outlook. The Korean dream is relevant to the priorities of young consumers of K-pop.

Fans and anti-fans

K-pop is notorious for its obsessive fans. These consume their favourite icons in minute detail. They are willing to fight for their preferred bands, using social media to promote and convert others to the cause. Because of their passion, fans have a lot of influence over the K-pop industry and its music brands. Keeping their support is necessary for success. Doing this can be exhausting. Fans have high expectations. Devoted K-pop followers are willing to give a lot to their preferred stars, and they demand a lot in return. Those that do not conform or perform correctly as per their expectations risk backlash. Alongside the fan phenomenon therefore, is a parallel phenomenon of anti-fans. Just as passionate, anti-fans attack artists they have singled out as not meeting their expectations. They harass aggressively, sending online and offline hate mail and threats. Anti-fans obsessively consume K-pop brands not because of love, but out of hate.

The dream's dark side

The Korean dream also has a dark side. The K-pop industry is notoriously controlling of its young protégés, who are not allowed to reveal details of their private lives except in carefully choreographed sound-bites designed to appeal to fans. Their sex lives are especially tightly regulated. Reasoning behind this is that fans discovering their idols are romantically attached, or sexually orientate away from them, might have the fantasy that they could one day be together, disrupted.

The process of becoming a K-pop figure is particularly gruelling. Music labels often recruit promising children who then live in dormitories as they are groomed, with no certainty of making the final cut (Tai, 2020). Potential stars are taken out of primary school to be trained. Academies charge to take on and teach aspiring stars. Televised competitions offer spots in manufactured groups. The K-pop production line is an intense one, as new icons are raised, promoted and micromanaged.

The consequences for K-pop performers themselves may be severe. The chances of making it in the industry are slim, with most aspiring icons failing to break through. For those few who do, the pressure to conform to an identity fabricated and packaged for fans may be at odds with individual's true self. To illustrate, Holland, one of the first K-pop singers to come out as gay, faced initially negative cultural and commercial consequences of doing so.

The dark side of K-pop has more recently become apparent. In 2019 the South Korean actor and pop singer Sulli died of an apparent suicide (Snapes, 2019). She had been known for standing up for herself and pushing back against fans and wider cultural conventions when their expectations and criticisms of her became too restrictive. Sulli reportedly had romantic relationships. This is something many male K-pop fans find unacceptable in the women they follow and want to themselves. Although her self-assertion earned Sulli many fans inspired by her feminism in a culture which expects women to be reserved, it also gained her plenty of negative criticism. Sulli was subject to long running abuse, particularly online.

Cyber bullying of those who differ from or challenge conventions has become a major issue in one of the world's most technologically advanced and connected countries. More generally, expressing individuality in South Korea is not always appreciated. Pressure to succeed and be loved for standing out is combined with pressure to conform and risk hatred for being different. This bipolar balancing act makes careers and life for K-pop icons difficult to manage.

Ironically, it may be this dark side of the Korean dream that connects with young listeners as much as the light. Significant pressure is on all young Koreans, not just K-pop icons, to both achieve in a highly competitive education and economic system, and follow cultural expectations. The burden to be successful and behave in a certain way is moreover felt by young people worldwide. The ruthless competition, punishing training and endless social media scrutiny of K-pop idols, as summarised by Wong (2018), are felt to greater or lesser extent by all young people. Both the Korean dream and the Korean nightmare are relevant to the cultural experiences of generations Y and Z. This is why K-pop has caught on with these as consumers.

Case questions

1. Why does K-pop resonate with so many contemporary youth consumers?
    Think about the themes packaged by K-pop songs and icons and how these are relevant to the routines and aspirations of listeners.

2   Are the apparent contradictions contained within K-pop a sales disadvantage or an advantage?
    Consider whether the divide between the glamour of K-pop icons on stage and the intense pressures upon these backstage is relevant to generation Y and Z consumers.
3   What other cultural phenomena have broken through with generations Y and Z?
    Think of examples from fashion, art, media, and analyse whether there are common themes within these that resonate with and are relevant to today's youth consumers.

Chapter summary

Relevance refers to breaking through into cultural consciousness, routines and aspirations. Relevance is not easy to obtain. As the brand lifecycle demonstrates, it is even more difficult to maintain. Nevertheless, marketing can be used to help achieve and sustain. These mean analysing and shifting cultural surroundings and the influences these have on consumers, especially young consumers, as well as evaluating current cultural phenomena and interpreting why these connect with certain consumer groups. Through such cultural research it may be possible to better judge how and why consumers think and act in particular ways, and therefore respond accordingly. In this way, following chapters will pick up contemporary consumer culture themes relating to the contradictory traits of generations Y and Z as both engaging with and withdrawing from their consumer surroundings.

References

Aaker, D. A. (2012). Win the brand relevance battle and then build competitor barriers. *California Management Review*, 54(2), 43–57.

Deloitte. (2018). *Welcome to generation Z*. Available at: https://www2.deloitte.com/content/dam/Deloitte/us/Documents/consumer-business/welcome-to-gen-z.pdf (accessed 12/06/20).

Holt, D. (2016). Branding in the age of social media. *Harvard Business Review*, 94(3), 40–50.

Kapferer, J.-N. (2012). *The new strategic brand management: Advanced insights and strategic thinking*. London: Kogan Page Publishers.

Kolbl, Z., Konecnik Ruzzier, M., & Kolar, T. (2015). Brand revitalization: Don't let your brands turn into sleepyheads. *Central European Business Review*, 4(2), 5–11.

Lehu, J. M. (2004). Back to life! Why brands grow old and sometimes die and what managers then do: An exploratory qualitative research put into the French context. *Journal of Marketing Communications*, 10(2), 133–152.

Mannheim, K. [(1928) 1993]. The problem of generations. *Psychoanalytic Review*, 57(3), 378–404.

Parker, K., & Igielnik, R. (2020). On the cusp of adulthood and facing an uncertain future: What we know about gen Z so far. *Pew Research Centre*, 14/05/20. Available at: https://www.pewsocialtrends.org/essay/on-the-cusp-of-adulthood-and-facing-an-uncertain-future-what-we-know-about-gen-z-so-far/ (accessed 12/06/20).

Shaw, E. H., & Jones, D. B. (2005). A history of schools of marketing thought. *Marketing Theory*, 5(3), 239–281.

Shin, H. (2009). Have you ever seen the rain? And who'll stop the rain?: The globalizing project of Korean pop (K-pop). *Inter-Asia Cultural Studies*, *10*(4), 507–523.

Snapes, L. (2019). Sulli, K-pop star and actor, found dead aged 25. *The Guardian*, 14/10/19. Available at: https://www.theguardian.com/music/2019/oct/14/sulli-k-pop-star-former-fx-member-found-dead-aged-25 (accessed 22/05/20).

Tai, C. (2020). Exploding the myths behind K-pop. *The Guardian*, 29/03/20. Available at: https://www.theguardian.com/global/2020/mar/29/behind-k-pops-perfect-smiles-and-dance-routines-are-tales-of-sexism-and-abuse (Accessed 22/05/20).

Wong, J. (2018). The punishing pressures behind K-pop perfection. *CBC News*, 24/02/18. Available at: https://www.cbc.ca/news/entertainment/kpop-hard-life-1.4545627 (accessed 22/05/20).

2
RECONSTRUCTION

Ideological consumer engagement – vegan extremism and BrewDog revolution

Welcome to the 21st century

The 21st century had barely begun when the September 11th terrorist attack occurred. News and politics have seemingly been dominated by associated debates ever since. Divisions around political and religious beliefs opened up by the attack and its aftermath have festered. Conspiracy theories, political malaise, competing nations, religious violence and the blaming of problems on immigrants or other easily victimised groups point towards times that are often polarised, confused and angry.

Then, in 2008, economies were thrown into crisis. Banks began to look over-exposed to the massive amounts of consumer debt that had built up over the decades prior. People trying to keep up with buying the latest goods and experiences had been doing so often on borrowed money. Economic recovery has in many places been slow, and in some has not yet arrived. Young people around the world have been hit especially hard. Many find themselves trapped in short-term employment, poor quality housing, putting decisions on hold.

More recently, the long-time background hum of climate change has become louder. In 2019, huge fires in the Amazon, Siberia and Australia were a frightening demonstration of how severe the impacts of climate crisis are starting to look. Yet even now, as people's homes burn, flood and sink beneath the waves, many people in positions of power do little to change, or refuse to admit the need to. Fierce divides have opened up over climate change. As elsewhere, splits between the attitudes of young and old have been notable.

Although it is still a fledgling century, only just out of its teens, the 21st has so far been characterised to significant extent by crisis and divisions over how to recognise and respond to these. The stresses brought by such things as terrorism, economic inequality and climate change are pressuring individuals and groups. Temptation is to retreat into denial, bad temper or blame shifting. Culture clashes and conflicts are everywhere. Online rivals troll and trick. Offline groups compete for influence. Consumers, consumption and marketing are implicated throughout.

Yet such stresses are also pushing people towards creative solutions. They are motivated and rising to challenges of things like climate change. Consumers are realising their individual power and finding new ways of working together. Engaging with more ethical and sustainable forms of consumption, they are driving businesses to adjust for the better. The importance of values and causes to contemporary consumers underlines their willingness to change old habits and challenge established assumptions.

If the 21st century is a period of uncertainty therefore, it is also one of ambition. The global consumer economy is more dynamic than ever before, thanks to the rapid development and interconnection of nations. East Asian markets in particular are a source of dynamic consumers, consumption and marketing. Technology has fostered radical changes in the connectivity and habits of global consumers. Online shopping, social media and mobile data barely existed at the start of the century, and now are second nature to billions. As old ways of being face decline, potential is there for new ideas and methods to take off.

Covid-19

At the end of 2019, and then through 2020, the global Covid-19 pandemic caused major disruption to national and global systems, as well as the day-to-day life of individual citizens. This flu-type virus spread rapidly around our interconnected world. Many countries responded with strict lock-downs to slow the spread of Covid-19. Citizens were advised to stay inside as much as possible. Public events were cancelled. Much of the economy shut down. Millions of jobs suspended. Many businesses faced an unprecedented fight for survival. Tensions over how best to manage the crisis emerged along familiar ideological lines. Also demonstrated was the ability of communities to come together and cope with a serious challenge. It will take time to see what the longer term effects of the lock-down will be. Commuting, working, leisure and consumption patterns may not return to how they were previously. Marketers are likely to emerge with new perspectives as a result.

Reconstruction: bringing ideology into consumption and marketing

Reconstruction is a term to describe the growing importance of ideology in contemporary consumption and marketing. This is a time of passionate debates around politics, culture and society. These conversations are increasingly brought into and expressed through consumption. Causes and issues are being engaged with enthusiasm, and sometimes anger, by consumers. People are looking to get more involved in such discussions through their consumption, and marketers have to be responsive.

Reconstruction implies building, breaking and rebuilding ideas, arguments and ways of living. Faced with many challenges and uncertainties, there is a growing drive to debate and try to change these. The methods and destinations of such conversations are not always agreed upon. Indeed, such discussions are often fractured, bad tempered and pan out unpredictably. However, that such dialogs are taking place is evidence of the importance of reconstruction to contemporary consumers.

Ideology shapes the meaning of consumption as an activity, and of things that are consumed. Referring to the belief structures of individuals, ideology might include the stories they have learned about what is right and wrong, the organisations and figures they look up to, or the social codes and cultural norms of groups they belong to. As such, ideology frames consumers' attitudes, behaviours and lifestyles. Consumption choices and actions are affected by the meanings associated with these. These meanings are increasingly important.

As conversations around ideology are mainstreamed, analysing the meanings of consumption is likewise.

Consumption is a rewarding pastime because it can help people to achieve various intentions. Purchases may have *utilitarian value* in that they help to meet a specific need, such as a new coat to keep warm when the winter arrives. It might be *emotional value* that is sought out. A new coat that makes feel attractive for instance, and cheers up if we were feeling a bit low. *Social value* is also important. That coat might be in a style that fits in with friends and helps express belonging to a particular group. There is also *ideological value*. Buying a specific coat is a means of expressing belief in a certain way of thinking, acting and living. A real fur coat may be entirely unacceptable. A vegan leather is one desirable.

Thus, consumption choices can be used to demonstrate values, ethics and beliefs. It is the ideological value of consumption which is increasingly important in today's marketplace. As contemporary consumers become more passionate about various causes and make efforts to express their values through their consumption, marketers have to respond. Brands for example are being caught up in and impacted by ideological discussions, whether they like it or not. Some brands use ideology to their advantage by developing a sense of vision that is meaningful to likeminded consumers. Lush, the soap and bath-bomb retailer, has built its brand around campaigning for particular causes. The brand's customers typically find these campaigns to be inspiring.

Clearly there are opportunities for marketers in relation to the rise of ideological consumption. Increasingly value-driven and actively ethical consumers suggest that brands may be able to build relationships through developing their ideological stances. Conversely, there is growing potential for clashes between consumers and brands where they are seen to disagree over or hold different values. Hence, ideological consumer trends need to be carefully monitored if they are to be worked with, or at least worked around.

The meaning of face masks

Products, services and experiences have in many cases been infused with ideological meanings. A stark recent example of this came from reports of retailers in the USA turning customers away for either wearing or not wearing face masks during the Covid-19 lock-down. For some, the meaning of face masks was a loss of freedom. For others, the meaning of face masks was protecting others. Illustrated in these instances is the sense that almost anything can be infused with meanings and that disagreements over different meaning interpretations can quickly escalate. Organisations can feel a need to pick sides in ideological debates over meaning. Some may even be willing to turn away customers over these as they pick sides.

Believe in something

Some organisations infuse ideological meaning into their brands very successfully. To illustrate, in 2018 Nike, the sportswear brand, launched an advertising campaign featuring Colin Kaepernick. 'Believe in something. Even if it means sacrificing everything' ran the text beside a picture of the former American football player. Immediately memes began popping up on the internet replacing Kaepernick with other public figures, or twisting the words of the message. If internet chatter is the gold standard of success in our digital culture, then Nike had succeeded in maximising its budget in this case.

The believe in something slogan cleverly played on Nike's longstanding positioning of its products as assisting consumers in becoming their best selves. Nike's customers emulate the pro athletes sponsored by the brand, even if just beating their own modest personal bests. Self-belief, assisted by the purchasing of stretchy fabric annotated with a little tick, is a central message of the brand. Yet in this case believe in something was referring to something beyond physical self-improvement.

Kaepernick became a political lightning rod in 2016, when he started to sit through, rather than stand for, the US national anthem at the start of games. A protest against racial injustice and systematic oppression in the United States, Kaepernick's stance rapidly gained massive attention in the nation's media and politics. Opting to kneel and take the knee during the national anthem caught on with other players. Praised by some for bringing attention to on-going racial tensions in the United States, for others, the protest showed a dangerous lack of respect.

That Nike would wade into such a fraught and politicised conversation around race is interesting. Traditionally, large brands have much to lose if they isolate sections of the public. Thus, they tend to avoid taking explicit ideological positions. General platitudes about things we can all agree on, such as the importance of being kind to our neighbours, are more typical. A company as mainstream as Nike adopting divisively meaningful advertising is therefore consequential.

With the benefit of hindsight, the believe in something campaign was highly successful. It has only become more culturally relevant over time. As the Black Lives Matter movement has progressed, and as racial inequality and structural racism in the United States and worldwide have become a bigger conversation, Nike's early involvement with this now seems forward thinking. The meaning behind believe in something as a slogan has connected with contemporary cultural themes and with consumers living through these.

The campaign works because it complements established themes already used by the Nike brand. Believe in something adds a political dimension to the longstanding Nike 'Believe' slogan, in that it engages with contemporary debate and asks people to interpret and add meaning themselves. In this campaign Nike links success on the field to not just physical effort (and great trainers) but also mental investment (and great trainers). Getting that gym body is no longer just about how many reps can be fit into a session, but what in your brain is driving you on to do this in the first place.

But don't believe in too little

Nike and Colin Kaepernick show that brands can successfully respond to the growing sense of belief in various causes that many people have. Nike is able to link its brand values of self-development through sport, with intellectual as well as physical strength. In doing so, the company has maintained its relevance for consumers who are being switched on to current affairs and are getting involved in intellectual as well as physical self-improvement.

Nevertheless, engaging with ideology is potentially hazardous for brands. Where people are switched on and committed to causes, they will not fall for pale attempts by businesses to get involved. Brands jumping on a bandwagon will be easily spotted and quickly dismissed. Marketing that invokes ideology has to do it with commitment.

Pepsi found this out with their 2017 'live for now' advert featuring Kendall Jenner. In this advert the reality TV personality is shown on a modelling shoot getting distracted by a peaceful protest movement occurring outside. Kendall then joins the protesters, who conveniently have plenty of cans of Pepsi on hand. The advert culminates with Kendall going up to a policeman monitoring the protest and giving him a Pepsi.

The almost immediate backlash to the advert saw people annoyed by the crass use of global protest movements, and in particular the Black Lives Matter marches occurring in many US cities at the time, to sell soda. The clumsy product placement, blunt stereotyping of protesters and starring role of a thin white model seemed to be a sanitised and whitewashed version of protest. Perhaps well intentioned, the advert drew ridicule. Pepsi was forced to apologise and pull the campaign.

Exploiting important issues for commercial purposes is not the way to garner public sympathy. If brands are to get involved, then they have to do so as genuinely as possible. This means commitment to researching, understanding and getting involved with supporting particular causes through significant actions. Lukewarm, cynical or tactless attempts to do so won't be tolerated by value-driven consumers.

Consumers have become more invested in ideological issues, and so are more cynical and critical regarding businesses attempts to associate with these. At the same time, consumers have become more knowledgeable thanks to new technology. Apps such as Progressive Shopper allow users to research which political parties different brands financially support. This means that partial or hypocritical values stances can be more easily identified and called out.

Or believe in too much

Where somebody believes in something, then sooner or later they are going to come across somebody who believes in something else. Consumers who are following one particular set of values may not gel with those who follow a different set. When they commit to ideological marketing, this polarisation leaves brands at risk of aligning not just with certain values and consumers, but against others. Such was discovered by Gillette.

Launched in January 2019 was Gillette's 'The best men can be' campaign. This was a play on the shaving brand's long running tagline 'The best a man can get'. Taking a strong value-driven stance, the campaign addressed toxic masculinity and its associations of bullying, sexism and sexual misconduct. It proposed that men need to hold each other accountable in addressing such behaviours. Gillette saw the campaign as encouraging the men of tomorrow to act and say the right thing.

'The best men can be' stance was an ambitious one for Gillette to take. It positioned the brand's values overtly in the highly charged ideological landscape of the contemporary United States and beyond. There was a strong negative backlash. 'The best men can be' advert became one of the most disliked videos on YouTube. Calls came for boycotts of the brand.

In setting out its stall, Gillette had apparently come on too strong. Many people did not agree with the issues being depicted. They did not share the political or social sentiment behind the campaign. Conservatives tend to be easily upset when challenged to be better. Even more moderate people seemed to shy away from the emphatic tone of the campaign.

Taking an ideological stance runs the risk of appealing to likeminded consumers, yet isolating others. To be committed to one cause may imply being opposed to another. In calling out toxic masculinity Gillette upset a lot of men who may be somewhat implicated. The ideals of the campaign were set high. Asking men to be better and do more, whilst certainly necessary, was quite demanding, particularly when associated with shopping for shaving foam. Asking too much of consumers can push them away.

Brands are increasingly being challenged to respond to current ideological debates and to set out their values. Often, it is no longer acceptable to be values neutral. Silence can leave open to accusations of not caring or of supporting a particular side. In order to take control therefore, brands stake out their ideological positions. Nonetheless, as found out by Gillette, doing so can open up fresh arguments.

Consumer case: vegan extremism

The increased importance of ideology to consumers, and the polarisation that can come with this, may be seen in the case of veganism. This is an ideology committed to very specific value-driven consumption and non-consumption. Fast-growing, veganism involves a diet and lifestyle that avoids all animal products. A surprisingly long list of items such as food, clothing, medicine and homewares are made with animal-derived ingredients. Vegans attempt to limit or eliminate their use of these. This asceticism comes from the belief that exploiting animals is wrong.

Three pillars uphold vegan ideology. First, a belief that an animal product free diet leads to better personal health. Second, that harvesting animals is cruel given that these have equal rights to life as humans. Third, that adopting a vegan diet will improve planetary sustainability. A sense of individual and collective belief thus drives the vegan movement and its associated lifestyle. This involves considerable effort in navigating consumption in line with vegan values.

The term 'vegan' was coined in 1944 by Donald Watson. He founded the Vegan Society in the United Kingdom and originally used the word to describe a non-dairy vegetarian diet. The term was later expanded as the doctrine that people should live without exploiting animals (Cross, 1951). Not all vegans interpret this viewpoint in the same way and there are variations in how it is applied by individuals in their day-to-day life and consumption. For example, whether it is morally acceptable to have pets is an issue debated amongst vegans. Thus, veganism is an established ideology with a strong but varied set of views, values and conversations around minimising human use of animals.

Recently, veganism has expanded in terms of visibility and popularity. The growth in vegan products has been significant. Meat-free food sales went up 40% between 2014 and 2019 in the United Kingdom for instance (Mintel, 2020). Spotting the commercial opportunity, major food chains, such as Burger King, have launched vegan options in response to rising experimentation with meat-free alternatives. This growing interest in veganism is especially marked amongst younger generations, with these more likely to identify as mostly vegan or vegetarian. In the United States recent data showed that some 12% of adults aged 18 to 49 are at least mostly vegan or vegetarian, compared with 5% among those aged 50 and older (Pew Research Centre, 2016). Meanwhile, citing statistics that a quarter of generation Y in the United States are vegetarian or vegan, *The Economist* labelled 2019 the year of the vegan (Parker, 2019).

The rapid growth of the vegan movement is interesting because of the commercial opportunities this presents. Plenty of brands have responded rapidly and to their advantage. To illustrate, Greggs, a British high street bakery chain known for its value pastries, gained plenty of media attention when it launched a vegan sausage roll in early 2019. The popularity of the new product was said to be behind sales and profits increases that year. More than this, veganism gives an insight into how contemporary consumers are willing to engage with ideological issues, and to make changes to their consumer routines as a result. This can be to quite an extreme extent.

Extremism is where partial personal interest and action become all-involving and public passion. The word extreme is applied in such cases because few people get caught up in causes and beliefs to such an extent. Generally speaking, people's interest in specific issues is partial, habitual and often passes. Ideology is somewhat important to most contemporary consumers, but other considerations such as price or convenience are considered essential as well. However, for some consumers ideology takes on greater significance. A strong moral stance is prioritised when making consumption or non-consumption decisions. Vegan extremism may be referred to as such, because vegan's firm beliefs and willingness to commit to these go far beyond the typical mainstream.

Convenient versus committed

For marketing managers, engaging with ideology in consumption is challenging for a number of reasons. There are often sensitivities, conflicts and disagreements over values and beliefs, which need negotiating. Illustrating, Fuentes and Fuentes (2017) show the tension for vegan food brands. On the one hand, they need to be seen as an animal product alternative in a more radical sense, in order to appeal to more serious vegans. These are brands that aim to disrupt the system and set out a radical values position to rally behind. At the same time, if animal product free brands want to appeal to non-vegans looking to try, they must be seen as convenient products that don't require significant changes in habits. These are brands that are friendly and sell as easy to fit into existing routines. Constructing a brand image that can accommodate both radical and milder opinions is a challenge. A good way of doing this can be to focus on a neutral activity that everyone can get behind. Vegan brands often highlight their health credentials. Positioned as low fat, high protein, and supporting gym body goals, is a way of sidestepping ideological issues altogether.

Case questions

1 What are the utilitarian, emotional, social and ideological values of vegan consumers?
   Outline these and evaluate the respective importance placed on each. Consider how this may influence their consumer perceptions and priorities.
2 How do meat-free brands appeal to extreme and less extreme consumers simultaneously?
   Consider the challenge of accommodating more radical and mainstream consumers. Look for examples of brands that succeed or fail in this balancing act.

Ideological marketing: doing it well

Faced with passionate and polarised consumers, marketers are challenged to tread carefully. They have to navigate ideological discussions with care, so as to avoid alienating customers or provoking backlash. Yet this does not mean ignoring current issues or not having a values stance. Indeed, failure to do so can leave open to criticism of inaction or being uncaring. Having a committed, genuine and well researched ideological position can reward brands with deeper and more meaningful customer connections.

The negative experiences of Pepsi and Gillette demonstrate that ideological marketing can go badly in various ways. Figuring out how brands such as these go wrong, and where others like Nike go right, is difficult. Marketing successes and marketing failures are unpredictable and contextual. Humans are emotional and behave in ways that can be surprising. Circumstances change, as businesses, people and ideological discussions evolve over time.

Nevertheless, some broad rules of thumb can be taken from analysing the hits and misses of various brands when engaging in ideological debates. Analysing past examples of successful and unsuccessful marketing helps to provide good practice guidelines. Briefly speaking, there might be summarised as three rules of thumb to follow when considering ideological marketing. Either by accident or design Nike seems to have fulfilled these, while Pepsi and Gillette did not.

1. *Ideological commit.* If a cause is to be engaged with, then this must be done thoroughly. Proper involvement with a cause is necessary. This means investing resources in support. Brands such as Pepsi, which only casually link themselves to certain issues, are unlikely to be convincing.
2. *Ideological fit.* Values and causes engaged with should fit with a brand. Nike's believe in something campaign works because it overlaps with the sportswear firm's longstanding brand associations of achieving personal best. Gillette's 'the best men can be' is less successful, because such a progressive stance is surprising coming from a previously apolitical brand, creating dissonance. Clear link needs to be between a brand's heritage and a particular moral issue.
3. *Ideological know it.* Ideological conversations are complicated and on-going. They take time to engage with and get a feel for. Know it means taking the time to research the themes and nuances of an issue, in order that these might be navigated with due care. Likewise, getting to know consumers and their ideological stances. Such understanding minimises the risks of misinterpretations or misunderstandings, as with Pepsi's poorly thought through advert.

Ideological marketing: doing it at all

It is not enough to just do ideological marketing well. Equally important is to consider whether it is worth doing at all. Before embarking on a values-laden marketing strategy, it is important to evaluate whether ideological issues are relevant to a particular product category or its consumers. There are reasons to avoid ideology in marketing altogether. Engaging with causes, values and beliefs in marketing always holds risks of clashes between different viewpoints. As issues can evolve rapidly, keeping up to date with them requires resources.

Consequently, where consumers are not actively concerned about issues, or where product categories are not exposed to current debates, it is reasonable to leave ideology alone. Opticians for example almost never make ideological claims about their products or associate their brands with particular causes. This is because consumers in this specific area are not typically looking for ideological self-expression through their spectacles purchases.

Nor are there contentious debates around eye care currently occurring. In such situations, bringing up ideological issues that have low awareness amongst consumers, or limited resonance with products, may be confusing and counterproductive.

However, there are plentiful opportunities around ideology that explain why marketers may wish to take an issues stance, despite the dangers and investments associated with this. Consumers that are more ideologically interested can be a source of competitive advantage. This is because products or brands sharing and supporting those same causes may be evaluated more positively. Consumers who support a particular cause are more likely to associate with a brand which does likewise.

Furthermore, brands may wish to engage with ideological marketing even where a particular product category is currently little implicated in ethical debates. This is because doing so may be a means of differentiation from competitors. If a brand is the first in a product category to assert an ideological stance, this might catch the attention of customers and be a means of standing out. Being the first optician to stand up for a certain cause may help to distinguish in the eyes of consumers.

An important role of marketing can be managing the boundary between organisations and ideology. A simple temperature and exposure check can assist in this process (Figure 2.1). This involves regularly checking consumers to gauge how fired up about an issue they currently are. Similarly, checking how exposed brands are to certain issues. By doing this regularly, brands can adjust. If the temperature begins to rise as ideological conversations develop, then a brand can respond in a timely manner.

To illustrate, a bottled water brand may have consumers who are moderately concerned about environmental issues. This may be an opportunity to build relationships by expressing similar values, for instance sponsorship of habitat regeneration around the water's geographic source. However, the product category of bottled water may be highly exposed to environmental criticisms. Associated with carbon emissions of production and transport, there is a high risk of bottled water becoming ideologically unacceptable for consumers, regardless of the standing of individual brands. To pre-empt this possible threat, initiatives, such as reducing packaging, should be taken early.

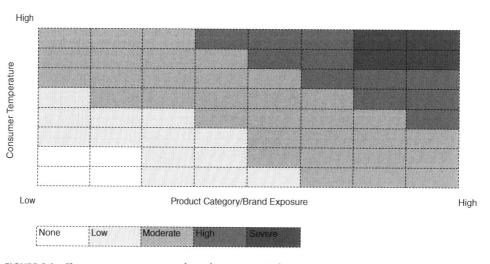

FIGURE 2.1 Consumer temperature-brand exposure index.

Ideological segmentation, targeting and positioning

Where it is relevant to a brand or product category, ideology can be a means of understanding consumers, defining markets and differentiating offerings. Segmentation, targeting and positioning (STP) is a framework used in marketing to profile consumers and divide markets. Doing this allows for a competitive position to be staked out. STP is an overlapping process, with the three stages complementing each other in analysing, deciding and executing marketing decision making.

- *Segmentation* is applied to both markets and consumers. Markets comprise products, services or experiences, and their associated brands, that make up a particular purchase category. Meanwhile, consumers are the different purchasers of products, services, experiences and their brands, in a particular market. Segmentation involves identifying and analysing these various markets and consumers in order to develop descriptive profiles.
- Breaking down markets and consumers into distinctive sub-categories that share similar traits is useful in that it develops understanding of nuances within these. *Targeting* is the process of using this understanding to identify the most attractive market and consumer segments. Various reasons may underpin evaluations of attractiveness. However, broadly speaking, marketers look to target their resources on areas of the market that have fewer competitors, or on consumer sub-groups who share similar values. Commercial success is more likely where a gap in the market can be identified and exploited.
- Having done this, *positioning* is the process of asserting a product, service or experience, and associated brand, in line with the market gap and consumer niche detected. This stage uses marketing tools to clearly position against other brands and in the mind of the consumer.

As ideology becomes increasingly important to consumers, then STP can be applied to values, causes and beliefs. STP in an ideological sense means reviewing markets and consumers in order to describe their beliefs, values and interpretations of meanings. Next, use this insight to identify potentially agreeable niche markets and consumers who may share likeminded ideological stances. Finally, align ideology with and alert these niches to a sense of shared values and common causes.

Where checks suggest that consumers' ideological temperature or brand exposure is high, then such a process is likely to be valuable. STP is a useful exercise for structuring analysis of competitors and consumers. Thinking about this in ideological terms helps to think strategically about consumer reconstruction.

Ideological perceptual mapping

Perceptual maps are a series of techniques for visually representing the STP process. They are used to depict consumer perceptions of brands and where they are placed within a market. The most common variables used are price and quality. Mapping consumer perceptions against these gives an idea of what consumers consider to be value, mainstream and luxury brands within a given market.

32 Ideological consumer engagement

However, alternative variables are selected to best represent a market. Where ideological considerations are important, then consumer perceptions can be mapped using appropriate variables. These might be inclusivity-exclusivity and equality-inequality, referring to breadth and accessibility of membership, respectively.

Ideology, in the sense of being concerned with values, causes, ethics and beliefs, is informed by these variables. Different viewpoints on issues or moral orientations might be captured by perceptions of inclusivity and equality. For example, whether a rule should be respected might depend on perceptions of how equal this is in the sense of being fair and appropriate. Likewise, respect may depend on whether a rule is inclusive of and applies to everyone, always, or just some people some of the time.

From these variables it may be possible to draw up a simple map for depicting consumers' ideological perceptions of brands within a market. Hereby, the equal-unequal continuum relates to the similarity or hierarchy of membership. Meanwhile, the inclusive-exclusive continuum refers to the breadth or narrowness of focus on such things as beliefs, values or issues, and of who these apply to. Figure 2.2 illustrates such an ideological perceptual map.

Using the ideological perceptual map it is possible to represent different types of brands that occupy alternative ideological positions according to the perceptions of consumers. These may be summarised as follows:

- *Apathetic brands* are those which have no or very little interest in ideological discussions. They are largely unaware of or put off by such conversations.

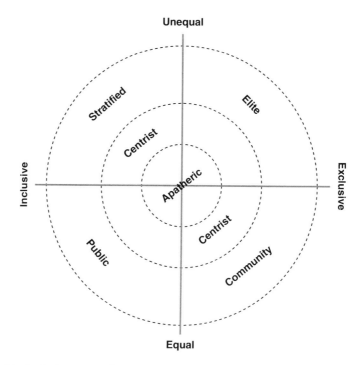

FIGURE 2.2 Ideological perceptual map.

- *Centrist brands* are those perceived to be ideologically moderate. They may orientate towards a certain cause or espouse particular values. However, their equal-unequal, inclusive-exclusive leanings are relatively gentle.
- *Public brands* are those that have perceptions as being strongly equal and inclusive. These brands are open to all and treat everybody the same.
- *Community brands* are equal in the sense of all members being of the same value. However, they are also exclusive in the sense that not everybody can necessarily become a member of the community. Particular attributes may be needed to join.
- *Stratified brands* are those which are inclusive in terms of membership, but which have a strong hierarchy within that membership. This hierarchy denotes that members are not all equal, with some holding more power and status than others.
- *Elite brands* are perceived as being exclusive in that they are available only to a few. They are also unequal in that they are positioned as superior to others.

From such a perceptual exercise it may be possible to better judge the ideological market positioning of a brand relative to its market competitors and consumers, and therefore to identify potential gaps in the marketplace. For example, if there is a glut of elite brands available, then a more competitive position might be to move in a more community-orientated direction. Doing so might maintain the exclusive focus of a brand, in terms of being closely identified with a narrow set of ideological issues and likeminded consumers. At the same time, reducing a sense of hierarchy amongst consumers might make for a more communal brand experience.

Commercial case: BrewDog's revolutionary rise

Beer is a product category whose consumers can hold strong and often divided views. In the United Kingdom, beer drinkers may have strong allegiances to particular brands and types of beer. A traditional split has been between mainstream beer drinkers and those who identify with 'real ale'. The former tends to consume mass produced beer made by large global businesses without really thinking much about it. The latter set themselves apart by their strong beliefs in what makes good beer. These drinkers are willing to invest energy and resources into finding brands that complement their values. Real ale fans typically identify with smaller brewers, making beer to more traditional standards.

Real ale fans are not the only consumers to feel strongly about their beer. The 'craft ale' movement is a similar beer following. Craft ale drinkers also seek out carefully made rather than mass produced products. However, there are significant differences between real and craft ale. The latter is creative rather than conservative. Craft ale is more to do with experimenting when making beer. New inspirations and fusions are popular, drawing upon techniques and ingredients sourced from other parts of the world or even different industries.

BrewDog is one of the most successful craft beer producers. Founded in 2007 by James Watt and Martin Dickie, the UK-based business was inspired by craft brewers of the United States, and their small, niche and highly creative approach to brewing (Henley, 2016). Unusual and varied products have characterised BrewDog from the outset. This has included super high alcohol premium beers, and unusual flavours with ingredients like chili or chocolate. The company has also produced unfamiliar combinations such as of lager and bitter. This experimental approach to the craft of beer in the United Kingdom was different, disruptive and highly successful. Within a year of starting up, BrewDog was winning industry awards and got their first major contract to supply at national supermarket giant Tesco.

Since starting up, the business has been one of the fastest-growing food and drinks producers and bar operators in Britain. Less than a decade after beginning, BrewDog had grown from two employees to 580, opened 30-odd highly successful bars across the United Kingdom, as well as 15 more around the world, and started exporting to more than 50 countries (Henley, 2016). The business was valued at over £1 billion in 2017. Competitors have in many cases been inspired by and emulated the experimental approach of the brewer. For a company which aimed to bring about a craft beer revolution, it seems to have succeeded.

BrewDog's success owes much to the brand's provocative marketing. Early on, limited edition premium beer was put inside stuffed animals in a publicity stunt that generated significant attention, as well as agitation from animal rights activists. The brand continued to build its profile through similar tactics. These included parachuting stuffed cats over the City of London as a protest against banking industry 'fat cats', and to promote their crowd funded rather than stock market business model. Meanwhile, products launched included Putin branded beer mocking Russian anti-LGBT legislation. Such actions called attention to the brand, established its iconoclastic values and divided observers into those who supported BrewDog's showmanship or were put off by it.

By using aggressive and provocative marketing, BrewDog has divided consumers, cleverly playing off those who identify with the brand's values from those who do not. Despite sharing enthusiasm for beer which is brewed carefully and unconventionally, real ale drinkers tend to be antipathetic towards BrewDog at best. Many of them see the company as embodying style over substance. Yet this is the point. BrewDog has taken an existing ideological conversation around beer, and added its own distinctive voice to the mix. It has isolated some, but also won many followers in the process.

Case questions

1. Why is taking a strong ideological position something many start-up brands do?
   Consider the ways ideology can be used to set out a niche position and increase awareness.
2. What is the ideological vision of a more mainstream beer brand such as Fosters?
   Think about the values, causes and beliefs espoused by alternative beer brands and why these might be the case.
3. How would you segment the beer market ideologically?
   Create a positioning map that outlines beer brands in your domestic market. Think about modifying ideological axes to best describe and segment this market.

Chapter summary

Increasing ideology of consumers is unavoidable, even if marketers might sometimes hope that it could be. Consumers are becoming more concerned with ideological value: the causes they support and beliefs they espouse when making purchases. Evidence of this comes from the rise of veganism. This demonstrates that even quite extreme consumption practices are becoming mainstream. Consequently, marketers need to engage proactively with ideology if they are to rise to associated challenges and seize possible opportunities. The experiences of brands such as Nike, Pepsi and Gillette demonstrate that any attempt at ideological marketing needs to be committed, fit with the brand and thoroughly researched. BrewDog and the C. J. Walker Manufacturing Company demonstrate contemporary and historical examples of best practice. Nonetheless, as the following chapter explores, not all consumers or all of the time are engaging with their surroundings. Indeed, the opposite trend, for pulling back from these, may be observed.

References

Cross, L. (1951). Veganism defined. *The Vegetarian World Forum*, 1(5), 6–7.

Fuentes, C., & Fuentes, M. (2017). Making a market for alternatives: Marketing devices and the qualification of a vegan milk substitute. *Journal of Marketing Management*, 33(7–8), 529–555.

Henley, J. (2016). The aggressive, outrageous, infuriating (and ingenious) rise of BrewDog. *The Guardian*. Available at: https://www.theguardian.com/lifeandstyle/2016/mar/24/the-aggressive-outrageous-infuriating-and-ingenious-rise-of-brewdog (accessed 17/02/20).

Mintel. (2020). *Plant-based push: UK sales of meat-free foods shoot up 40% between 2015–2019*. Retrieved from https://www.mintel.com/press-centre/food-and-drink/plant-based-push-uk-sales-of-meat-free-foods-shoot-up-40-between-2014-19 (accessed 17/02/20).

Parker, J. (2019). The year of the vegan. Where millennials lead, businesses and governments will follow. *The Economist*. Available at: https://worldin2019.economist.com/theyearofthevegan (accessed 17/02/20).

Pew Research Centre. (2016). *The new food fights: U.S. public divides over food science*. Available at: https://www.pewresearch.org/internet/wp-content/uploads/sites/9/2016/11/PS_2016.12.001_Food-Science_FINAL.pdf (accessed 17/02/20).

Watson, D. (1944). Concerning ourselves. *The Vegan News*, 1(3), 1–4.

3
REASSURANCE

Consumer nostalgia and never growing up – Otaku, Pokémon, Lego and Hikikomori

Reassurance: consumption in the age of anxiety

Reassurance is a theme around consumers experiencing uncertainty and their responses to this. Much of the time contemporary consumers are ambitious and outgoing. They may be frequently prepared to challenge values they do not agree with and also to get more involved in making changes they wish to see. However, such reconstruction can be tiring. Some consumers may not have the energy or resources to confront uncertainty and its consequences. An alternative response is to retreat from uncertainty into reassuring distractions and comforts.

Contemporary consumers are confronted with various anxiety driving issues such as ideological divides. Outlining how times of uncertainty cause anxiety, the academic Jane Parish (2000) coined the term 'age of anxiety'. Parish describes how people react by looking for comforting answers in such things as conspiracy theories. The anxieties, underlying uncertainties and reactions noted by Parish appear as relevant today as they were 20 years earlier. Day-to-day existence and longer term goals can be affected by anxiety. This can permeate consumer routines and aspirations, influencing their attitudes, behaviours and lifestyles.

Seeking distraction from anxiety, consumers may retreat into specific interests shared with likeminded others. Fandoms may provide a comforting sense of focus on a particular passion. Indulging in nostalgic consumption that looks back to a supposedly simpler past can also reassure. Merchandise brands that sell child and teen items to adults demonstrate how the past can be continually relived through consumption.

As such, some consumers, some of the time, are looking to withdraw into more specific interests and familiar experiences. The reassurance of close focus and nostalgic remembering may be valuable to those consumers suffering from feelings of anxiety. A sense of much needed stability can come from pursuing these types of focused or backward looking interests.

Nevertheless, too much withdrawal may be problematic in that potentially rewarding new interests and wider experiences may be missed out on. Likewise, the personal and

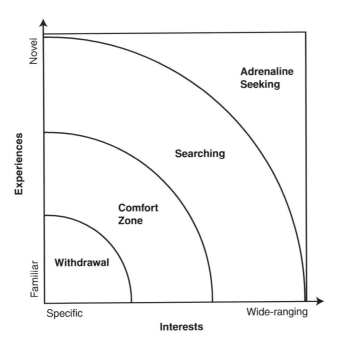

FIGURE 3.1 Degrees of consumer reassurance.

collective growth and positive change can come from confronting issues. Rather than engaging with the world more broadly, reassurance suggests shutting it out. The relevance, role and responsibility of marketing in this context are interesting to reflect upon.

As summarised in Figure 3.1, consumption can facilitate various degrees of consumer reassurance. These may include relatively extreme withdrawal into obsessively niche and repetitive consumption. Otaku fandoms discussed in this chapter may represent this category. Less extreme are more comfort-orientated purchases, as broader geek consumers may tend towards. Consumption can also facilitate more outgoing tendencies. Search can be for unfamiliar and varied types of products, services and experiences, even to particularly adventurously challenging or exciting purchases that push far out of comfort zones.

Extended adolescence

Reassurance is a broad consumer issue. However, it relates especially to the tendency of individuals within generation Y to experience an extended adolescence. (The jury is still out on whether generation Z behave similarly in this respect.) This involves such things as continuing to live with parents, working temporary jobs and pursuing travel over extended periods. Rather than settling down and acting like a grownup, in the established cultural sense, Y's adolescent traits can be seen in their attitudes, behaviours, lifestyles and identities. Generation Y continues well into their twenties and thirties thinking of themselves, pursuing interests and living in much the same way as they did a decade ago.

Harking back to the descriptions of this generational cohort as contradictory, this style of living seems to arise from a mixture of self-confidence and self-doubt. On the one hand, generation Y appears to enjoy their unencumbered lifestyles. They spend money on the stuff they like such as hobbies and associated merchandise. Spoilt for consumer choice meanwhile, generation Y might prefer to indulge living in the here and now, rather than trying to save for mortgages and pensions long into an uncertain future.

Y consumers are also self-confident and open minded in their temperament. Able to resist the pressure of previous generations to follow strict career, saving and spending patterns, instead, this cohort pursue more independent and personally rewarding styles of living. This means that they feel better able to indulge their interests and to stick with what they enjoy doing, whether this seems especially grown up or not. The importance of work and having children is questioned by millennials, who often decide to prioritise self-development and self-pleasure instead. This may see more emphasis on things like pursuit of further education or continuing to play video games, over career advancement or romantic settling down.

Yet, on the other hand, members of generation Y may have no alternative to living adolescent lifestyles, whether they want to or not. With reliable work and affordable housing difficult to come by, it takes generation Y a lot more effort to accomplish the same signs of adulthood as previous generations. Young people may feel frustrated that they are not able to measure up to how their parents and grandparents were at a similar age. With their strong sense of values, they may be exhausted by pushing for ideological changes that are slow to arrive. Somewhat mollycoddled and gentle, they can struggle to succeed in ruthless education and employment landscapes.

Furthermore, the effort it takes to be an adult can seem off putting. The opportunities to be an adult may be hard to come by. Turning away from these challenges, or making lack of opportunity seem like a choice rather than an imposition, the alternative is to avoid adulthood altogether. Being adolescent may have its disadvantages, for example a lack of financial security or personal independence. However, it has advantages of fewer obligations and more time for self-indulgence. By choice or not, generation Y seems to be retreating from growing up. Instead they are seeking reassurance through continuing with adolescent interests and lifestyles long-term.

This phenomenon is not restricted to generation Y. Reassurance has significant implications for consumption and marketers across all age groups and international locations. Where consumer lifestyles are changing to reflect an extended or perhaps even permanent adolescence, then this raises opportunities and challenges for the appropriateness of goods and services. Big one-off purchases linked with growing up, such as a car, may be falling from favour. More frequent self-indulgent consumption, such as of daily treats or pursuing niche hobbies, may be the new normal. Rather than consumption as part of aspirational reaching for rites of passage therefore, this is consumption as comforting distraction from these rites of passage, which are either not wanted, not relevant or not possible, for many consumers today.

Consumer case study: Otaku

Otaku is a Japanese term used to describe someone who has obsessive interests that they pursue. This obsession is supposedly to the detriment of their social skills, although this latter aspect may now be seen as somewhat unfair. Although otaku may be awkward with established social norms, many have excellent social skills and strong friendship networks based around their shared interests. These interests are typically linked to computers and computer games, manga comic books and anime.

Essayist Akio Nakamori used and defined the word otaku in 1983. Recounting his visit to a comic convention he described the eccentricities of the crowd attending. "They're like those kids — every class has one — who never got enough exercise, who spent recess holed up in the classroom, lurking in the shadows obsessing over a shogi board or whatever." Using often derogatory language, reflecting the initially negative attitudes towards the otaku that have softened somewhat over time, Nakamori summarises a large but until this point mostly ignored group of people.

According to Nakamori, otaku were comprised of those teenagers unnoticed or bullied at school. They were the poor kids from families without a well-respected surname, those who were less academically or physically gifted. Associated with being socially awkward and introverted, otaku are a product of Japan's at times rigid and hierarchical social structures. Nakamori's description captures the general disdain for people who fall outside of conventions of beauty and success, even from a very young age. With poor social standing, looked down upon by mainstream society, otaku protect themselves by withdrawing into private spaces.

Found in all cultures, in some ways social norms and expectations are especially burdensome in Japan. Here, family and group reputation is tied to looking good, doing well and acting as expected. Even in contemporary Japan for example, burdensome gender norms mean that women are expected to dress and act a certain way at home, whilst at work and when out in public. Of course, in all cultures women face heightened such expectations, but Japanese nuances present their own idiosyncratic set.

Compounding this, in 1990 Japan entered an economic recession. What is now termed the 'lost decade' saw a reduction in employment opportunities for the young. Once prestigious company jobs working for one of Japan's major conglomerates, which were always highly competitive to obtain, became even harder to find. The social pressure to gain a good job and make families proud increased further. So too did the disappointment heaped on those unable to get such work. Feelings of uncertainty, anxiety and failure might likely increase in such a situation.

The temptation to pull back from all of this pressure is understandable. Under stress to conform culturally or compete economically, some may choose to withdraw into their own worlds. Otaku culture has gradually become more prominent and widespread as increasing numbers of Japanese have pulled back from strict social mores and difficult economic situations. Otaku has become the de facto term in Japan for individuals who pursue their hobbies with a single-minded passion bordering on obsession. Such obsessive focus allows otaku to sidestep the strict conventions and economic competitiveness of Japanese society. Otaku are able to develop their own self-contained individual and social identity quite apart from their difficult surroundings.

Shūkatsu

'Shūkatsu' roughly translates as job hunting activity, and refers to the year-long process Japanese final year students go through as they try to secure a job prior to graduation. Shūkatsu, a system devised in the 1950s by Japan's business lobby, is the traditional recruiting practice across Japan. The shūkatsu season is vital for students, whose social status can be elevated by the outcome of their job hunt. However, as reported by Shibata (2019), the system is changing. As the number of graduates' declines, businesses are recruiting promising employees without waiting for a shūkatsu period. It is reported that young graduates often have to turn down multiple job offers from businesses fighting to find fresh employees (Economist, 2020). In addition, Japanese young people are increasingly looking for alternative careers that are more personally meaningful. Japanese culture may in some ways be quite rigid, but it is subject to change like any other. As elsewhere, young people are often amongst the protagonists most involved in transformation.

Otaku going global

The otaku phenomenon has spread far beyond Japan. Japanese experiences of economic stagnation, burden of expectation on young people and restrictive social norms are significant. They are however not unique to this part of the world. Globally, many are similarly affected by circumstances that are uncertain, stressful, limiting and anxiety inducing. Climate change for example is an unfolding crisis that affects all of us everywhere.

Sociocultural, economic and environmental anxieties are widespread in the contemporary world. In many cases global youth is engaged with trying to bring about change. Engaging with ideology and more involved consumption are evidence of an outgoing cohort who seek to make a difference to and leave their mark on making the world a better place in their image.

In such ways, consumers, particularly young ones, are demanding brands align with their outlooks and expectations. 'Cancel culture' for instance refers to a willingness to cut out those brands which are not agreed with. Noisy demonstrations and campaigns assert viewpoints and try to bring about change. Engaged with ideology and enthusiastic to join debates, millennials are often confrontational consumers.

Concurrently, signs are of generations Y and Z withdrawing from such confrontations. Clashes are fatiguing. Those with rival ideologies push back. Change is slow and setbacks along the way frustrating. Pulling back from fights or because of disappointments is inviting. Cancel culture might be applicable to millennials internally as well as externally.

As pioneered by the otaku in 1980s Japan, withdrawing from difficult macro surroundings into more tightly controlled micro ones can be an appealing prospect. Such phenomena as the huge growth of digital fandoms demonstrate that many consumers are indeed tending to focus on specific obsessions. In such niche focus and grouping with likeminded others, they are becoming akin to otaku.

With more people seemingly withdrawing into their interests, challenge is for marketers to respond. Introverted consumers have different needs to extrovert ones. Rather than getting out in the world and trying the latest thing or buying something new, following familiar patterns and focused interests becomes more important. The rise of geek culture gives an insight into what this might look like.

What type of otaku are you?

Nakamori asked readers at the end of his essay 'what type of otaku are you'? This question reminds that we all have interests, and that we all can use these for reassurance. Otaku tendencies and interests can be observed amongst consumers worldwide. The expansion of online fandoms, communities that come together around a particular shared passion, reveals how otaku culture has influenced the overall cultural mainstream. Geek cultures meanwhile, often draw inspiration from their Japanese counterparts in relation to their similar interests in gaming and comics. Perhaps more broadly, consumers in general are coming to realise that they often do not fit in with conventional norms or expectations. This sense of being slightly outside of the norm, looking for identity and belonging, is something that motivates many contemporary consumers overall.

The geek dollar

Otaku remain relatively unknown outside of Japan. However, geek cultures, often much inspired by Japanese otaku references, are well established worldwide. Broadly involving enthusiasm for specific cultural references, particularly those around computer games and comic books, geek culture displays an obsession with the details of these. This phenomenon was initiated in North America by generation X, who grew up with access to and consuming Marvel or DC comics, Star Wars and Spielberg films, Nintendo and Atari games.

Over the past decade, geek culture has become increasingly mainstream. Television shows such as Big Bang Theory have made geek references accessible and appealing to wider audiences. Moreover, geek qualities are increasingly appraised positively. Old established geek stereotypes are of an extended adolescence. This includes an introverted lifestyle of living with parents, playing with media and tech, eating take out and hanging with like-minded friends. These traits have gone from being seen derogatorily to being normal and even attractive lifestyle choices.

New products and services have made it easier to pursue such inward focused lifestyles. Streaming allows for a surfeit of games, films and television shows to be watched anytime for example. At the same time, it has become easier to indulge hobbies by streamlining other activities. Food delivery services for instance make already fast food even faster, leaving with more time to box set binge. Finally, connecting with likeminded others through new technology increases opportunities to share specific interests. Where Nakamori presciently saw that all Japanese were to some extent otaku, so more broadly all millennials are geeks.

With geek cultural events, such as the famous San Diego Comic Con, now attracting hundreds of thousands of attendees during their running, the size of geek culture and the commercial scale of their combined spending power cannot be ignored. The resulting pursuit of the 'geek dollar' is much like that for 'pink pound'. This trended in the 1990s, when marketers realised that there are significant numbers of LGBTQ people in the world. Moreover, LGBTQ people had been largely ignored by the mainstream up to then, because of negative prevailing attitudes towards them. Opportunity was therefore ripe to connect with an otherwise neglected consumer demographic. Pioneering brands such as Absolut Vodka linked with gay customers. These built enduring relationships with members of a community that appreciated being belatedly recognised.

This is now similarly the case for mainstream brands when dealing with geeks. These have also often been ignored by mainstream marketing, hence leaving opportunities for brands to establish relationships with an underappreciated niche. Understanding and linking with geeks can thus bring about success. Primark for example, the Irish clothing retailer, has stocked gaming-related T-shirts for a number of years, steadily increasing the number of geek enthusiasts in their stores. This move has tempted gaming enthusiasts into a shop they might otherwise have overlooked. Meanwhile, non-gamers can still enjoy well-known references such as Pac Man on their clothing.

Primark has been clever because geeks have often had a limited interest in traditional shopping. Malls or high streets tend not to reach out to this group in the past. They might even have made them feel unwelcome by carrying traditional representations of 'cool' teenage archetypes. The prep boys and sorority girls invoked by Hollister for instance would likely pick on the nerds. Hence, such consumers have gone to specialist retailers to purchase relevant goods and services. As with other subcultures, geek culture has a rich tradition of independent producers that have arisen to meet the specific demands of their community and to create welcoming community spaces where there otherwise aren't any. Brands that reach out to geeks may benefit from both connecting with an undervalued consumer demographic, and tapping into the rich cultural resources built up by that group over time.

> **Star Wars' sexless universe**
> A mainstay of geek culture, the Star Wars film franchise is an ongoing commercial phenomenon. Since the first film in 1977, an array of sequels, prequels and spin offs have kept a merchandising empire afloat. The devotion of the franchise's most ardent followers is a force to be reckoned with. The success of Star Wars is owed to many things. However, an important feature of the franchise is that it is largely devoid of sexuality. Leia and Solo's relationship is the only romantic one properly defined, and even this remains chaste save a few glances and brief mouth-closed kisses. This lack of sex may be reassuring for consumer cohorts who appear to not be especially interested in seeing. Research has suggested that gen Y and Z in the USA are having less sex and are likely to remain sexually inactive for longer than older generations (Twenge, Sherman & Wells, 2017). Such ambivalence may seem surprising given the relaxed attitudes towards sex and sexuality of millennials. Yet, it may be that these liberal stances undermine the importance of sex. The philosopher Michel Foucault argued that it is the denial and restriction of sex that leads to unhealthy and hypocritical obsession with it. Once sex is permitted more openly then it loses its taboo power.

Commercial case: Pokémon don't go

The on-going cultural appeal of Star Wars and similar geek brands is interesting in that these give insight into fans' attitudes, behaviours and lifestyles. Lists of the world's most successful media franchises highlight the consumer empires that can be built on the back of dedicated fandoms. Pokémon, Hello Kitty, Winnie the Pooh, Mickey Mouse and Star Wars are estimated to be the five most valuable franchises of all time. Manga comics, led by Anpanman, videogame series such as Mario and the Marvel and Harry Potter print and film franchises are other multibillion-dollar juggernauts. All of these brands owe at least passing connection to otaku and geek followings. Indeed, some are almost unknown outside of dedicated circles despite having revenue profiles the size of major stock-market listed enterprises.

One of the most popular within and without geek culture is the merchandising behemoth Pokémon, created by video game designers Satoshi Tajiri and Ken Sugimori. Launched in 1996 on the original Nintendo Game Boy, Pokémon rapidly became a global phenomenon. The original and its sequels have become one of bestselling video game franchises ever. Associated mobile games, cartoons, films, music, trading cards, comics and toys have placed Pokémon amongst the world's most successful merchandise lines. The concept continues to pull in worldwide revenues from new and long-term loyal consumers. Indeed, over 20 years since its debut, Pokémon games remain major releases. The cartoon series continues to be made after 1,000 episodes and counting.

The premise of Pokémon is simple. Players collect cute cartoon monsters. Every so often a new generation of these is released, keeping an open-ended quest. Whether in a game world, wandering around with a mobile on GPS or gathering individual cards, the collecting is a simplistic but addictive activity. On top of this, players can battle their pocket monsters against each other. Pokémon can be upgraded, evolved or trained. There is very little depth to the concept. It is cheerfully superficial. Children can quickly pick up the few rules and actions that underpin.

The appeal of the Pokémon franchise is arguably its insubstantial and repetitive nature. Its protagonists are cute but vacuous. There is limited depth to supporting ideology. As pointed out by Bainbridge (2014), even Pokémon promotes a particular ideology of conserving and consuming nature; ideology permeates everything! Values, beliefs and current affairs are mostly absent from the colourful franchise however. Meanwhile, there is almost zero character or story development. The sophistication, subversive humour, irony or subtly adult references associated with other cross-generational children's franchises, such as the Simpsons, do not appear.

It might be expected therefore for followers to age out once they got to a certain maturity. Nevertheless, the longstanding commitment of many within the Pokémon fandom belies its simplicity. The franchise manages to continue to connect with players who were children when it first exploded onto the market. Now adults, they remain invested in Pokémon, still caring about the brand, collecting the merchandise and involved in the parallel universe where every so often more cutesy creatures are released. Spending time observing passers-by in any medium to large city centre, those wearing Pokémon branded items quickly rack up. Players of Pokémon Go, a GPS location-based freemium mobile phone game, are a frequent sight even years after launch.

The persistence of playing Pokémon into adulthood is an interesting insight into the mind-set of generation Y. This is a cohort comfortably holding on to childhood references and continuing with associated activities. To some extent these references may get updated in line with adult freedoms. Pokémon tattoos are popular amongst the fandom for example. Yet, staying so engaged physically, emotionally and intellectually with a child-orientated theme is particularly prevalent amongst contemporary youth. It may be that the reassurance of a simplistic, repetitive, familiar and nostalgic franchise is what a generation that came of age during an age of anxiety is looking for. Likewise, it may be that cohorts who have been unable to grow up thanks to socioeconomic restrictions have never felt the need or had the opportunity to step beyond their childhood frames of reference.

Never growing up
The world's major merchandise brands, including Pokémon, and their associated products, tend to be child or young adult orientated. Yet, these brands are wildly popular with adults. Millions of grown-ups like to wear Hello Kitty backpacks, visit Disneyland, and watch the latest Avengers movie. Many such consumers stay embedded within their preferred merchandise franchises year after year with little sign of leaving. Traditionally, consumers would be expected to grow out of certain habits and associated products. This no longer seems to be the case. The transition to adulthood, in the traditional sense of getting a stable career and then starting a family, seems to be weakened. More consumers are staying more childlike, for longer.

> **Case questions**
>
> 1 Why do some generation Y consumers connect with Pokémon?
>   Consider the attitudes, behaviours, lifestyles and identities of this cohort and how these may intersect with Pokémon's brand values.
> 2 How important is repetition and familiarity to consumers in general?
>   Think about the routines and aspirations of other groups of consumers in different consumer contexts. Discuss whether millennials consuming Pokémon are all that distinctive from other types of consumers.

Nostalgia: consumers gazing backward

It is interesting to consider why otaku themes have caught on. The otaku and associated geek cultures may be restricted to certain niche consumers who gravitate towards particular interests. However, similar themes of retreat into comforting small fantasy worlds can be seen in broader cultural trends such as the rise of nostalgia. Nostalgia refers to the looking back towards an idealised imagined past. This past is usually just out of reach, either before the lifetime of the person doing the remembering, or associated with their childhood. This distance allows space for romanticising of remembering. Nostalgia indulges memories that are selective and distorted.

Implying that things were better in the past than they are now, nostalgia is reassuring in that it transports away from present uncertainties. Walder (2014) outlines for example how nostalgia in post-apartheid South Africa may be symptomatic of a time of uncertainty. Despite the apartheid period being a divided and difficult one, it is remembered by some as having a sense of certainty that contrasts with the more disordered South African society that has followed. Looking back to a falsely comforting past downplays the difficult realities of the time and embellishes the positive aspects.

Nostalgia is in this sense of romantic remembering selective and dishonest. In early modern Europe nostalgia was classified as a form of mental illness (Sanchez & Brown, 1994). Nostalgia was associated with negatives including being unable to keep up with the times. To not participate in scientific and social advances was to miss out on the positives of a changing world. Staying trapped in the past meant to deny the reality and possibilities of one's own surroundings.

Generally speaking, taking a rose-tinted look back at the past has become more commonplace and acceptable. Nostalgic looking back can be comforting and a source of community sharing. Research suggests that nostalgia has the capacity to boost social bonds, provide reassurance and increase self-esteem (Zhou et al., 2012). It can also help to provide a sense of meaning in life (Routledge et al., 2011). Romanticising the past may have a helpful role to play therefore in providing needed individual and collective reassurance.

Leone (2015) suggests that nostalgia has become a major consumer trend, as evidenced by the hipster and vintage movements. Requiring a commitment to specific fashion, music and drinking, hipsters are united in these respects by an affinity for vintage styling and throwback consumption. Skinny jeans, Converse trainers, check shirts and wide brim hats are their rehabilitated garments of choice. A return to guitar rock and folk music typifies their soundtrack. They drink craft beer that eschews the corporate mainstream and takes a more traditionalist approach to sourcing and production. Hipsters have a taste for things that look to the past for inspiration.

Hipsters are interesting because they tend to be younger consumers. Highlighted here is the enthusiasm of generation Y for nostalgia, despite their relatively young age. Returning to childhood references is something members of this cohort do a lot. The enjoyment of looking back fits descriptions of generation Y as unable to grow up. For generation Y nostalgia seems to be a part of extended adolescence. Although they are now adults, filling their time with childhood references and activities means they do not have to feel as if they are.

Nostalgia and marketing

Nostalgia is a trend that has infiltrated marketing. Advertising for instance often features themes intended to trigger memories of the past. Tesco, the British supermarket giant, celebrated its 2019 centenary using CGI versions of television personalities from previous decades for example. More than merely reminding consumers of the past, such nostalgia is used to bring up the positive emotions associated with this. Nostalgia involves romanticising, whereby things are remembered more fondly than they actually were at the time. By triggering certain positive associations using nostalgic references, marketers hope to link their products to these.

The ways in which nostalgia is used in marketing vary. There are different sorts and uses of nostalgia. For instance, nostalgia may refer to gazing back to the recent past which individuals themselves lived through. Indeed, 1990s cultural references are already being mined for commercial purposes. Alternatively, nostalgia can stretch back to a more distant past not directly experienced. The 1920s remain popular because of its wealth of cultural references that continue to be enjoyable.

To better make sense of nostalgia within marketing, it is helpful to break up according to the different types that may be drawn upon. Figure 3.2 does this in a simple matrix format. Axes capture three dimensions of nostalgia:

- **Recent or distant** refers to the timescale of nostalgia references, which can range from a few years ago to antiquity. Recent nostalgia tends to be for a specific decade came of age in. Thus, boomers look fondly back to the 1960s and may consume associated brands and products when looking for a nostalgia hit. Distant nostalgia goes beyond an individual's lifetime, to more historical past that may be of interest. In Britain, gazing back to Second World War (WWII) has become something of a national pastime, despite most British people being born long after the war ended.
- **Experienced or overheard** refers to whether that being recalled was directly experienced or not. This relates to recent or distant, in that events beyond a person's lifetime can only have been overheard. This is through stories shared via word of mouth, cultural myths, museums, books and other records. Within a lifetime, events and issues may have been directly or indirectly experienced. People who went to raves in late 90s experienced this phenomenon currently being mined by fashion and television. Others might not have been to a rave personally, but been around as they took place.
- **Fake or folk** relates to whether remembering is of a real event or activity, or one that was made up. Fake nostalgia is for something that took place in a parallel universe such as that of a videogame fondly recalled. Fake nostalgia also involves things that never really happened, reimagined as a hypothetical. What if the Nazis won WWII is a

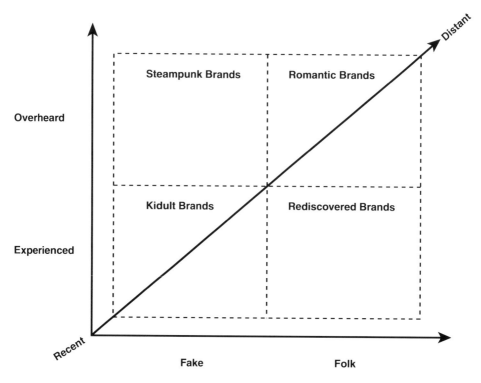

FIGURE 3.2 Nostalgia brand matrix.

popular fabricated nostalgia in films and television. Folk nostalgia is around things that happened in real life such as the infamous Woodstock festival that boomers often refer to. Although folk nostalgia derives from actual events, it can nonetheless be manipulated and elaborated through memory, and so is not necessarily any more real than fake.

Nostalgia brands

Using these three axes for determining types of nostalgia, it is then possible to plot and categorise different types of brands that relate to these (Figure 3.2). Nostalgic brands are those that look back to their and their consumers' pasts, recent or distinct, experienced or overheard, fake or folk. Different types of brands nevertheless place particular emphasis whilst doing so. These may be summarised variously:

- **Steampunk brands** mash up historical and contemporary references, as well as actual and imagined ones. Steampunk is a subculture that draws inspiration from the Victorian era, but which then reimagines in a contemporary setting. This mash-up of real and fake, distant and recent influences, allows for flexible remembering and creative reimagining of the past. Artisanal food and drink brands, such as Jack Daniels whiskey, often feature this type of nostalgia. These fuse recent and distant ideas about such things as manufacturing techniques, with their own specific brand identity. Emphasised is a rustic brand heritage that invokes a mixture of real and possibly imaginary elements.

- **Romantic brands** are those that tap into a distant past and then remember is a selective way that flatters the brand being associated. In 2014 the British supermarket chain Sainsbury ran a Christmas advert set in the WW1 trenches. The real events of 100 years previous, when soldiers on opposing sides briefly suspended hostilities to play a game of football, were reimagined to plug the grocer. The sanitised and sentimentalised advert romanticised history.
- **Kidult brands** are those that link with relatively recent childhood memories and experiences. Often it is brands that were used or lusted after as children, now hoping to maintain or reignite a connection, such as Nintendo or Disneyland. These types of brands bring back feelings associated with the often carefree and enjoyable time that is childhood. Using this to make consumers feel good, they hope to initiate an exchange relationship.
- **Rediscovered brands** are those brought back from the past into current popularity. Where they may have been somewhat forgotten about and slipped into irrelevance, then reminding consumers of their heritage can trigger positive emotions. Celebrating a brand's history can aid this. Fiat with its reborn 500 city car for example drew upon its product heritage to develop a product that resonates with many buyers too young to remember the original, but swayed by the retro references nonetheless.

Understanding that not all nostalgia is the same, and that different brands may use in different ways, helps to better represent the nuances of nostalgia marketing. Although reminding consumers of the past may be a way to kindle positive emotions and connections, the past is not remembered or evaluated in the same way across individuals or groups. For example, sixties pop music may bring back fond memories for boomers of their youth. Yet, this might simultaneously irritate silent generation elders who associate with rebellious children. Care therefore needs to be taken to understand the attitudes of target consumers towards the references being brought up.

Commercial case: Lego come back

Nostalgia is an important part of the Lego brand. Not only are the plastic bricks themselves a reminder of childhood, but they can be used to recreate further memories. A visit to a Lego store is to be bombarded with pop cultural references. The iconic little blocks have been made into everything from the Central Perk coffee shop in Friends to the Upside down portrayed in Stranger Things. References to pop culture past icons, such as the Mini Cooper, are complemented by current attention getters, a kit to build the Bugatti Chiron for instance.

In essence, Lego sells 3D jigsaw puzzles. More open-ended boxes of bricks that can be put together spontaneously now occupy precious little floor-space in a Lego store. Priority is given over to set pieces with varying levels of difficulty to recreate. There is possibly no product sector less exciting than jigsaw puzzles. If you asked a thirty-something whether they would like to spend their time and money on a jigsaw, they would likely politely decline, even if that puzzle had the magic words 'Disney', 'Star Wars' or 'Harry Potter' printed on it, talismans that seem largely guaranteed to part millennials from their money.

Yet thirty-somethings are willing to spend large sums on the Lego variations upon these themes. A plastic brick Hogwarts castle or Star Wars space craft made from knobbly blocks costs significant amounts. Smaller sets are still pricey. There is even an aftermarket trading of already assembled models, for a premium, for those who don't have the time to put one brick on top of another. Only a cohort that is time heavy and that prioritises leisure time could be convinced to part with such significant amounts for little piles of plastic.

Recognising this customer opportunity, the current positioning of Lego is extremely successful. After a difficult period during the early 2000s, with Lego almost bankrupted in 2004 after a period of unsuccessful over-expansion (Trautman, 2013), the toy brand refocused itself around its core customers. Interestingly this is not necessarily children. Although clever marketing has positioned Lego bricks as an educational toy over the years, parents can rarely afford to spend such sums on their children. The section of Lego stores devoted to traditional children's play sets is limited. Rather, Lego has targeted 'big kids', grown up adult children who want to play and who have significant disposable income to dedicate to this. Antorini, Muniz and Askildsen (2012: 74) explain:

> For decades, Lego's colourful plastic bricks were developed for and used by children who played alone or with a few playmates. As the children grew up, they generally outgrew their interest in Lego products. However, beginning in the late 1990s, two things happened: (1) the company introduced a series of new products that appealed to older users, such as Lego Star Wars and Lego Mindstorms; and (2) the Internet enabled people to connect in completely new ways, prompting many adults to return to Lego play and transforming their play experiences into a serious and demanding adult hobby.

Lego has repositioned its product accordingly. This was done by co-opting of pop culture. By linking with current and recently nostalgic references, Lego has made itself seem trendy and relevant again. Lego computer games and movies have brought the brand out of the toy-box and positioned as a viable purchase for adults. The upbeat humour and just a splash of irony of these appeal to millennials. The licencing deals with media conglomerates and intellectual property magnates have seen the comforting childhood references of generation Y converted into playful and tactile brick format.

Combining these reminders with a beloved childhood toy results in a super hit of nostalgia that is difficult to resist. Lego's pop culture references are arguably, like all such pastiches, lazy, unoriginal, introverted and reductive. A Lego Death Star is a plastic facsimile of a model from a sci-fi film. It is an expensive puzzle whose only reason for existing is the highly tangential link that has been made between the click together cubes and a 40-year-old film franchise established through clever marketing. Yet this is seemingly exactly what many contemporary consumers are looking for, reassurance through wallowing in nostalgia and continuing to play with childhood toys and references well into adulthood.

Looking back, but with contemporary eyes

Lego has rejuvenated its appeal by taking a classic toy concept and reimagining it through the lens of contemporary consumer culture. The product itself has changed little. However, the way they are interacted with has been thoroughly updated. Many Lego play sets are now more in line with collector's pieces. They are expensive, complex and meant to be put on display. Constant new and special editions maintain interest. Tapping pop culture references associated with positive nostalgia these keep the brand culturally relevant. In these ways Lego has been able to legitimise its appeal to adults as much as children.

Whilst doing this, Lego has reconsidered itself from a current cultural viewpoint. An up to date sense of humour is used when packaging and selling Lego. Involving plenty of pastiche, Lego is able to affectionately play with the pop cultural elements it builds around. Lego Batman parodies the original, making it more playful and child-friendly, whilst adding in-jokes for fans. The brand does not seem to take itself too seriously and this works well for young adults who share similar outlook. Balancing earnestness and irony, Lego has found a tone of voice and sense of humour that is relevant to today's generation Y and Z consumers.

Contrasting with Lego's regained relevance is another global toy brand that has struggled to connect with contemporary consumers in the same way. Barbie, launched in 1959, remains one of the largest toy brands in the world. The eponymous doll anchors a wide range of plastic companions, accessories and wider merchandise that has seen the pink Barbie logo appear on everything from movies to home furnishings.

Nevertheless, Barbie has struggled with stagnating sales in its long established markets like the United States (Timms, 2015). The reasons for this relative lack of success are varied and include such things as new competitors and shifting consumer habits. However, a part of Barbie's struggle seems to be the dissonance between current cultural values and the brand's heritage. For some, the pneumatically proportioned, platinum blonde Barbie doll has become a questionable childhood role-model. Looking back to Barbie's past is to survey a product landscape that is littered with problematic concepts from a contemporary perspective.

Conscious of this, Barbie has worked hard to update its current image. New dolls with different skin tones, body shapes and disabilities have been launched. These efforts to be more inclusive seem to have had some success in terms of overall sales, which have picked up over recent years, and particularly regards positive media coverage and online comments.

Yet Barbie remains a product that is seen as largely for young girls. It is trapped in a narrow market segment and struggles to be relevant beyond. It also receives criticism for being targeted at young girls. The messaging, tone of voice and consumer targeting of Barbie have all become somewhat muddied, not so much because Barbie has changed, but because the world around her has.

Case questions

1. Why do millennials connect with Lego and its products?
   Think about the ways in which Lego is relevant to generation Y and Z routines and aspirations.
2. How do environmental surroundings influence millennial consumers' purchasing of Lego and similar brands?
   Consider PESTLE trends and how these may underlie a tendency of generations Y and Z towards reassuring consumption such as of childish or nostalgic brands.
3. Lego revitalised itself by looking at its current products through contemporary eyes and updating them accordingly. Can Barbie do similar?
   Consider ways in which the Barbie doll might be able to tap into nostalgia and get consumers to rethink about the brand as it currently is?

Consumer case: Hikikomori

If a certain narrowness may be associated with contemporary consumers, who look to stay within reassuring bubbles, then more extreme restriction is noteworthy in some cases. Hikikomori is a Japanese word that translates as 'pulling inward' and 'being confined'. It is used to describe people who experience acute social withdrawal. The extent of this withdrawal can vary, but refers to those individuals who have very few friends or contacts, and who largely retreat from social spheres into their homes. Hikikomori rarely, sometimes never, go outside. The word captures extreme forms of socially introverted behaviours that often leave hikikomori dependent on family members as care givers.

The term hikikomori was developed by the Japanese psychologist Tamaki Saitō, who has written about the phenomenon and explored why it is occurring in Japan. Saitō (2012) describes the condition as like an adolescence without end. Hikikomori retreat into their bedrooms, fail to make a life outside of the home and rely on their parents to continue providing for them. Estimates vary widely, but suggestions are of around a million people in Japan who are hikikomori. Typically, younger adults in their late twenties and early thirties are more likely to become hikikomori, which typically happens as a gradual process.

The reasons for extreme social withdrawal may be varied. Links have been made to underlying psychological conditions or to experiencing psychological stress. For instance, encountering a major setback at school or work might begin the process of withdrawal. As seen in relation to the otaku, psychological stress may be particularly prevalent in Japan as a nation with a difficult economic system, high population density and singular culture. Alan Teo (2010), an expert on hikikomori, has suggested that the strict social codes of Japan place significant pressure on individuals to measure up. If they do not, then social retreat may be a coping strategy (Teo, Stufflebam & Kato, 2014).

It has been suggested that hikikomori often start out as futōkō, or school refusers. School refusal is a significant issue in Japan, where many children insist on dropping out of traditional state schools (Cerantola, 2019). This refusal is linked to schools being highly regimented and achievement orientated. They are not necessarily welcoming spaces for unconventional individuals. Fitting in at Japanese schools is important and these frequently impose strict social codes. Some children feel unable to fit in and drop out from school.

The phenomena of otaku, hikikomori and futōkō are prominent enough in Japan to have dedicated terms come to describe them. As discussed, some of the traits of Japanese culture may lend themselves to the emergence of these issues. Yet they are not restricted to Japan. Research by Kato, Kanba and Teo (2018) for example has illustrated the spread of hikikomori-alike persons in other parts of the world. As with otaku, Japan may be a pioneer in terms of experiencing issues that are now similarly affecting people worldwide, and with similar individual consequences.

Although hikikomori are a relatively small and extreme minority, social withdrawal in a milder sense may be a more widespread trait in contemporary society. It is easier than ever before to minimise human interaction thanks to digital technology. Our work, play, shopping and associated relationships are now often mediated by technology. Online reviews take the place of the salesperson's pitch. Self-service checkouts have replaced staff-customer exchanges. Delivery drones even threaten to substitute the drivers who present a friendly informative face on the doorstep. Whether we are conscious of it or not, many of us are becoming increasingly hikikomori.

Reassurance and consumption

As with otaku and geek cultures, hikikomori represent a withdrawal coping strategy. This pulling back from the outside world is a means of self-preservation. Consumer narrowness and nostalgia relate back to the extended adolescence and unwillingness to adult of many individuals in contemporary societies. Both help to provide reassurances against uncertainty. Difficult decisions may be put off. Uncomfortable circumstances can be distracted from. Adolescents are not expected to be fully formed, assured of their identity or entirely independent yet, albeit significant downsides of such a coping strategy include missed opportunities for self-development and lost connections with others.

Where withdrawal is becoming more of a theme therefore, marketers need to be conscious of how this affects consumption. To illustrate, if consumer routines and aspirations are informed by reassurance, then these may likely become more introverted. On the one hand, this means consumption that takes a narrower focus, concentrating around niche interests with their associated groups and activities. On the other hand, consumption become more inward looking and backward gazing. Such may be seen through an interest in nostalgia that revisits past references rather than looking forward to the future.

Consumer introversion is an opportunity and a challenge for marketers. There is an established tendency to associate consumption with extroversion. Hereby, acquiring products may be suggested as a means of impressing others through their conspicuous display. Taking part in experiences meanwhile might be inferred as a way to connect with attractive others. Such themes of social status and socialising could be less relevant to a new wave of introverted consumers. This calls for a rethinking of marketing content and communications in order to make relevant to the distinct priorities of consumer reassurance.

For example, tourism marketing could re-evaluate the packaging and promotion of travel consumption. Generally speaking, tourism is sold as an outgoing and adventurous activity, through which novel interactions with people, places and self are potentially obtained. To greater or lesser extent this is anathema to those consumers desiring reassurance through the comfortingly familiar, narrow and nostalgic.

Reconsidering tourism therefore, the question may be asked as to whether it is possible to have a vacation without leaving one's own home? Examples of how this might be so arose during the Covid-19 lockdown. Tourism was one of the worst affected industries during this period as people could not travel to consume spaces. Creative thinking by some tourism organisations allowed them to continue operating. Museums and galleries for instance provided virtual tours of their shut down spaces. In many cases these provided imaginative interpretations of and virtual interactions with exhibits. Such digital tours gave viewers new experiences such as tools to zoom in ultra-close to and magnify the surface of paintings, alongside expert commentary. They also permitted tours to be taken at a personalised pace, in solitude and from the comfort of home.

New possibilities and priorities for consumption are therefore arising that may complement an introverted turn amongst consumers. Taking the time to reflect and reconsider current offerings, it may be possible to develop appropriate products, services and experiences, as well as accompanying marketing, which are adapted to the desires of more introverted consumers. What is more, doing so could help to maintain or even develop social, educational and other contacts with consumer groups who might otherwise feel increasingly unconfident, overlooked and withdrawn.

What type of hikikomori are you?

Paraphrasing Nakamori, who asked his readers their type of otaku, the question might similarly be related to the type of hikikomori readers of this text might be. As with otaku, hikikomori is a social phenomenon that is not confined to Japan. Worldwide, people may be pulling inward. Technological developments facilitate more introverted exchanges, not least in relation to consumption. As the digital realm expands and becomes more sophisticated, virtual existence may become more encompassing. Advances in artificial intelligence, robotics and game simulations, may mean that social needs are increasingly served through technological rather than human interactions. Culturally, fragmentation means that individuals and groups are retreating into likeminded clusters. Those who do not share very similar attitudes and behaviours can be shut out. In addition, economic stratifications means that people are tending to increasingly associate with those from similar economic backgrounds. Different classes live in distinctive areas, attend different schools, consume in different ways and places. Opportunities to push out of technologically, culturally or economically introverted immediate surroundings, are in some cases declining.

Chapter summary

The otaku, geek and hikikomori cultures outlined in this chapter may help to provide insights into a tendency towards reassurance amongst some current consumers. As reviewed in Chapter 2, some consumers are increasingly active, involved and engaged with and through their consumption with wider surroundings and changing these. This chapter however outlines that others may pull back from and retreat into comforting narrow interests and nostalgia. This may be particularly associated with younger consumers. A trait of generation Y is their extended adolescence. Members of this generation tend to wait much longer than their elders to settle down, find a partner and start a family. They may consequently not outgrow related consumption habits. Illustrated therefore is one dimension of the contradictory nature of today's consumers. These seek reassurance and repetition at the same time as they are often radical and novel. Whichever emphasis of consumers, outgoing or pulling back, the next chapter looks at dynamics of how they express these.

References

Antorini, Y. M., Muñiz Jr., A. M., & Askildsen, T. (2012). Collaborating with customer communities: Lessons from the LEGO Group. *MIT Sloan Management Review*, 53(3), 73.

Bainbridge, J. (2014). 'It is a Pokémon world': The Pokémon franchise and the environment. *International Journal of Cultural Studies*, 17(4), 399–414.

Cerantola, A. (2019). Why so many Japanese children refuse to go to school. *BBC News*, 23/12/19. Available at: https://www.bbc.co.uk/news/world-asia-50693777 (accessed, 29/05/20).

Economist. (2020). Japan's new industry: Turning down jobs, 30/04/20. Available at: https://www.economist.com/asia/2020/04/30/japans-new-industry-turning-down-jobs (accessed 26/05/20).

Kato, T. A., Kanba, S., & Teo, A. R. (2018). Hikikomori: Experience in Japan and international relevance. *World Psychiatry*, 17(1), 105.

Leone, M. (2015). Longing for the past: A semiotic reading of the role of nostalgia in present-day consumption trends. *Social Semiotics*, 25(1), 1–15.

Nakamori, A. (1983). Otaku Research# 1: This city is full of Otaku. Trans. Matt Alt. *Néojaponisme*. Japan: Manga Burikko.

Parish, J. (2000). The age of anxiety. *The Sociological Review*, 48(2 suppl), 1–16.

Routledge, C., Wildschut, T., Sedikides, C., & Juhl, J. (2013). Nostalgia as a resource for psychological health and well-being. *Social and Personality Psychology Compass*, 7(11), 808–818.

Saitō, T. (2012) *Social withdrawal: Adolescence without end*. Trans. Jeffrey Angles. Minneapolis: University of Minnesota Press.

Sanchez, G. C., & Brown, T. N. (1994). Nostalgia: A Swiss disease. *The American Journal of Psychiatry*, 151(11), 1715–1716.

Shibata, M. (2019). Why Japan's 'shūkatsu' job-seeking system is changing. *BBC Generation Project*, 21/08/19. Available at: https://www.bbc.com/worklife/article/20190731-why-japans-shkatsu-is-disappearing-for-japanese-youth (accessed 27/05/20).

Teo, A. R. (2010). A new form of social withdrawal in Japan: A review of hikikomori. *International Journal of Social Psychiatry*, 56(2), 178–185.

Teo, A., Stufflebam, K., & Kato, T. (2014). The intersection of culture and solitude: The Hikikomori phenomenon in Japan. In Coplan, Robert J., & Bowker, Julie C. (eds.). *The handbook of solitude: Psychological perspectives on social isolation, social withdrawal, and being alone*. Hoboken, NJ: Wiley-Blackwell, pp. 445–460.

Timms, M. (2015). Life in plastic, not so fantastic: The tale of Barbie's decline. *The New Economy*, 7 January 2015. Available at: https://www.theneweconomy.com/business/life-in-plastic-not-so-fantastic-barbies-great-decline

Trautman, T. (2013). The Year of the Lego. *The New Yorker*, 11/11/13. Available at: https://www.newyorker.com/business/currency/the-year-of-the-lego

Walder, D. (2014). Hysterical nostalgia in the postcolony: From coming home to district 9. *Consumption Markets & Culture*, 17(2), 143–157.

Zhou, X., Wildschut, T., Sedikides, C., Shi, K., & Feng, C. (2012). Nostalgia: The gift that keeps on giving. *Journal of Consumer Research*, 39(1), 39–50.

4
REINVENTION

Evolving consumer identities – observing RuPaul's drag race fans and reading Taylor Swift's lyrics

Introducing consumers

'Consumer' is the term used to describe someone as they go about consumption: the acquiring, using and having of products, services or experiences. This consumption is for personal reasons such as meeting the utilitarian, emotional, social or ideological needs of an individual or their immediate group. For instance, purchasing a laptop might enable an individual to fulfil their work or leisure commitments. A consumer therefore purchases products, services or experiences to satisfy (or at least attempt to satisfy) various personal needs and desires. The search for outcomes to fulfil these needs and desires drives consumer actions, which, in turn, are shaped by surrounding context (Figure 4.1).

At a fundamental level consumption addresses peoples' needs. Needs are the basic requirements of a healthy life such as food or shelter. Discussion in marketing often refers to meeting customer needs. This means providing basic goods and essential services that fulfil these. 'Bottom of the pyramid' for example is a phrase used to summarise marketing products, services and experiences that are relevant to the needs of and accessible for consumers that have fewer economic resources.

Bottom of the pyramid (BoP) refers to the distribution of wealth amongst consumers. The very wealthiest few are at the narrow top of the pyramid. Meanwhile, a large majority with very little disposable income form the broad base. Illustrating this, research by Oxfam (2019) estimated that in 2018 the richest 26 people in the world had as much wealth as the poorest half of humanity, i.e. 3.6 billion people. According to Oxfam, almost half of the world's population live on less than $5.50 per day.

BoP marketing addresses those poorer consumers, who although individually have limited resources collectively represent a significant market. Like all consumers, those at the base of the pyramid have needs and desires. Understanding these is important if solutions are to be relevant. Those who have few resources may have quite different priorities from those who are more comfortable. In particular, BoP consumers require solutions that are affordable. This means developing and delivering low cost products, services and experiences. For instance, selling things like laundry detergent in single use sachets may make this necessary

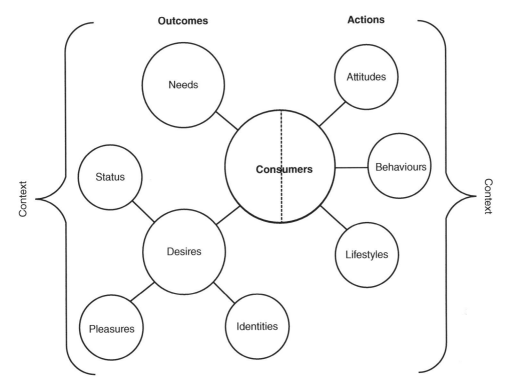

FIGURE 4.1 Overview of consumer outcomes, actions and context.

product more accessible. When it comes to BoP consumers, marketers can provide insights into and create corresponding solutions for mutually beneficial exchange relationships.

Consumer outcomes

Meeting essential needs is an important outcome for many consumers much of the time. Nevertheless, in many developed economies at least, most people's needs are met relatively easily. Having acquired the basics, many consumers have resources left over. Disposable income is money available to spend on non-essential items, such as small pleasures and bigger luxuries, nevertheless important to overall quality of life. Beyond fundamental needs therefore, consumption can be used to complement a wider range of human experiences. These are desires, outcomes sought out by consumers that are not necessarily essential for life, but which do make it more enjoyable. Consumer desires may be categorised into pleasures, status and identities. Through consuming products, services and experiences, consumers hope to obtain these non-essential but rewarding outcomes.

- *Pleasures* include sensations, relating to bodily feelings, emotions, involving inner moods, and intellects, referring to engaging cognitive states. Consumers can use the acquiring and use of items to stimulate these. A smart-watch for instance is a tactile item that can be pleasing to touch, can trigger feelings of pride when wearing and involves brainpower when using. Likewise, consumption as a process can arouse sensations, emotions and intellects. Online shopping for example can be visually rewarding, contribute to an inner state of anticipation and employ mental powers in researching.

- *Status* refers to the social standing of the individual in relation to others. This relates to perceptions of the self by peers. Consumption can be a source of increased social status such as through the conspicuous display of wealth associated with purchasing expensive goods. Standing amongst peers may rise as a result.
- *Identity* relates to sense of self at both individual and group levels. This comprises the distinctive characteristics that define individual uniqueness and commonality with similar others. Consumers can develop and express a sense of who they are through their consumption. For example, purchasing a particular experience, such as a holiday, might assert certain cultural values and help to link with likeminded others.

Consumer actions

Consumers are therefore motivated to consume by the pursuit of various essential needs and non-essential but important desires. Consumerism supposes that pleasures, status and identity can be obtained and shared with others through using and owning items. In turn, consumers engage with consumption through actions. These are decisions they take about what, where and how to consume, that then manifest in particular consumption. This includes the ways in which products, services and experiences are evaluated, interacted with, purchased or not purchased, used and disposed of. Attitudes, behaviours and lifestyles influence consumer actions and manifest through these.

- *Attitudes* include the ways that consumers think, their interpretations of events and outlook on issues. This includes thinking about consumption, the sense and style of which is informed by consumer's attitudes. Attitudes relate to the intellectual ways that individuals engage with consumption such as their opinions on a product's quality or evaluation of a service experience. Consumption can both serve and challenge people's attitudes. For example, buying something that fits in with existing viewpoints may help to reaffirm them. However, coming across something alternative, such as a tasty meat-free option, may cause to rethink. Perhaps an alternative diet might suddenly seem more possible.
- *Behaviours* are how people interact with their surroundings. This includes their expressions and routines. Behaviours refer to the ways that people engage with consumption such as through their browsing and purchasing habits. As with attitudes, consumption can both serve and challenge people's behaviours. The rise of online shopping for example has disrupted many consumers' long established habits for browsing and buying items in physical stores.
- *Lifestyles* refer to the ways that consumption goes beyond framing day-to-day ways of living, and towards doing so for the overall shape and meaning of lifespans. Thus, short-term attitudes responding to current affairs, and behavioural routines around daily or weekly habits, cumulatively and over longer time periods become more ingrained lifestyles. Longer term, purpose and meaning in life can come from consumption. Aspiring to own certain things for example can frame ways of setting up a work-leisure balance around this.

Consumer context

It is important to note that in respect of outcomes and actions consumers are shaped by the surroundings in which they exist. Known as context, this is the particular setting in which consumers come to understand their needs and desires. In different contexts these will likely be very different, because although humans share many universal needs and desires, these are also affected by unique circumstances. Environmental analysis, such as that structured by the widely adopted PEST tool, can be used to scope out the surroundings of a certain group of consumers and evaluate how these may influence their consumption.

BoP consumers for example face a particular set of circumstances. These influence the outcomes they look for through consumption, and the consumer actions they take in pursuit of these. The limited economic resources available to BoP consumers mean that some consumer desires or behaviours may not be possible for those on lower incomes. Unable to afford expensive products, services or experiences, creative alternatives must be developed in order to connect with such consumers. Albeit looking at broader trends affecting the BoP context, such as developments in mobile internet, may add complexity to such an impression.

Thus, the outcomes that motivate consumers are informed by their surroundings. Pleasures, status and identity are shaped by such things as the attitudes of peers. For instance, priority may be given to certain products, services or experiences as a source of social status, when peers place greater value on those. If owning designer brands is desirable amongst social circles, then this may more likely be emulated.

At the same time, context frames ways of pursuing needs and desires through consumption. Consumer actions are influenced by the availability, set up and emphasis of consumption surroundings. Attitudes, behaviours and lifestyles are shaped by such things as the cultural norms of a place or people. Consumers follow the guidance of peers and institutions regarding what are deemed acceptable manifestations of consumption.

Reinvention and consumer identities

Consumers' needs and desires often relate to identity. Sense of individual self and group belonging is a consumer outcome sought. Identity is what many consumers seek much of the time through their acquiring and using of items. Consumption is useful for developing identity because it offers outlets for exploring and asserting this through expressing particular attitudes, behaviours and lifestyles. For example, a metrosexual identity may be developed through consuming such things as male make-up. Doing so is a way to state a particular set of characteristics to oneself and to others. Buying and using male make-up suggest an affinity with certain ways of thinking, acting and living.

Attitudes relate to the values and ideology of a person. Beliefs about what is right and wrong, normal and aspirational, frame how a person thinks of themselves and who they feel they should associate with. Behaviours meanwhile are attitudes put into action through words and deeds. Sense of self comes from the actions one has taken in the past, is doing in the present and intends to do in the future. Identity additionally arises through lifestyles. The established surroundings, routines and habits of lived experience frame individual uniqueness. Daily life frames how one thinks and acts.

Because it links with attitudes, behaviours and lifestyles, consumption relates to identity as well. It is part of finding, refining and expressing sense of self. Who people are comes partly from what they do as consumers. The things that they desire and what they acquire help to reinforce and develop their identity. Purchasing specific products, services and experiences demonstrates personal values and attributes. For instance, buying a certain type of car helps to project a particular style of person to the world and back at the self.

Brands and products try to link themselves with particular identities in the hope that these are what customers might be aiming for and attracted to. A hint of shared identity characteristics or aspirations can make to feel welcome. There is a greater chance of a connection being triggered between a brand and a consumer where the latter feels they are understood, valued and represented. Lotus sells pure sports cars for people with a passion for auto engineering and driving. Audi serves those who aspire towards conventional markers of success. In this way, consumption choices help people to define their identity. Consumers gravitate towards products, services, experiences and their associated brands, with which they feel some sort of an affinity.

Consumption and aspects of identity

If consumers look to develop and express their identity through consumption, then there are a number of ways in which the purchase, ownership and display of products, services or experiences enables this. Consumption can be used for symbolism, learning and connections, all of which inform identity work.

- *Symbolism* relates to the display of certain values through public demonstrations of consumption. Wearing particular styles or brands of clothing for example is a public representation of sense of self. Personal characteristics, financial situation and ideology of the wearer are all demonstrated through fashions purchased and worn.
- *Learning* about the self may be facilitated by consumption, which provides opportunities to gain new experiences. These can extend or challenge identity and provide the materials to further develop or reinvent this.
- *Connections* may be made with likeminded others, and through them oneself. Consumption provides opportunities to find and fit in with groups, such as tribes that share similar ideological values, or fandoms that pursue same passions. Identities are developed through membership of groups that provide inspiration and space to share.

These aspects of identity can all be explored and developed through consumption. To illustrate, deciding on a preferred lunch venue, involving thinking around such things as the atmosphere of a space, format of service delivery, style of cuisine, time taken and whether to eat alone or with others all develops and expresses a sense of self, provide opportunities for personal learning and may facilitate connections with others.

Identity aspects can moreover be changed, played and experimented with through consumption. It is very easy to try out new food venues and see how they may complement or contradict sense of self. Swapping street food for the workplace canteen at lunchtimes might lead to new and different social connections that draw into an alternative tribe. Because consumer options are so varied, trying out new products, services or experiences is readily available. So too is trying out new identity aspects that accompany these.

Consumption can therefore play a role in identity invention and also reinvention. Conscious and unconscious decisions over who to be can play out through marketplace choices and the opportunities these allow for symbolism, learning and connections.

Identity: work, patterns and paths

Through their links with particular products, services and experiences, consumers hope to find out more about themselves. This search for self is on-going because consumer identity is not fixed. Rather, it is a work in progress. Illustrating this fluidity, results from a study by Harris et al. (2016) suggest that lifelong stability of personality is generally quite low. The authors collected data on six personality characteristics: self-confidence, perseverance, stability of moods, conscientiousness, originality and desire to excel. These were measured in a sample of respondents aged 77. They compared these answers with data collected on those same respondents when they were children. The authors found that over the intervening 60 years participant's personalities changed significantly across different traits.

People continually reflect upon, reassert and reinvent themselves as a response to their surroundings. In line with the feedback of peers for example, self-confidence can ebb and flow. Meanwhile, changes in circumstances mean that sense of self progresses. Becoming a parent for instance challenges how one thinks of and enacts oneself. Finally, as people gain more experiences, self-perception can alter. New knowledge can stimulate shifts in attitudes. Throughout these shifting surroundings, circumstances and experiences, consumption is a means of identity work.

People often gain a sense of who they are from replicating established patterns. When consuming they emulate the choices of peers for example. Through such repetitive ways of conducting oneself, identity is promulgated. Longer term meanwhile, established paths are often followed. People pursue desires, attitudes, behaviours and lifestyles that are set out in surroundings. Established ways of doing things are followed. Hence, individual identity comes in large part from repeating patterns and sticking to set paths.

Consumption can facilitate these. Shopping is frequently habitual and purchases a means of conforming to what is familiar. Yet, patterns and paths can be disrupted. Various internal and external shocks can cause the individual to step outside of and question their attitudes, behaviours and lifestyles. These and accompanying identities can be re-set. Consumption can facilitate this as well. Purchasing education for instance may expose to new ways of thinking and being that inspire a change in sense of self. Consequently, consumption can play a role in both repeating and breaking patterns.

Habit versus loyalty

Looking at patterns and paths it can be seen that consumers are often habitual. This means that they buy things on a somewhat repetitive basis. Much of the time this is unconscious. Consumers follow established habits without particularly pausing to think about. Frequency of consumption denotes habit in the sense that more regular purchasing of a brand implies an established routine. Habitual customers prioritise cost, convenience and consistency. They have set shopping patterns and want these to be as effortless as possible. Indeed, any disruption to this pattern, such as an item not being in stock, can cause them to rethink and possibly break the habit. Habitual consumption is therefore at risk from external factors. Failures in a supply chain may leave shelves empty for instance. Such external disruptions are largely beyond the control of an organisation.

By contrast, loyalty is a state that implies a strong and enduring sense of connection between a consumer and a product, service or experience and associated brand. This involves affection and awareness. Loyal customers have deeper positive feelings towards and keep track of a brand, even if they only occasionally purchase it. Cold remedies for instance may only be purchased every few years when the customer develops symptoms. This is not habitual consumption as there is no set pattern for getting a cold. However, when symptoms come, a familiar and trusted brand may always be the go to. Even where cheaper or newer options are available, a loyal cold remedy customer sticks with the brand they like and know.

Loyal consumers prioritise values, service and promise. Where these are important, they use products, organisations and brands that they feel affectionate towards. Underpinning this affection, loyal customers may find specific brands highly relevant to their aspirations or ideological outlook. They also remember reliable consumption experiences such as consistently good quality customer service. This leaves them feeling positively disposed. Loyal customers trust the promise associated with a particular good or service to be relevant and reliable. Loyal consumption is therefore at risk from internal factors. Failures in terms of living up to values, service or promise expectations can damage customer loyalty. Such internal disappointments are largely within the control of an organisation.

Marketers try to encourage customer loyalty because this tends to be more enduring than simple habit. Disruptions are inevitable. These might be from major one-off events such as economic downturns, health pandemics or natural disasters. Alternately, gradual consumer lifestyle and competitive marketplace changes, such as the growth of online shopping, might interrupt old patterns. What is more, competitors can hope to disrupt habitual consumption through aggressive promotions of their own. It is core loyal customers who will tend to see a business through difficult periods of disruption or competition, because of their more enduring appreciation of what that business offers.

Habitual loyalty

A sweet spot for marketers is the intersection of consumer habit and loyalty (Figure 4.2). Where regular consumption patterns coincide with positive consumer feelings, then organisations have the double benefit of consistent and committed customers.

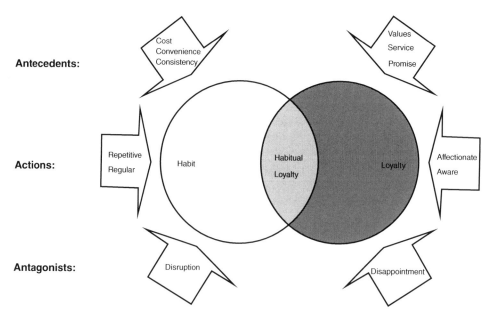

FIGURE 4.2 Consumer habits and loyalties.

To maintain such a situation requires a lot of work. Customer patterns need to be supported through practical steps, such as making a purchase exchange as time efficient as possible. Simultaneously, affections need to be kept up through emotional steps, such as putting a personal spin on a purchase interaction. Habitual loyal customers are desirable therefore, but they are also demanding.

Consumer case: RuPaul's drag race

An example of consumers who are most definitely loyal, as opposed to just habitual, is fandoms. Made up of dedicated followers of particular issues or icons, fandoms have become increasingly prominent thanks to new technologies that connect niche groups and their interests. Online, likeminded individuals can come together in order to share their common interest, as well as to articulate and build communal identities around these. Fan tribes swap materials for identity inspiration, formation and affirmation. This can be observed in relation to fans of a wide variety of consumable goods including reality television.

RuPaul's Drag Race is an American reality television show first aired in 2009. The premise of Drag Race is a competition to be crowned 'America's next drag superstar'. This title is awarded to the contestant who best epitomises the show's mantra of 'charisma, uniqueness, nerve, and talent'. The eponymous RuPaul, a veteran drag queen, has a triple role as host, mentor and judge, alongside a panel of regular and guest critics. These decide who progresses and who is eliminated via weekly challenges themed around various traditions and skills of drag. In addition, each week all of the contestants model a themed runway look. Based on the quality of that week's challenge and couture a winner is picked.

Initially a cult programme amongst a primarily LGBTQ audience, Drag Race has over the years become increasingly mainstream. Alongside Drag Race, which began airing in 2009, are a number of linked television programmes. Drag Race All Stars is where prominent contestants from previous series return to compete. Thai, British and Canadian spin off series have been launched, and a range of web series are hosted by former contestants. Beyond the television shows meanwhile, there is a wide variety of live shows, merchandise and events. With over 100 contestants having participated, Drag Race has spurred the careers of many individual drag performers, each with their own outputs.

The Drag Race online fandom is notoriously committed to the show. Fandoms offer a means of expressing and developing particular identities around specific passions. Fans become members of a tribe. This membership is a source of personal identity and social status. It is important to fans sense of self and their sense of belonging.

Drag Race fans

Fandoms are therefore examples of dedicated consumer communities committed to a particular cause. These form tribes with a strong sense of shared identity. This is developed around consumption of a common interest such as a TV show. Fandoms are places where members can experiment with identities, finding inspiration for these from likeminded others, sharing references and performing before the group. This is the case with the Drag Race community. Online fans of the series bond over shared sense of identity that comes from the symbolism, learning and connections facilitated by the community. Fans also blur identities, gaining confidence as part of a group to express themselves. They additionally break up over identities into new niche fandoms. How consumption of a cultural product, alone or together, can assist consumer's self-invention and reinvention is expressed below.

Identity bonding
- Drag is a cultural expression closely associated with gay people. There is long tradition in gay culture of drag queens and kings having prominent community positions. The frequently marginalised LGBTQ community is brought forward and celebrated by Drag Race. By portraying different types of identity on screen, including those which are normally hidden or negatively stereotyped, the program helps viewers figure out their own identities. Seeing unconventional gender and sexual identities represented is talked about by online fans as informative and empowering. Watching these be celebrated gives fans confidence in their own identities.

Identity blurring
- Drag Race also gives followers the opportunity to experiment with alternative identities. Consumed by viewers is drag. This is an art-form where men dress as women and vice versa. This type of gender bending is still seen in many societies as unacceptable. The program's mash ups of masculinity, sexuality, and gender are appreciated for blurring identity assumptions. Inspired by watching the program, fans may likewise feel more able to try out different identity combinations.

Identity breaking
- Fractures between Drag Race fans may be observed online. Identity breaks come from disagreements over how identity bonding or blurring should take place, for instance whether depictions of identities on Drag Race are accurate or otherwise, and whether incomers into the fandom are considered respectful and so welcomed, or less so. For the most part these disagreements are talked through with respect and good humour. Nevertheless, in time, these identity disagreements may lead to deeper identity breaks. Splits into different sub-fandoms occur. These might be those who move onto different social media platforms for example, or those who bond over a specific type of fan identity. As such, the shared identity of the Drag Race tribe may break into sub-tribes with their own more closely felt sense of shared traits.

Case questions

1. How do consumers of RuPaul's Drag Race use the program to build identity?
   Think about the individual and collective resources and relationships that come from immersion in the program and its fandom.
2. How do the interactions of Drag Race fans online support identity experimentation and reinvention?
   Consider how fans break down as well as build up aspects of identity, such as gender or sexuality stereotypes, and what this means for identity development.

Culturally appropriate versus cultural appropriation

Consumer's identity reinvention may draw on various cultural resources. As with fans of Drag Race for example, exploring LGTBQ culture may be inspiring for many people. Marketing managers are similarly inspired. Studying cultures is a source of new ideas at the same time as it gives insights about group members. These exchanges between marketing and culture can be mutually rewarding, if managed carefully. When they draw upon culture for inspirations, marketers need to ask a number of questions such as:

- What culture is being referenced?
- Is this culture's creativity being exploited without due respect and recognition?
- Does the brand or product have any underlying connection with the culture being referenced?
- Is this a positive referencing of underlying culture or a voyeuristic, even negative one?

Asking these questions will help to ensure that marketing is culturally appropriate. This is in the sense of getting involved in a particular culture, sharing the creative outputs and values of that culture, and potentially helping to raise its profile in a positive manner. Cultural appropriation refers to taking ideas and inspiration from sources and then using these for own purposes. For example, Tinson and Nuttal (2010) highlight UK high school proms as an example of adopting and adapting a cultural practice into the fabric of local youth culture. A US cultural tradition, proms have been enthusiastically embraced by UK teenagers.

Such cultural appropriation can be mutually respectful and stimulating. Cultures benefit from exchanges. To illustrate, Canavan (2016) talks about tourism culture. This sees a fusion of hosts' and guests' cultures where they come together in holiday destinations. The results of hosts and guests interacting with each other are new and unique tourism cultures. These are a blend of different influences and tend to be open minded and entrepreneurial. Both hosts and guests benefit from this tourism culture, and this is an important part of the appeal of holiday hotspots.

Cultural appropriation can henceforth be positive. However, it can also be voyeuristic. This is in the sense of intrusions by outsiders into cultures, without adequate respect, commitment or communication accompanying this. Appropriation can bring a sense of fetishizing a culture by boiling it down to a few exotic aspects. Appropriation can also be exploitative in terms of using cultures for purposes of self-pleasure without giving anything back. Black cultures for example are often referenced for musical inspiration. Yet this process can be exploitative rather than mutually rewarding, where black artists are not given due credit or equal opportunities.

Cultural subversion and La Sape

Cultural appropriation can be subversive. This is in the sense that taking established cultural references, and then playing around with these, can be a means of questioning and resisting them, as drag does with gender norms. Thompson and Haykto (1997) review how consumers often develop personalised fashions that resist dominant ideas of how people should dress. Taking inspiration from different styles, consumers can subvert cultural dress codes and better express themselves. The La Sape fashion culture is a heightened example of this. Popular in parts of Africa, La Sape is dress code where smart and colourful clothes are worn. Taking inspiration from the elegant dress of 1920's western dandies, La Sape is a way of resisting the poverty and conflict of parts of Africa through elaborate clothing. It also subverts Africa's colonial legacy by taking the dress code of the oppressor and reinventing it for local circumstances. Cultural appropriation is in this case an act of subversive self-expression.

4 C's culture checklist

Cultural appreciation is a valuable source of inspiration for marketers. However, cultural appropriation can be a problem in that a lack of respect may earn brands a bad reputation amongst the communities they draw upon. Judging the balance between these positions is not always easy, and the conversation is always on-going as ideas change. Is Kim Kardashian getting cornrows culturally appropriate or cultural appropriation? What about brands tapping into LGBTQ imagery during pride month? Marketers need to tread carefully if they are to stand on the positive side of cultural appropriation as involving mutually rewarding exchanges. Being inspired by different cultures to explore own identity is positive. Ripping them off to do so is not. Balances of power and sincerity of mind-set are important to these discussions of appropriate appropriation. The 4 C's are a quick checklist for marketers to follow when engaging with cultures.

1. **Confidence** refers to the strength of a culture being referenced. Some cultures, such as that of the United States, are high profile, well known and have many members. This means they are resilient and can stand up for themselves. Confident cultures can be more easily worked with for marketing purposes. Yet some cultures, such as the LGBTQ community, are lower profile, less well known and have fewer members. Such cultures that fall outside of the mainstream are vulnerable to being misunderstood. To avoid this, they need to be treated with sensitivity by marketers.
2. **Commonality** means the link between a product or brand and a cultural reference. Marketing works better where these links are genuine. RuPaul's Drag Race is a hugely successful product within the LGBT community because it heavily features gay people. Drag Race is made in large part by gay people for gay people.
3. **Commitment** relates to how involved a product or brand is with the culture it is referencing. This commitment may be considered in terms of consistency and longevity of commitment. To illustrate, where some brands occasionally get on board with gay culture, during pride month for instance, others do so year-round. Absolut Vodka has spent decades representing gay people in its advertising.
4. **Celebration** of culture is what marketers should always aim for when referencing. Cultures are not better or worse than each other, just different. It is risky to denigrate culture in marketing. This may leave individuals and groups feeling put down and unwanted. Not only is doing this ungenerous, but it raises the potential for fallout in terms of resulting resistance and conflict. Instead, appreciating cultural influences and references is a positive step to take.

Commercial case: Taylor Swift's lyrical reinventions

Many brands have been criticised for inappropriate cultural appropriation. One of these has been Taylor Swift, judged as referencing such things as classical ballet without due qualifications to do so. Regardless, Swift is one of the most successful musical artists of the 21st century so far. Song-writing and performing from her early teens, she broke into the mainstream as the best-selling musician of 2008 (Grigoriadis, 2009). An unexceptional singer and uncoordinated dancer, Swift nonetheless has become a huge and enduring commercial success. Her 2014 single 'Shake it off' has been watched over two and half billion times on YouTube alone. Over the course of her career so far, Taylor has won multiple awards, toured globally, sold millions of records and been the centre of her own feature length documentary.

Beyond her listener base, Swift has generated plenty of attention and debate not just around her music, but regards her image, politics and what she represents. When the singer finally waded into political commentary in October 2018, her social media comments outlining why her fans should register to vote ahead of upcoming US mid-term elections seemed relatively banal. Yet the reaction generated by the singer's post was dramatic. Global media coverage followed, as did numerous op-eds analysing, and even a direct response from the then president who said that he now enjoyed her music about 25% less. A reportedly significant increase in voter registration numbers in her home state of Tennessee was attributed to her intervention. Swift therefore hits a cultural nerve and generates conversations beyond what even her level of fame would normally suggest.

Accompanying this commercial and cultural success, Taylor Swift is notable for her deep and enduring connection with her listeners. Swift's fans are known to be especially dedicated to the singer. Her 'Swifties', one of the first waves of fandoms given a dedicated name to denote their loyalty, have followed her closely from an early age. They have grown up with the singer as her country style has evolved into more mainstream pop. Swift seemingly captures the cultural context, pressures and priorities of her age group, like no other artist. 'Shake it off' for example is a song that embodies how her young fans are not going to take being defined and disenfranchised by older generations any longer.

As such, Swift connects deeply with the identities of generations Y and Z and their growing self-confidence exploring and asserting this. Shake it off is a formidable statement of self. In the song, Swift makes clear that she, and only she, will define herself. Here and elsewhere, Taylor Swift's lyrics provide insight into the identities of young adult music consumers. Those consumers who connect with her brand, products and messages do so because they share a sense of mutual identity. Accordingly, listening to Swift is a valuable research tool for marketers looking to gain understanding of youth cohorts.

Identity reinventions

Taylor Swift's song lyrics seem to be especially concerned with the singer herself. Although Swift sings about romantic others, friends and rivals, she does so from her point of view and in terms of how others see or affect her. As such, Swift may demonstrate a typically generation Y and Z tendency towards being self-focussed at the same time as being highly concerned with the opinions of others. In addition, Taylor's lyrics demonstrate an artist highly involved in managing her public image. The singer refutes, co-opts and manipulates outsider's perceptions of herself. In this way, Taylor echoes generation Y and Z characteristics of being highly involved in their own reputation management through such things as online staging and image enhancing consumption. This lyrical emphasis can be captured in three particular themes of the pop star outlined below.

Romance and revenge
- Recognised by Canavan and McCamley (2020) is that romance and revenge are powerful motifs within many of Taylor Swift's songs. Her early releases tended towards romantic storytelling. In these, references are to classical figures such as the Romeo-Juliet theme of 'Love Story' (2008). The singer's more recent songs have developed themes of revenge as well as romance. In Swift's lyrics she is often wronged by third parties. The song 'Bad Blood' (2015) for example describes a friendship turning sour, possibly referring to her at the time reported feud with fellow singer Katy Perry. Perhaps the most obvious example of this revenge tendency relates to the singer's long-running clash with Kanye West and his wife Kim Kardashian. This has been slowly picked over in songs that hint at Swift's sense of betrayal and fantasising about revenge.

Fantasising out loud
- The stories contained in Taylor Swift's song lyrics are often a semi-explicit fabulation of reality. 'Blank Space' (2014) for instance is a daydream inviting a lover into a relationship and then imagining how this might then pan out. This is typical of Taylor's hypothesising style that blurs reality and fiction, past, present and future. Listeners don't know what exactly is fantastical and what is real. Swift likes to bring up oblique references that stir up conversations. Rumours circulated in late 2019 that one of the rings she wears in the video for 'Look what you made me do' is a replica of one stolen at gunpoint from Kim Kardashian in a highly publicised 2016 incident. True or not, the possibility of such a suggestion illustrates the air of mystery crafted by Swift around herself, and how compelling this is for listeners.

Controlling the narrative
- Beyond documenting her personal life, and embellishing this through daydreaming out loud, it seems important to Swift that her versions of events are taken seriously. Taylor is renowned for turning her real-life romantic liaisons, social circle dynamics and professional disputes into song-writing material. Lyrics recall the turbulence of her personal or professional life and give her account of events. Swift remembers slights against her, and develops into lyrics that respond to and refute these. Those who cross or disagree with the singer are dismissed. 'Shake it off' (2014) repeats the derogatory comments thrown at Swift's persona, then cheerfully waves these away. 'I did something bad' (2017) more aggressively imagines taking down an opponent. 'You need to calm down' (2019) mockingly dismisses conservative ideology. Swift closely monitors her self-image. Disagreeable opinions, relationship clashes, professional disputes are all pulled apart and Taylor's point of view on these asserted in their place.

Case questions

1   What can be read through Taylor Swift's song lyrics about contemporary consumers and consumption?
    Consider the consumer culture insights to be gained from studying the singer's work. Think about what themes are present in Swift's lyrics and why these resonate with her listeners.
2   Other than Taylor Swift, what other recording artists might be useful in gaining possible insights into contemporary consumer culture?
    Think about other artists who may represent similar or distinctive themes. Consider also how different artists working in different genres may speak to different groups of listeners.

Chapter summary

This chapter looked at the role of consumption in collective and individual identity projects. Amongst various possible consumer outcomes and actions, consumption can be used to reinforce and reflect sense of self. Consumption moreover allows for experimentation with different identities. Trying out new versions of self can be enjoyable and rewarding, as is apparent from following RuPaul's Drag Race fans online. The materials provided by the show inspire fans to experiment with and express their identities. Meanwhile, consumption can be used to assert desired identity by projecting certain values and narratives. Taylor Swift's willingness to dismiss or co-opt the views of others, of which she is vigilant, may speak to ways her listeners construct their identities likewise. As the next chapter will review, careful identity management is important in contemporary surroundings, particularly digital ones.

References

Canavan, B. (2016). Tourism culture: Nexus, characteristics, context and sustainability. *Tourism Management, 53,* 229–243.

Canavan, B., & McCamley, C. (2020). The passing of the postmodern in pop? Epochal consumption and marketing from Madonna, through Gaga, to Taylor. *Journal of Business Research, 107,* 222–230.

Grigoriadis, V. (2009). The very pink, very perfect life of Taylor Swift. *Rolling Stone.* Available online: https://www.rollingstone.com/music/news/the-very-pink-very-perfect-life-of-taylor-swift-20090305 (accessed 29/01/18).

Harris, M. A., Brett, C. E., Johnson, W., & Deary, I. J. (2016). Personality stability from age 14 to age 77 years. *Psychology and Aging, 31*(8), 862.

Oxfam. (2019). Public good or private wealth? Oxfam briefing paper – January 2019. Available at: https://oxfamilibrary.openrepository.com/bitstream/handle/10546/620599/bp-public-good-or-private-wealth-210119-summ-en.pdf?utm_source=indepth (accessed 09/06/20).

Thompson, C. J., & Haytko, D. L. (1997). Speaking of fashion: Consumers' uses of fashion discourses and the appropriation of countervailing cultural meanings. *Journal of Consumer Research, 24*(1), 15–42.

Tinson, J., & Nuttall, P. (2010). Exploring appropriation of global cultural rituals. *Journal of Marketing Management, 26*(11–12), 1074–1090.

5
REPUTATION

Building and breaking brands offline and online – Halo Top, Angelababy and Fan Bingbing

Reputation: brand aura and appeal

Reputation is about social status and standing. These relate to how the individual, an organisation or a specific group is perceived by society. Such things as businesses, brands, products, fandoms and consumer communities have particular reputations and levels of social standing. The perceptions of society towards these stem from their particular associations. These are the things thought and felt when encountered. Associations come from a mixture of overlapping sources (see Figure 5.1).

Sources of reputation include the *background* to an individual, organisation or group as it currently is. This comes from their past actions and values. Likewise, the *vision* of these refers to their outlook on the desired future. In turn, *actions* are the past and present things that are done by individuals, organisations or groups. These are the behaviours and performances they are known for. *Values* relate to the historical and contemporary attitudes held by individuals, organisations or groups. This includes the causes supported, principles followed and thoughts admired by individuals, organisations or groups.

Because individuals, organisations and groups are connected with particular consumption, products and brands, their reputations intermingle. The associations of vegan consumers overlap with those of meat-free alternative brands. Vegan's reputation amongst wider society may likely shape the reputation of these brands and vice versa. This is one reason why brand managers try to associate with consumer subcultures that are seen as having positive attributes more broadly and why they may shy away from linking with those that have more controversial reputations.

Ultimately, reputation may be summarised as the aura around a particular individual, organisation or group, as well as their linked consumption, products and brands. Aura comprises the feelings and thoughts triggered spontaneously when these are come across. Aura either appeals to bystanders, or it does not. Positive or negative appeal may encourage or undermine interaction with an individual, organisation or group. Reputation is therefore a powerful means of shaping the reactions of and connections with others.

To illustrate, the reputation of the police differs across countries and communities. Their associations as an organisation may be perceived quite differently and appeal to some far

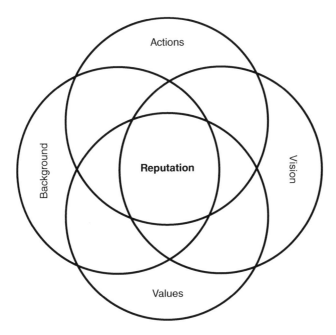

FIGURE 5.1 Sources of brand reputation.

more than others. Feelings and thoughts triggered by seeing a police vehicle vary markedly. So too, willingness to trust and desire to connect with the police diverge widely. The aura and appeal of an individual, organisation or group depend on the specific society evaluating.

Managing reputation

The reputation of the police depends on interpretations of their associations. These will differ across social groups. Some may feel more of an affinity with their background and past actions. Others might not think their vision or current values appropriate. Things like previous experience, knowledge and ideological proximity influence how reputation is perceived.

As such, there is no guarantee that aura will be interpreted in a specific way. Nor that it will appeal to certain groups. Understanding needs to be of the alternative feelings and thoughts that can be triggered by an individual, organisation or group. Why this is the case, whether this is an issue and how to change the situation are considerations for marketers.

Reputation must be crafted in order to modify, develop and project a certain type of aura that may have a desired effect on others. For example, a reputation for generosity may be useful for a business leader looking to inspire affection amongst employees. If this is the case, then investment needs to be into understanding the background, vision, actions and values that different groups of employees will perceive as generous. Once this is understood, then efforts can be made to commit to such reputation associations.

Marketers spend a lot of time building the reputation of brands. This involves celebrating their heritage, sharing their vision, managing their actions and promoting their values. The reasons for doing this are that brand reputation is a crucial part of successful exchange relationships. Stakeholders are more likely to interact with brands that have a reputation they trust and admire. Indeed, a large part of the value of many major firms, such as Apple, comes from their strong brand reputation as much as it does their expertise at making or selling particular items.

Managing reputation is an on-going process because societies and their perceptions evolve over time. Reputation management involves updating and projecting associations. Vision needs to be updated in line with changing surroundings for example. Meanwhile, values may need modifying in line with shifting ideological conversations. Reputations are also shaped through external events. Reviews, mistakes, misunderstandings and other such actions can undermine aura and appeal. Reputation management therefore also involves responding to such issues timely and appropriately.

> **Public shaming**
> The potential for reputation damaging missteps to be made public has grown significantly that to digital technologies. These have interconnected individuals, organisations and information like never before. This means that brands' backgrounds, visions, actions and values can rapidly be picked up, evaluated and commented on. Mistakes can be quickly identified and amplified. For all the time that it takes marketers to carefully craft a brand's reputation, a single mistake can quickly go viral and undo this. United Airlines for example, received unwanted media attention and plenty of online criticism in 2017, when footage of a passenger being forcibly removed from a flight went viral. Social standing can be rapidly undermined by these events.

Brand reputation

For marketers, reputation is all important. A strong reputation underpins exchange relationships between stakeholders. Reputation relates to levels of trust in a relationship. An established reputation comes from clear and consistent associations. Where background, vision, actions and values are well known, these inform stakeholders what to expect from a particular exchange relationship. Consequently, reputation influences whether stakeholders want to enter or continue a relationship.

Brand reputation is closely associated with trust in a brand. Where stakeholders feel a stronger sense of trust then they are more willing to enter relationships and more likely to commit more to these. Trust is particularly important when it comes to more involved exchanges, those that require greater investment of resources. When stakeholders commit significant time, intellectual effort or money to an exchange, they seek reassurance that this will be respected. The aura of a brand can help to provide such reassurance.

To illustrate, Tesla has an aura around its brand that gains adoration from a large sub-set of automotive consumers. They connect with the background, vision, actions and values of Tesla and its founder Elon Musk. As a result, customers are often willing to pay significant sums to buy vehicles from a relatively new car brand over more established rivals. More than this, they will often put up with long waiting times for products to arrive and other inconveniences, because the Tesla brand has such strong appeal.

Conversely, a lack of trust in a brand may undermine the ability to form new relationships, by putting off prospective customers. Where associations are unclear, inconsistent or just problematic, then the thoughts and feelings triggered upon encountering a brand may be ambivalent. A poor or unreliable reputation can also weaken existing relationships with current customers, potentially to the point of these being irreparably damaged and broken.

Facebook exemplifies the problems of a tarnished brand reputation. Recent controversies around the privacy of users have undermined trust in the reliability or security of the social media platform. The aura around and appeal of the brand is perhaps less than it once was. In the medium- to long-term this could have significant implications for the brand's ability to initiate and maintain exchange relationships with stakeholders.

Reputation versus tribalism

Important through reputation is, it is not everything. There are plenty of examples in contemporary consumer culture of brands that have a terrible reputation, but are highly successful nonetheless. Donald Trump for example, with a background of business failures, record of unpleasant actions on camera towards opponents, and history of divisive values statements, has a toxic political reputation. Yet, Trump became president of the USA and remains connected with a consistent core of supporters. To help explain this, a study by Veloutsou and Moutinho (2009) found that tribalism is often more important than reputation when it comes to brand relationships. They conclude that people are more likely to have a relationship with a brand that is linked with their community, regardless of how positive or negative its overall reputation.

Commercial case: Halo Top

New brands face a struggle to establish reputations as they are unknown quantities. Their social perceptions and status do not exist. However, new brands can rapidly break through into sociocultural consciousness and become known for positive associations. Such has been the case for Halo Top, whose brand aura and appeal have allowed it to expand rapidly. Only founded in 2011, by 2016 Halo Top was one of the leading ice cream brands in the United States and valued at around $2 billion (Cassidy, 2018). This amazingly quick ascendency resulted from Halo Tops' ability to define a clear and relevant USP and then to build a positive reputation around this through clever marketing. This has allowed a start-up brand to take on powerful established competitors and carve out a significant niche of the market.

Halo Top sells low calorie ice cream, made with sweeteners rather than sugar. Halo conquered the market by offering similar flavours to rivals, such as cookies and cream or sea salt caramel, but with the twist of having fewer calories (Buckley, 2019). The brand's attention grabbing packaging declares how many calories are in an entire tub; 360, 320, 280, the numbers seem amazing. The idea of guilt free ice cream is highly relevant to many consumers. But at the outset, Halo Top, as a new brand, had to raise awareness of its unique offering with a limited budget.

Halo Top became a hit through word of mouth, picked up and talked about by rapidly growing numbers of people who learned about the brand from peers and influencers (Wohl, 2017). The tubs would often quickly sell out when they turned up in stores as people in the know bought as many as they could fit into their freezers. This all added up to an aura around Halo Top as something that must be good.

The ice cream brand built up this reputation with online marketing. Halo hired small scale online influencers with a few thousand followers. These were used to post about the brand and help accumulate further interest amongst their followers. Halo also used targeted ads, reasoning that these were more cost effective and less easily ignored than traditional billboard advertising. Really pushing the brand over the top in terms of awareness however, an article in GQ magazine on the ten day Halo Top diet (Snow, 2016), went viral, and helped to capture wide public attention.

In order to maintain and grow interest the brand persistently brings out new flavours and tub sizes. It accompanies these with notably odd advertising. A 2017 commercial featuring an ice cream feeding robot was much talked about as disturbingly strange. Halo Top also has a lot of followers across its quirky and continually updated social media pages. These are used to keep fans up to date with latest developments and propagate the brand's values and personality. Halo Top is an excellent example of how new challenger brands are able to succeed by using social media to connect directly with consumers.

Brand narrative: telling a good backstory

Brand narrative refers to the story that a brand shares about itself. Such stories explain where the brand comes from, why it is here now and where it is going. Actions and values can be highlighted. Sharing these details is therefore an opportunity to manage reputation and connect with consumers who may find such details informative or inspiring. Almost all brands feature a narrative, some more prominently than others. Halo Top for example shares a story on its website that outlines the brand's product development. Focus for the ice cream maker is on its product story, the first idea, later developments and latest updates.

There are two key ingredients that go into a good brand narrative, even fewer than go into making ice cream. These outline where a brand is from, highlighting certain traits and events from its backstory, and using these to associate with particular attributes and values.

- *Provenance* relates to the place where a brand comes from. This is the physical, as in geographic, place where a brand originated. Playing up the local or national identity of where a firm was founded or is based is something many brand backstory's do. This roots in a distinct place and associates with the attributes of that place. Being from France for example brings to mind a certain sense of style and particular outlook on life.
- *Heritage* relates to the temporal, as in time-based, place where a brand comes from, as well as key events from the history of its existence. Emphasising the time period founded during links a brand to particular references. Victorian links for instance might suggest associations with craftsmanship of that era.

Compared with many brands, including rivals such as Ben and Jerry's, the Halo Top story is quite brief and focusses on products. Perhaps this is because Halo Top is such a short lived brand. It has relatively fewer historical materials to draw upon when describing its backstory. This brevity could be a mistake however. A more detailed brand narrative offers opportunities to outline such things as brand purpose, to demonstrate sense of values and to emphasise expertise. Through these, narratives can be used to build aura and make a more enduring connection with consumers by triggering emotional or ideological responses.

Ben and Jerry's offer an example of brand narrative being used to make a deeper connection with customers. The brand's website features an interactive timeline that takes the reader through the decades since its founding in 1978. Key moments from Ben and Jerry's history are brought forward. Going beyond the products, these vignettes stress the quirky and caring nature of the ice cream business from its outset. Ben and Jerry's support for good causes, their sense of fun represented in annual free ice cream days and launches of experimental flavours are all brought up. Doing so helps to reinforce the sense of where Ben and Jerry's comes from and what it currently stands for. The brand's reputation is reinforced by its narrative.

The Ben and Jerry's story is an interesting one that features unusual protagonists (the eponymous founders Ben and Jerry who set the firm up in a former gas station), and over 40 years of existence to draw upon. But Ben and Jerry's crafts these into a compelling brand narrative that succinctly shares those parts of the story that it wants to sell: values, creativity and fun. This narrative backs up and adds depth to the Ben and Jerry's brand as depicted in colourful and jokey packaging. It enhances what and who the ice cream firm represents. A good brand narrative is like a nugget of cookie dough; it is something tasty to dig into. Halo Tops' brand backstory is, a bit like criticisms of some of its ice cream, slightly unsatisfying.

> **Case questions**
>
> 1 What are the reputation associations of Halo Top?
>   *Evaluate the background, vision, actions and values of the brand.*
> 2 Could a more sophisticated brand narrative add to the overall reputation of the Halo Top brand?
>   *Look into the brand's background and identify interesting parts of this that might be brought forward. Think about how these might be used to make a more emotional or ideological connection with consumers.*

Social media marketing: building and breaking reputations

Halo Top is an example of how brands may begin to build or loose reputations online. The ice cream maker has carefully worked with influencers and used its social media pages to build its brand aura. This is a smart strategy. In contemporary culture social status and reputation associations are very often built and broken online. Aura around and appeal of brands can be curated through carefully crafted content and well managed communications. Played correctly, social media can be a means of gaining positive awareness and building a brand that is enjoyed and followed widely. Played badly however, and social media can be a source of negative awareness, reputational damage and even notoriety.

Social media is distinguished by two features. First, it allows interactions. Social media sites connect users to other users. They provide forums for initiating and holding conversations such as through swapping text, photographic or video messages. This interaction includes with brands that have an online presence. Importantly, connections via social media are two way. Through social media, brands can talk to followers, share information and respond rapidly to queries or current events.

Burger King for example is well known for its quick witted online presence. It regularly replies to other users' compliments or criticisms in a humorous way. Illustrating this, the firm's 'explains a lot' reply to Kanye West's tweet that McDonald's was his favourite restaurant tickled plenty of users, who liked and shared extensively. The brand's jokey commentary is enjoyable to follow and helps to build goodwill towards the fast food chain.

Second, social media allows content generation. Social media sites provide spaces and tools for users to consume the content of others, and to produce and share their own. In this way social media sites connect users to content, including the content of brands that have an online presence. Thus, brands can share details about themselves. Their background, vision, actions and values can be outlined and updated. Opportunity is also to pick up on content shared by other users, and to gain insight into their thoughts, activities and opinions. As such, social media content give users and brands the opportunity to know each other better.

Again, Burger King is known for generating interesting online content. The business has run campaigns such as its 2014 'cheat on beef' promotion. This saw consumers in New Zealand invited to a specially converted motel where they could cheat on beef by eating BK chicken burgers. Motel customers were asked to film themselves and upload their seedy stays to BK's social media (Beltrone, 2014). The associated content shared by the brand and its customers helped to create online brand buzz.

Commercial case: Angelababy

Online influencers are an excellent illustration of the ability to build reputations through social media. Influencers brand themselves. Crafting identities for public consumption, their personality is what appeals to, connects with and is consumed by followers. Top influencers may have millions of subscribers. They can generate significant revenue from sponsored content, endorsements and merchandise. The underpinning for all of these is a willingness of online audiences to interact with influencer's and connect with their content.

One of the largest of all influencer brands is Angelababy. Although relatively unheard of outside of her home market, this influencer is undoubtedly one of the most successful. A model, actress, reality television personality and musician, Angela Yeung Wing, who goes by the stage name Angelababy, is most significant for her online presence. A hugely popular celebrity inside China, Angelababy has over 100 million followers on Weibo, the largest social media platform in the country.

In China, influencers are known as 'Key Opinion Leaders' (KOLs) or 'Wanghong's', which translates to 'online successes' (OMR, 2018). Hundreds of thousands of wanghongs help to drive the domestic Chinese economy. They promote and recommend products, services and experiences to their followers, and drive sales of sponsored goods. Wanghong's influence is measured in the sales they drive as much as it is likes or followers. Selling the most of a certain item in the shortest time possible is a key KOL metric. Angelababy has helped brands such as Maybelline to sell huge numbers of products shortly after she uploads her endorsement.

The significance of KOL's in China, as with influencers elsewhere, is that these forge a connection with their online followers. People keep up to date with Angelababy because of her entertaining lifestyle. Her posts, commentary and livestreams engage followers and build relationships with them. The influencer has been described as the Chinese Kim Kardashian. She is similarly known for sharing in detail online her glamorous life. Her 2015 wedding to actor Huang Xiaoming for example, live-streamed for fans, was said to have cost over $30 million. Such social media sharing is what underpins the Angelababy brand. The most successful influencers interact regularly with their followers and produce content that is both entertaining and seems intimate.

This connection means that Angelababy and her fellow KOLs are better liked and more trusted by their followers than professional marketers. Followers feel like they get know their favourite KOLs in detail. Because they share so much with their fans, KOLs have a reputation for being more transparent and honest. This intimacy and trust are less likely to be established through traditional advertising. Hoping to piggyback on KOL's reputations therefore, and the relationships based off of them, brands will pay for the privilege. Dozens of major labels, including Audi and Viktor & Rolf, have used Angelababy in campaigns. Having built a brand reputation of her own, Angelababy is able to lend this to other brands looking for some of her aura to rub off on them.

Brand authenticity

Angelababy is popular with followers because of her perceived authenticity. In business research, the term 'authenticity' is used to refer to the genuineness, reality or truth of something (Kennick, 1985). Authenticity has also been defined in terms of sincerity, innocence and originality (Fine, 2003). As such, authentic brands are those that are perceived as being truthful and genuine in what they stand for. Their background, actions and values are honest and believable. Authenticity is important for brands because it relates to consumer trust. Consumers who feel that a brand is open, honest and sincere may be more likely to believe what a brand claims to represent, and thus more willing to enter into exchange relationships with them.

In trying to seem authentic, brands will try to emphasise that their backstory, actions and values are genuine. A sense of something as authentic can be related to concepts such as being seen as natural, honest, simple and unspun. Brands can attempt to project these through the marketing content and communications they produce. For instance, many brands try to highlight naturalness through their logo design, packaging or brand narratives. These can be used to frame a brand's reputation associations, for example actions such as being handmade or values around caring about the environment. Because people associate nature with honesty, naturalness may be a useful thing to play up in order to be seen as authentic.

By contrast, being unnatural relates to being heavily adulterated and altered. This includes products, services and experiences that have been overly tampered with, modified and are no longer close to the original from which they were inspired. Consumers are often wary of such intense manufacture. Whereas nature is associated with being clean, pure and good, highly manufactured items may be linked with pollution and corruption. For example, significant consumer suspicion is of highly processed foods, likewise of factory farmed produce or foodstuffs that contain GMO ingredients. Such food products can be seen as less healthy, trustworthy or desirable.

However, claims of being natural may be inaccurate, partial and misleading. Food brands for instance are not always transparent regarding their supply chains or ingredients. Looking at a cereal packet, the ingredients list will often highlight good natural ingredients such as being made with 20% fruits and nuts. However that list will then fail to give a percentage for the amount of sugar involved. Indeed, sugar is often listed under several different terms, perhaps to confuse the reader about how much is included in the recipe.

Such small acts cover up the bad or less natural components of the product. Whilst they may be perfectly legal and not outright dishonest, these types of acts are not fully open or honest. They risk eroding the authenticity of the brand. Consumers are increasingly aware of such tactics used by brands to seem more authentic, or less inauthentic, than they actually are. The genuineness of brands' commitment to values espoused is inspected more critically. The honesty of their claims is reviewed more carefully. Being inauthentic, in the sense of being false, uncommitted or dishonest, is more readily picked up thanks to online networks.

> **Case questions**
>
> 1. How do Angelababy and other influencers use social media to build their reputations?
>   *Think about the interactions and content potential of social media and how this is used by influencers to gain and maintain interest in their brands.*
> 2. Why do influencers have a better reputation for honesty than more traditional forms of marketing?
>   *Consider, using examples where possible, how influencers build a strong reputation and make connections with their followers.*

Social media exchange relationships

As illustrated by Angelababy and other influencers of varying scale, social media facilitates relationship building. This includes the exchange relationships that are the focus of marketing. There are a number of reasons why relationships are supported through social media. First, the easy interactions and content swaps facilitated by social media can support the development of stronger relationships between brands and consumers. Rather than a one-way reception of messages from producer to consumer, social media facilitates consumer interaction. Likewise, instead of passive processing of content, users can get more actively involved. Social media users can share, comment, critique and give feedback. They can also produce their own.

Online relationships are also more spontaneous. This means that these can have an informality that might not be possible in traditional contexts such as a sales desk. There is not the pressure to have to interact, but the possibility is there if interest arises. An amusing tweet can trigger a conversation. An emergent question can be quickly shared. Social media relationships are popular in large part because they are quick, easy, fun and fit into moments spent waiting for the microwave.

In addition, online connections tend to be considered more trustworthy. Consumers are savvy regards the intentions of marketers. They know that advertising serves a purpose. Online exchanges and content seem to overcome some of these barriers. Because they are able to get to know a brand through its social media in more depth, over time, consumers feel less like they are seeing only carefully presented messages. It may be changing somewhat, thanks to various data privacy scandals over recent years, but users tend to view social media interactions as transparent and honest.

Finally, a presence on social media is an opportunity to gather information on customers' tastes. The likes, shares and uploads of users may be observed, and insights into their personality gained accordingly. This information can then be used to maintain and deepen relationships. Finding out that followers of your or rival brands are liking and subscribing to vegan pages for example may inspire to rethink own product offering.

Therefore, social media provides a place where brands can interact with, listen to, influence and learn about their customers. Stronger exchange relationships can result. Brands using these relationship management advantages can build a positive reputation based on their being more responsive, involved, open and relevant towards followers. These stronger relationships are not just with individual customers. At a group level social media can be used to nurture consumer communities. Opportunities are for groups of likeminded consumers to come together and follow certain interests, as well as associated brands. Consumer awareness, ideas and feedback can be shared. Community members motivate, educate and inspire each other. This all has the effect of heightening consumer connections with a brand.

Zoflora ladies

Zoflora is a relatively low priced household cleaning fluid. The floral scented concentrate is diluted and used to clean surfaces. Not initially the most exciting of items, Zoflora nevertheless has a vibrant brand community across various social media. Online followers, mostly female, enthuse about the brand. They review its products, upload content regards its place in their household chores, and even launch businesses selling such things as personalised spray bottles. Users describe how important Zoflora is to their personal identities. Being known as the Zoflora lady at work for example, because of always having a bottle of the stuff handy. Members of Zoflora brand communities seem to be inspired by social media influencers who have built their reputation around cleaning. Mrs Hinch and similar such influencers upload content centred on household management tips and reviews. A vibrant online cleaning community is the result. As previously noted, consumer communities are important drivers of brands' success. These communities frequently advocate on behalf of the brands they are enthusiastic about. They amplify the content and communications of brands, increasing reach. Consumer communities contribute ideas and materials of their own meanwhile. As such, brand aura benefits from vibrant consumer communities.

Commercial case: Fan BingBing

Social media may be a source of reputation building, through engaging fans in relationships. However, the potential is for engagement to turn hostile and for relationships and reputations to be undermined by negativity. Social media facilitates and augments reputation destruction at least as much as it enables its fabrication. This dual edged experience might be observed in relation to a second influencer. Fan Bingbing is a Chinese actress, model, singer and online influencer, and arguably the most famous celebrity in China. Fan has acted in many domestic and international films since her breakthrough in the highly successful 2003 Chinese comedy-action film Cell Phone. This movie helped propel her to being one of the most recognisable entertainers in the country.

Social media augmented Fan Bingbing's celebrity status. With tens of millions of followers across her social media, the entertainer has significant brand recognition and clout. Bingbing is a brand name engaged with millions of online users who interact with and consume her content. As a significant off and online influencer, Fan worked with dozens of designer brands, such as Louis Vuitton and Chopard, as an ambassador. They desired links with a figure so well known, glamorous and who had such a large and engaged online following. Reportedly, brands would raise their prices shortly before a Fan Bingbing led endorsement, knowing that she would create a surge in demand amongst fans who wanted to emulate her.

Nevertheless, such a powerful and profitable reputation was not impregnable. In July 2018 at the height of her fame, Fan Bingbing disappeared. Her public appearances stopped. Her social media went quiet. Upcoming films she was due to appear in were delayed from release. No announcement or explanation was provided. Whether Fan had officially vanished or not was never stated. However, people quickly began to realise that there was no trace of the most famous woman in China. Brands, ever sensitive to staying on the right side of the Chinese government, sensed something was off and began to drop her (Myers, 2018). Rumours circulated online of whether Fan was in prison or had fled abroad. Foreign media began to pick up on the story.

Just as suddenly as she disappeared, Fan reappeared on 3 October 2018, three months after she first went missing. In an apparent explanation, the entertainer issued an apology via her social media for not setting a good example to society and asked for forgiveness. At the same time, Chinese authorities reported the actress was guilty of underreporting her income in order to avoid taxes. They announced fines on her and her businesses of $131 million dollars in back taxes and penalties.

This tax avoidance scandal had started earlier that year in the month's leading up to her disappearance. In May 2018 accusations were made on Weibo by Cui Yongyuan, a famed TV host known for his feud with the director of Cell Phone and the upcoming Cell Phone 2. Jeong (2019), who documents the Fan Bingbing story in detail, describes how Cui's initial accusation was that Fan had been paid far more to appear in Cell Phone 2 than had been officially reported. This opened Fan Bingbing up to much online gossip about her fabulous wealth and supposed corruption. Although she initially carried on as normal, over the course of the next month the gossip around Fan continued to grow, culminating in her eventual arrest and punishment. Bingbing's reputation was augmented online, but so too was it destroyed.

Social ranking

The experience of Fan Bingbing reveals a lot about the importance of reputation in China. Jeong outlines how Fan Bingbing has an enduring connection with her generation Y fans, who have grown up with over her 20 year acting career, and feel connected as a result. They see Fan as not only beautiful and successful but also admirably kind, hardworking and independent. These qualities speak to the aspirations of millennial Chinese. The sudden and unexplained disappearance of one of the most famous and well liked celebrities in China was therefore a powerful symbol that nobody is beyond the reach of the Chinese Communist Party (CCP).

In China, there is a need to comply with the country's social rules, as dictated by the CCP. China has been working towards a system of social ranking that measures all citizens based on their behaviour. This reportedly goes into micro detail, with such things as spending too frivolously or even playing computer games being noted and counting against people's social ranking assessment (Nittle, 2018). It seems likely that higher social rankings may be rewarded, with for example access to better jobs. Meanwhile, lower social rankings could face the threat of sanctions (Ma, 2018). In a country where the CCP is powerful and sets strict rules on social, cultural and political conduct, and where social standing is highly important to getting various opportunities, people need to be carefully conscious of their reputation.

Fan Bingbing seems to have been a useful example to make this point to Chinese citizens overall. In a 2018 social ranking of 100 top celebrities in China conducted by the Chinese Academy of Social Sciences, Fan Bingbing ranked at the bottom (Liya, 2018). Her social and cultural status did not fit the expectations of Chinese leaders. The consequences of this poor rating for Fan were made clear by her disappearance, and by extension were made clear to her fellow nationals. All Chinese need to be mindful of their public reputations if they want to stay on the right side of the government and avoid negative consequences. Jeong notes that since returning to public life, Fan Bingbing has carefully presented herself in line with CCP ideology.

In China, social reputation is monitored and rated by the CCP. Whilst this may seem dystopian, and indeed it is, to some extent at least such ranking systems occur in all parts of the world. In capitalist economies for example, credit rating is all important to determining ability to obtain the financing necessary to participate in consumerism and acquire social status through conspicuous consumption. Meanwhile, hierarchies around such things as class, age, gender, sexuality, ethnicity or religion are all heavily influential in various places as to how somebody is publically perceived and treated.

Henceforth, the question arises as to what extent individuals have power over constructing their own reputation, through such things as social media, and to what extent this is regulated by external circumstances. Social media influencers such as Angelababy are able to build well known and hugely profitable reputations. Yet, as Fan Bingbing's experience demonstrates, they are also exposed to having those reputations torn down. General social media users, consumers and citizens witness this dynamic and are influenced by it. They see profitable reputations being made and unmade online. In contemporary culture therefore, pressure is not only to build a positive reputation but also to avoid a negative one.

Case questions

1. Why would brands drop Fan Bingbing after her disappearance?
   Think about how brands try to manage their reputation and what might be considered as threats to this.
2. What factors contribute to social reputation where you are from?
   Evaluate different sources of social standing in your origin culture and consider how these may shape the ways that people manage their reputations through such things as social media.

Consumption under surveillance

The rise of social media has accompanied an increased consciousness of being constantly observed. Anyone with a footprint thereupon is easily traceable. Their heritage, actions and values are online for all to see. As various cases covered in the media have demonstrated, this ease of being observed online can have consequences. People have lost jobs because of old social media posts coming to light considered inappropriate. Advice to students and prospective job applicants is to clean up old social media and to present a professional image on current sites.

Nevertheless, the pervasive reach of digital technology is difficult to manage. Beyond social media, where users at least have some degree of control over their interactions and content, digital technology is continually tracking consumers. GPS and mobile data for example monitor the geographical location of individuals. Their physical routes and wandered paths are recorded. In addition, browser histories record digital routes and paths. Such things as online searches and purchases are logged and used to build up a detailed impression of attitudes, behaviours and lifestyles.

Such surveillance can be convenient. Cookies used to track online browsing may help to improve website user experiences by tailoring recommendations and making sponsored content more relevant. Nevertheless, this surveillance can become creepy. There is something unsettling about the always watching, ever listening devices that have become indispensable pieces of our lives. Phones that listen in on conversations and then bring up associated adverts the next time a browser is opened for example are an unwelcome reminder that our most personal exchanges are being mined for commercial purposes.

Such surveillance often takes place without making clear that it is occurring. The ability of technology users to give informed consent to their being monitored and their data monetised is debateable. Notoriously long user agreements for software and apps are ticked unread. Cookies consent statements on websites are swatted away like irritating mosquitoes. As early as 2004, Zwick and Dholakia recognised that consumers display tactics for managing their identity online such as adjusting privacy settings or choosing which details to share. However, the authors contend that such actions are largely ineffective and provide only the perception of sovereignty. Zwick and Dholakia conclude that only full access to databases, not the mere ability to tweak profiles, allows for maintenance of control over identity.

Data mining of consumers is extensive and largely invisible. The sovereignty of the individual consumer online is tenuous. So far, consumers seem to be a mixture of unaware and unbothered by this. It may be that trading a certain amount of privacy is accepted in return for convenience. However, consumer acceptance of their data being accessed and exploited may decrease. There are already signs of this happening, with a number of campaigners and industry figures suggesting that ownership and control of data will become a debate of growing importance.

Onlyfans

Onlyfans and similar platforms are sexually explicit social media. Users interact with sexual content created and shared by other users. They pay for the privilege. In order to generate income, performers need to curate their online reputation. They solicit the attention of potential followers through discounts and special offers. On other platforms, particularly Twitter, they share taster video clips and links to their paywall protected content. By interacting with potential customers, and by producing and uploading their most intimate moments, Onlyfans brands are made. Such sites are perhaps the ultimate expression of how social media has facilitated a shift from private to public. Even most intimate moments are now shared in the hope of being monetised or even just noticed.

Consumer empowerment

The rise of social media and other related digital technologies raise questions over consumer empowerment. In short, empowerment means gaining mastery over one's life. This can be related to the things that facilitate self-mastery, or that may undermine. Zimmerman (2000) describes how actions, activities or structures may be empowering, and the outcome of such processes result in a level of being empowered. To illustrate, consumption can be empowering as an activity. It provides opportunities to meet essential needs important to quality of life such as healthy food. Consumption can also help people to enjoy life by pursuing pleasures such as entertainment.

In turn, the digital realm may empower consumers. The connections to others and access to information that social media provides might enable consumers to make more careful decisions. They can benefit from reading reviews, soliciting the opinions of others and staying up to date with latest developments. In short, consumers do not have to take brand's reputations at face value. They can readily evaluate these themselves. In turn, conscious of maintaining their reputations brands may be more responsive to consumers who they know are watching.

At the same time, social media and similar technologies have disempowered consumers who face their personal data being widely accessed, shared and exploited without clear consent. As such, consumers are subject to surveillance themselves. Their backstory, vision, actions and values are open to analysis and critique. Conscious of this, some consumers are starting to become more cautious when it comes to their online behaviour or their use of digital technology.

Whether consumers will continue to accept such surveillance is debateable. People have strategies for dealing with power relationships, and particularly imbalances or encroachments. Consumers can take action to resist and to rebalance these. Disengagement and hostile engagement can be used as strategies to protect or push back against intrusions upon consumer sovereignty.

It is therefore important for marketers to respect the empowerment of contemporary consumers. This means being conscious of their ability to observe, analyse and discuss marketing content and communications. Being sensitive and consistent with these will ideally avoid misunderstandings or confrontations that can harm brand reputation. In addition, mindful of disempowering consumers, marketers need to respect the boundaries of consumers' privacy and control. Positive reputations are and will increasingly be built on honesty and integrity when it comes to mutual surveillance.

Chapter summary

Reputation is essential to brands. A strong reputation is a source of higher social standing and trust. Brands such as Halo Top that are able to build an aura around themselves may be more likely to connect with consumers. Hence, reputation management through such things as brand narratives or social media engagement is an important aspect of marketing practice. As every individual increasingly becomes akin to a brand, thanks to their digital fingerprint, reputation management is now something conducted by consumers as well as marketers. Inspired by the successes and traumas of social media influencers, such as Angelababy and Fan Bingbing, consumers are conscious of being under surveillance. This awareness may influence their engaging with refraction as a means to regain some power. As the next chapter outlines, refraction can be used to manipulate and mythologise viewers, helping to create and disseminate preferred narratives.

References

Beltrone, G. (2014). Burger King has people 'Cheat on Beef' with chicken burgers at an actual motel. *AdWeek*, 28/03/14. Available at: https://www.adweek.com/creativity/burger-king-has-people-cheat-beef-chicken-burgers-actual-motel-156601/ (accessed 19/06/20).

Buckley, T. (2019). The ice cream wars heat up: Upstart halo top is eating into Ben & Jerry's parent Unilever's lead. The giant is countering with its own high-protein, probiotic treat. *Bloomberg Businessweek*, 4599, 14.

Cassidy, A. (2018). The man who created a $2bn ice cream firm in his kitchen. *BBC News*, 02/07/2018. Available at: https://www.bbc.co.uk/news/business-44614104 (accessed 15/05/2020).

Fine, G. A. (2003). Crafting authenticity: The validation of identity in self-taught art. *Theory and Society*, 32(2), 153–180.

Jeong, M. (2019). "The big error was that she was caught": The untold story behind the mysterious disappearance of Fan Bingbing, the world's biggest movie star. *Vanity Fair*, 26/03/19. Available at: https://www.vanityfair.com/hollywood/2019/03/the-untold-story-disappearance-of-fan-bingbing-worlds-biggest-movie-star (accessed 04/06/20).

Kennick, W. E. (1985). Art and inauthenticity. *The Journal of Aesthetics and Art Criticism*, 44(1), 3–12.

Liya, F. (2018). Chinese celebrities given social responsibility rankings. *Sixth Tone*, 04/09/20. Available at: http://www.sixthtone.com/news/1002871/chinese-celebrities-given-social-responsibility-rankings (accessed 04/06/20).

Ma, A. (2018). China has started ranking citizens with a creepy 'social credit' system — here's what you can do wrong, and the embarrassing, demeaning ways they can punish you. *Business Insider*, 29/10/18. Available at: https://www.businessinsider.com/china-social-credit-system-punishments-and-rewards-explained-2018-4?r=US&IR=T (Accessed 04/06/20).

Nittle, N. (2018). Spend "frivolously" and be penalized under China's new social credit system. *Vox*, 02/11/18. Available at: https://www.vox.com/the-goods/2018/11/2/18057450/china-social-credit-score-spend-frivolously-video-games (accessed 04/06/20).

OMR. (2018). China's crazy influencer industry: A German stands out amidst clone factories and billion-dollar revenues. *Medium*, 25/09/18. Available at: https://medium.com/@omrockstars/chinas-crazy-influencer-industry-a-german-stands-out-amidst-clone-factories-and-billion-dollar-c9a2f632de54 (accessed 02/06/20).

Snow, S. (2016). What it's like to eat nothing but this magical, healthy ice cream for 10 days? *GQ*, 28/01/16. Available at: https://www.gq.com/story/halo-top-ice-cream-review-diet

Veloutsou, C., & Moutinho, L. (2009). Brand relationships through brand reputation and brand tribalism. *Journal of Business Research*, 62(3), 314–322.

Wohl, J. (2017). How halo top is conquering the ice cream biz—without ads. *Advertising Age*, 88(5), 8.

Zimmerman, M. A. (2000). Empowerment theory. In Rappaport, J.; & Seidman, E. (eds.). *Handbook of community psychology*. New York: Springer. pp. 43–63.

Zwick, D., & Dholakia, N. (2004). Whose identity is it anyway? Consumer representation in the age of database marketing. *Journal of Macromarketing*, 24(1), 31–43.

6
REFRACTION

Alternative realities and marketing fairy tales – myths around dropshipping, meerkats and backpackers

Reality as complicated and malleable

In February 2002, the then United States Secretary of Defense, Donald Rumsfeld, delivered what would become an infamous response to a press briefing enquiry. Questioned on the lack of evidence linking the government of Iraq to weapons of mass destruction, Rumsfeld made the following statement:

> Reports that say that something hasn't happened are always interesting to me, because as we know, there are known knowns; there are things we know we know. We also know there are known unknowns; that is to say we know there are some things we do not know. But there are also unknown unknowns; the ones we don't know we don't know.

Much mocked at the time, this comment has nonetheless come to be assessed in a different light. Indeed, Rumsfeld may have been insightful in his description of knowledge. The idea of knowledge as being limited in various ways is an interesting one to explore. The philosopher Slavoj Žižek (2005) engages with this when analysing Rumsfeld's comment, adding that beyond these three categories, there is a fourth. Žižek describes this as the unknown known that which we intentionally refuse to acknowledge that we know.

Rumsfeld's description of what is known-known, known-unknown and unknown-unknown, along with Žižek's unknown known, is an unwittingly perceptive comment on the limitations of knowledge and lack of knowledge. These limitations have perhaps become more apparent in the years since. The uncertainty of various selective knowns and unknowns has infiltrated our ways of thinking at large. Speculation, paranoia, conspiracy and fantasy have moved from fringes into wider public consciousness.

Now, it is increasingly difficult to assert what is known and what is unknown. The digital realm is increasingly implicated in this confusion of knowledge. On the one hand, we have via the internet a wealth of information at our fingertips. On the other hand, the quality of that information is deeply uncertain. Deepfakes, bots, puppet accounts and other online manipulators pump out content to fit particular agendas. Commercial motives for example often hide behind apparently spontaneous content. Online it is difficult to know what is real. With the virtual and physical worlds intertwined, this uncertainty is leaking from the digital realm into everything else as well.

The result is an age of consumer conspiracy. Mixed, alternative and competing messages are multiplying. This can make it hard for consumers to know what sources to trust. In an era of fake news, marketers face difficulties getting their messages across. The media landscape is not only ever more fragmented; it also hosts competing claims over what is real and what is fake. Brands risk getting lost in this disorder. Conspiracy theories have proliferated and can pose a challenge to organisations that come in for criticism.

Yet this is also an age of consumer possibility. Digital technologies have empowered consumers to acquire knowledge, and also taught them to treat it with distrust. Consumers can investigate and challenge versions of events, truth claims and promises, like never before. This is leading to savvier and more demanding customers. What is more, consumers are harnessing digital technology to craft their own versions of reality. Online, it is possible to live out heightened versions of self. By selectively resenting and editing public image it is possible to create convincing myths that alter and extend actual consumption.

#Deepfakes

Deepfakes are unreal media images or videos in which a person in an existing image or video is replaced with someone else's likeness. Artificial media images have long existed. Photo shopped celebrity magazine spreads for example. However, deepfakes are distinguished by how convincing the image or video can be made to feel thanks to advanced machine learning technology. This believability has led to concerns about viewers being tricked into believing faked content. For example, politicians may be deepfaked saying something they never did, in order to lose the respect of voters. Deepfake pornography, often involving celebrities, is another worrying application. In both these respects manipulation of content is not new or restricted to high tech digital applications. Selective reporting of political speeches or erotic fan fiction have long existed. Deepfakes do show however, how much more sophisticated and widespread bogus content might become. As it does, this increases wariness about what can be taken as reality.

Making our own reality and alternative facts

Following on from Rumsfeld, two other much commented upon insights into political mind-sets have been informative when considering how knowledge of reality is shifting. The first of these was brought to attention in a 2004 article in the New York Times Magazine. Here, the journalist Ron Suskind was investigating the inner workings of the George W. Bush Whitehouse. During the course of this investigation, Suskind shared a quote from an unnamed political aide:

> The aide said that guys like me were 'in what we call the reality-based community, 'which he defined as people who 'believe that solutions emerge from your judicious study of discernible reality.' [...] 'That's not the way the world really works anymore, 'he continued. 'We're an empire now, and when we act, we create our own reality.

And while you're studying that reality - judiciously, as you will - we'll act again, creating other new realities, which you can study too, and that's how things will sort out. We're history's actors... and you, all of you, will be left to just study what we do'.

The veracity of the quote and who said it have been contested. Whitehouse insiders denied that such a thing was said with the journalist present. Suskind defended that it had. Either way, Suskind's article picked up on an interesting idea. This is the sense that reality, in terms of widely shared and accepted knowledge, truths, stories and values, can be made. Rather than studying what is happening in order to establish the facts, which takes time, just going out and acting may assert facts, real or not. By the time they have been studied and proved or disproved, things have moved on and those actions have already helped influence people.

The second of these political insights happened in January 2017, when Kellyanne Conway used the term 'alternative facts' during a televised press briefing. The Presidential Counsellor defended statements made by the White House about the size of President Trump's inauguration crowd. Despite plentiful evidence, including photographs and metro journey data that showed the crowd as significantly smaller than that for Barack Obama's first inauguration, Conway defended the false claim that Trump attracted more followers. She mentioned the Trump team as having alternative facts to those being put forward by critics.

Conway's use of alternative facts was rapidly pulled apart by political commentators. They were aghast at the idea that provable facts could just be dismissed, and provable lies asserted, by politicians in a democratic system. Yet again, despite the initial shock of such a bald term, alternative facts are an interesting description of knowledge and reality as debateable. They are also a reminder that strong arguments backed up by evidence are not always enough to convince people of a particular version of reality. After all, billions of humans believe in God, despite the lack of evidence for and compelling arguments against God's existence.

A loose relationship with reality is perhaps quite normal in politics, where politicians have always tried to put forward particular viewpoints and spin issues in as favourable a way as possible. Nevertheless, the increasingly open discussion of reality in politics is noteworthy. As highly visible members of society, politicians have influence over wider public attitudes and behaviours. If political leaders are questioning established truths and propagating made up alternatives, then it may not be surprising if such conversations catch on in other domains as well.

In the 21st century it has become normal to challenge established assumptions that are inconvenient, even where the evidence for doing so is highly insubstantial, as with Conway's alternative facts. Meanwhile, creating new reality through actions, as Suskind overheard, is becoming more possible at an everyday level. Both alternative and made realities are permitted by new technology in particular. Online there is endless content, including information to back up any possible alternative reality. Moreover, if that information does not yet exist, then it can easily be produced, shared and used to make up a new reality. The digital realm has made it easy to counter argue, subvert, manipulate or propose preferred theories. There has never been so much potential for making new and alternate realities.

Vranyo
Vranyo is a Russian word that loosely translates as white lies or half-lies. In Russian culture, these vranyo are told not so much with the intention of maliciously deceiving,

but instead for suppressing unpleasant parts of the truth. Vranyo are something of a fantasy, exaggerating certain aspects and overlooking others as desired. With vranyo, the fantasy is often openly so. The person telling the lie knows it is a lie. So too the listener. Both also know that the other knows. However, the lie is mutually bought into regardless and the fantasy perpetuated. Vranyo is something of a subtle mutual dance. Illustrating this in action, Vladimir Putin has been associated with vranyo by a number of commentators. His winning appearances at judo tournaments or ice hockey matches are simultaneously clearly faked set pieces and widely accepted evidence of his strong leadership. With vranyo, the lies are often as important and informative as the truth.

Virtual realities

The limits to and manipulation of reality, proliferation of alternative facts and propagation of vranyo are all turbocharged by the internet. Online, it is possible to freely assemble and distribute opinions. Anyone with wifi can do so. This freedom of expression is one of the greatest assets of the internet. It potentially gives voice to everyone, including those long excluded from mainstream media. Digital journalists and online users have documented for example police abuse of black people in the United States, shining a light on an often hidden issue. Yet that same internet freedom has meant that anything can be shared online, including hate speech, conspiracy theories, malicious content and accidental or deliberate misinformation. The anonymity and interconnectedness of the internet mean that it is difficult to verify information sources or ascertain motivations.

Whether personal or purposeful, the proliferation of partial and false information online is becoming an acute problem. An extreme consequence of this can be seen in a wave of lynching in parts of India targeting the Muslim community, fuelled by accusations made over the WhatsApp messenger service (Madrigal, 2018). Longstanding local tensions between Hindus and Muslims predate the appearance of WhatsApp in India. However, these platforms have been used by vested interests to spread false information and whip up a reaction that serves their purposes. Increasingly, ideological conflicts are being made worse by their playing out online. Digital media can be used to discredit opponents through a variety of tactics that seek to control perceptions of reality:

- *Manipulating reality* includes activities to modify and twist stories to suit particular purposes. Selectively editing and presenting data can be used to change the believability or emphasis of a story. Cropping photographs, videos clips or quotes for example, or taking these out of context, are ways of shifting the impression of an event, discussion or statement.
- *Asserting reality* is the process of sharing a particular viewpoint or version of events. Online, the most popular story is what trends, not the most honest or rigorous. Hence, gaming digital platforms is a way of pushing forward certain stories, as when armies of paid followers like and share sponsored content.
- **Supressing reality** is the action taken to silence dissenting opinions. Cyber bullying has been linked to a number of suicides. Revenge porn, the releasing of intimate images in order to humiliate someone, can likewise have consequences for victims. Fear of such harassment has the effect of pushing out different voices and stifling debate.

Virtual reality is less dramatic than often depicted in science fiction films or slick videogame marketing. It is however more insidious. Instead of immersive fantasy simulations accessed via headsets, smaller enhancements and twists play out on phone and laptop screens. Algorithmically filtered news feeds orientate content in a certain direction. Social network contacts present themselves in a flattering light. Controversial posts generate interactions and become more visible. The consequence is an online virtual reality that is geared towards certain attributes. This is a selective reality, an augmented reality and increasingly a personalised reality, where the boundaries between control and manipulation are becoming more opaque.

#CoronaChallenge

Amidst the initial global shutdown associated with the spread of Covid-19, the #CoronaChallenge trended (originally, Covid-19 was named coronavirus). This saw a number of young social media influencers and users taking up deliberately stupid and provocative acts, such as coughing in people's faces. Part of this, the TikTok star Ava Louise courted controversy, when she filmed herself licking a toilet seat on a flight. Strong reaction to and condemnation of such videos followed. Understandably viewers were upset during a time of uncertainty and stress. However, the reaction to a small number of teenagers being stupid, as teenagers are prone to being, and of a few influencers seeking attention, as their business model demands, was perhaps, as so many things on the internet are, disproportionate. In reality almost nobody took up the #CoronaChallenge. The problem of the online realm is that trending stories gather momentum and shape perspectives, whether they are all that broadly representative, or not.

Consumer case: building the backpacker myth

Distortions of reality that exaggerate, romanticise or perhaps entirely fabricate can be found in relation to consumers and consumption. Amongst backpackers for example, there can be a tendency to emphasise preferred facts and make own realities. Backpackers are a specific tourist niche who tend to travel for extended periods of time, stay in relatively basic accommodation and where the journey itself is often as important as reaching a particular destination. There is a strong backpacker subculture which may be found online and offline. As with other consumer communities, backpackers develop a sense of cohesive identity around their shared interest.

Backpackers have distinctive consumption characteristics. They tend to spend less money day-to-day, but because they go away for longer periods, cumulatively backpackers may invest a significant amount in their travel. Backpackers are also willing to go off the beaten track and put up with more rudimentary infrastructure. They will often visit and stay in places other tourists would not want to.

Indeed, status for backpackers comes from visiting more exotic and unusual locations. The length and difficulty of time spent on the road are considered important. In addition, connecting with local people and cultures is emphasised amongst the backpacker community. These backpacker traits help to set apart from regular tourists. Doing so is important to.

Therefore, demonstrating consumption of more challenging and adventurous, or culturally sensitive experiences, gains status amongst fellow backpackers. Consumer symbols and stories obtained from this specific type of travel can be used by backpackers to acquire social standing. Backpackers have a vested interest in describing themselves in a certain way. Emphasising particular attitudes, behaviours and lifestyles through consumption can help to gain prestige. Those products, services and experiences purchased that complement social standing may be played up. More mundane parts of tourism consumption that do not help build consumer status are less likely to be shared.

Canavan (2018) suggests that status building may be observed amongst backpackers in their self-conscious attempts to position themselves as desirable travellers who are ambitious, adventurous and original. For Canavan, these attempts at image building particularly take place online, with social media used to selectively promote a classic backpacker identity. This is carefully presented in line with what is valued by the wider backpacker community. Using local transport is highlighted online for instance, as a means of seeming more adventurous and willing to live like a local. However, use of airplanes, which is inevitably the case much of the time, is rarely featured, because this does not add status.

As such backpacking consumers present refractions of reality. These are distortions of actual consumer experiences that gradually alter reality for those who observe and those who fabricate. Backpackers may promote certain consumption choices, and downplay others, altering the impression of what actually took place. Such myth making is something that many tourists indulge and that digital technologies encourage. It is tempting to present oneself on holiday as more interesting than the reality might have been. An image is cropped to get rid of the other guests and make look more exotic. Highpoints are shared, not the lowlights. Social media is about editing and exaggerating in ways that are conducive to social status seeking. Social media vranyo allows consumers to project a faintly fantastical version of themselves.

Case questions

1 How can consumers manipulate their consumption to make this seem more significant in a certain way?
    Think about the tools and techniques available to contemporary consumers for editing, distorting, selectively representing or heightening their consumption.
2 Why might consumers choose to present their consumption in an exaggerated way?
    Consider the outcomes sought by consumers such as identity and social standing. Evaluate how not just consumption but the presentation of consumption may help to fulfil these.

Refraction: manipulating reality

Refraction is the term used to describe light waves (also sound, liquid and other waves) being deflected in passing through the interface between one medium and another such as air and then water. Such mediums have varying density; water is thicker than air. As light passes through different densities its appearance alters. The change in direction of the wave is a result of its travelling at different speeds through the different mediums.

Refraction manipulates light and has the effect of an optical illusion. It is because of refraction that objects under water appear closer than they actually are. Refraction is also responsible for natural optical phenomena such as rainbows or mirages, where light is distorted and appears altered to the human eye.

Refraction is a useful analogy for the manipulation of more than waves. Reality, in terms of knowledge, truths and facts, can similarly be deflected through the different mediums that these pass through. Mediums, such as word of mouth, institutions, influencers and media, pick up and share realities. An idea that originates somewhere can be picked up and shared globally through such things as social media newsfeeds. As this occurs, the original source may be refracted. Its appearance might be altered. Multiple variations, augmentations and alternatives may emerge.

Different mediums can present knowledge, facts and truths in various ways. Gossip can heighten and exaggerate content. Officials can try to put a positive spin on events. Selective reporting can play up certain aspects and not others. Surroundings can be cropped away. Interpretations can put a particular spin on the original. Alternative interpretations, subversions and proposed alternatives fragment the singularity of reality into multiple possibilities. As such, as an idea passes through different mediums it can be manipulated into appearing quite different from its original context (Figure 6.1).

Although such manipulations take place in various mediums, social media is particularly notorious for distorting reality. Online, digital presentations can be used to create and project a desired outward impression. These might be truthful, entirely fabricated or somewhere in-between. Selective presentation, editing and filtering are all readily available online. Simple tools built into popular applications can alter and enhance original images, comments and versions of events.

Indeed, users are encouraged to refract reality as a standard part of the social media experience. Online drama, exaggerated beauty stereotypes, claims to lifestyles of luxury, such distortions of more mundane or nuanced truths are present throughout social media. Users get pulled into the illusions being crafted. Myths are created, promoted, self-convinced and made real. Eventually, what is truth, half-truth or entirely fabricated merge. They become so blurred as to become indeterminate. On social media, what is real or a refraction is difficult to ascertain.

Commercial case: the BS reality of dropshipping

An illustration of how social media refraction has been adopted by marketers comes from the world of dropshipping. This is a recently emerged phenomenon, whereby so called

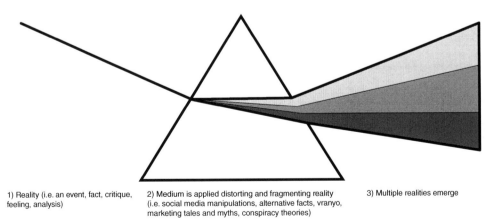

1) Reality (i.e. an event, fact, critique, feeling, analysis)   2) Medium is applied distorting and fragmenting reality (i.e. social media manipulations, alternative facts, vranyo, marketing tales and myths, conspiracy theories)   3) Multiple realities emerge

FIGURE 6.1 Reality refraction.

dropshippers act as middle persons between manufacturers and consumers. This is all done online. Dropshippers search large digital marketplaces, such as Ebay or Ali Express, for niche products that they think consumers might be interested in, for example Bento lunchboxes. They then create virtual stores where these products can be ordered, and pay for targeted ads on platforms, particularly Facebook, promoting items to potential customers. Once orders arrive, the dropshipper buys from the original seller and send to the customer's address, pocketing a small mark up in the process.

Dropshipping is a simple and low cost business model. All that is needed is a small amount of capital to buy targeted ads and access to the internet. Dropshipping hubs, such as Chiang Mai and Bali, have experienced influxes of young people looking to start up their own businesses in places with low living costs. These exotic locations have also helped turn an odd internet side-line into a seemingly glamorous lifestyle opportunity. International migrants have flocked to dropshipping hubs in order to get involved in the prospects apparently on offer.

Belying its simple premise, dropshipping is presented to outsiders as a glitzy profession where individuals have the opportunity to get rich quick. Many dropshippers are active on social media, where they use various platforms not only to advertise their products but also to build personal brands. Posing inside luxury villas, leaning on the hood of supercars, displaying their muscles, tans and designer outfits, these young self-described entrepreneurs encourage others to follow in their footsteps. It is all social media refraction, enhancing a far less glamorous reality, in the hope of convincing others. The lifestyle of a dropshipper is made to look as appealing as possible.

This is because an important side-line for many dropshippers is offering coaching services. People can pay to learn how to set up an online store and begin ordering products. The incredibly simple, fast way to make money, as the ubiquitous YouTube adverts always exclaim in their titles, nevertheless needs prospective entrepreneurs to follow specific sets of rules, and to pay for the privilege.

These coaching services are vital because there is seemingly little money to be made in dropshipping itself. Media investigations, such as that by Kale (2020), have called the aura around the activity bullshit. The expensive cars in the YouTube promotions are hired for the day. The bling watches are fake. The exclusive lifestyle is a myth based on credit. Meanwhile, the actual profits to be made are slim. Mark ups on items have to be small in order to keep prices competitive whilst still covering costs. It is also hard and uncertain work, with no guarantee that particular products or targeted ad campaigns will pay off. It seems that most dropshippers work long hours for a relatively modest annual income.

More than this, dropshipping has elements of being a marketing scam. The products displayed in targeted ads often have little resemblance to the reality that arrives weeks later through the post. Many dropshippers can lose out when dissatisfied customers ask for refunds. In 2016, Buzzfeed investigated the long and murky supply chains behind such unsatisfying orders (Maheshwari & Fu, 2016). They found common incidences of photos being stolen, designs ripped off and fake profiles set up. With little regulation, it is difficult for those who get sucked into the too-good-to-be-true refractions of dropshipping, whether as entrepreneurs or customers, to get what they hoped for.

Snake oil scams and Ponzi schemes

Dropshipping is not the first area of commerce to be built on more dubious foundations than the associated marketing lets on. 'Snake oil salesperson' is an old term from the late 1800's. It was used to describe travelling merchants who would try to sell medicinal cures (including those supposedly made from snakes) using elaborate claims regarding their effectiveness. Meanwhile, Ponzi schemes, names after the 1920s fraudster Charles Ponzi who at the time ran one of the biggest, are based on luring investors to put money into a particular business. Their money is used to cover up the fact that the business has little to no sales coming in; all of the supposed profits come from investors. Thus more and more investors need to be recruited if the scheme is to keep going. Eventually, when new investors run out, the scam collapses. Snake oil and Ponzi schemes are forms of fraud. They refract reality, extremely and dishonestly so, in order to appeal to consumers.

Case questions

1. If the reality of dropshipping is less glamorous than online presentations would suggest, then what other industries refract reality to manipulate stakeholder perceptions, and how do they do this?
    Consider marketing tools and techniques used for initiating and managing exchange relationships in a variety of contexts.
2. Do some business sectors, product categories or brands manipulate reality more than others?
    Using examples, think about how truthful marketing content and communications are. Discuss why this honesty-dishonesty might be the case.

Telling tall tales: marketing myth making

Dropshippers join a fantasy lifestyle associated with this business practice. Following the social media stories of their peers, dropshippers similarly create their own mythical lifestyles. These refract the reality of a career that involves hard work, uncertain pay and challenges of making a sales breakthrough. These aspects of the job are all downplayed. Instead the glamour, beauty and independence of dropshipping are emphasised. In embellishing these aspects the dropshipper lifestyle is mythologised. It becomes something more than the mundane reality, but more of an idealisation, aspiration or fantasy.

As such, dropshippers are crafting fairy tales through the selective narratives they develop and share. They are telling stories from their personal point of view, documenting their surroundings and blending real and fantasy elements into a purposeful narrative. These four features are recognised components of fairy tales. These are a specific type of storytelling concerned with the experience of a focal protagonist, the interface of reality and fantasy, influence of surroundings and with a lesson to be drawn from:

1. First, fairy tales look at the individual storyteller, who is typically interwoven into a tale as both narrator and protagonist. Many fairy tales are written from the perspective of the individual heroine or hero as they go about a particular quest. Their journey, the obstacles faced and the outcome of this are rooted in the other three aspects of such stories. Online, dropshippers share their personal journeys. They tell stories about their livelihood and lifestyle.

2   Second, fairy tales deal with interpretations of reality and fantasy. These blend elements that might be real, such as poverty, with those that are fantastical such as the use of magic. It is the blending of both that informs the protagonist's journey. Rumpelstiltskin for example is a tale of female exploitation, but uses magic to illustrate and as allegory for this. Dropshipper narratives try to be both tempting and convincing. They include apparently real details, such as information regarding business practices, with probably fantastical exaggerations such as of the money to be made.

3   Third, fairy tales place the protagonist in their sociocultural surroundings. Stories are heavily influenced by the context in which they are told. Although they contain timeless elements, explaining their enduring appeal, fairy tales are updated in line with the times that they are told in. Croft (2006) for example shows how the Hansel and Gretel story evolves over time in line with surroundings. Parental fears over child safety are timeless, but the influences on these fears can change depending on context. Dropshippers make their stories relevant to contemporary surroundings of young people. They play on their economic insecurities by emphasising the financial wealth and freedom that can come from this career.

4   Fourth, fairy tales tend to contain a lesson that is taken from them. They serve a purpose such as outlining the consequences of a particular type of behaviour, or underscoring the roles that certain types of protagonist are supposed to play. Princesses for instance are expected to act in an expected way if they are to get their happily ever after. So too dropshippers will get the livelihood and lifestyle depicted in the online fairy tales, if only they follow the system being proscribed.

Fairy tales and marketing

All cultures tell fairy tales in some form or another, with often broad similarities in terms of structure and content. Ziolkowski (2010) argues that these are one of the few literary genres shared by people of all ages and social classes in all Western countries. These stories are moreover intertwined with childhood. In Western countries in particular, such figures as Hans Christian Anderson are presented as suitable for children, with great commercial success.

Consequently, fairy tales are a source of shared experience for most humans, and one which connects deeply with childhood. Hearing 'once upon a time…' is a trigger that most people will immediately recognise, and one that brings to mind certain images, memories and emotions. This makes fairy tales a powerful resource for marketers, and it is one which is used accordingly. Tapping into fairy-tale motifs is an opportunity to connect with the stories and meanings which we share from an early age. Marketers do this through two methods: fakelore and folklure:

- This link between fairy tales and marketing was recognised by Dorson (1971). He coined the terms 'fakelore' and 'folklure' to describe the different methods used by marketers for exploiting the materials of fairy tales. The first of these, ***fakelore***, refers to the presentation of spurious or synthetic writings under the claim that they are genuine folklore. Plenty of adverts present made up backstories. Twix chocolate bars for example with their right Twix versus left Twix ads, featuring duelling Victorian brothers, are an obviously fakelore but funny nonetheless.

- Second, *folklure* relates to what Sullenberger (1974: 53) describes as "the calculated association of folkloristic concepts with manufactured products, usually through one form or another of the media, in the sole interest of commercial gain". Illustrating such marketing co-option, Green (2007) considers the figure of the fairy tale trickster as used often within breakfast cereal marketing. Children are familiar with fairy stories. They are exposed to storybooks, cartoons and films. Within these, it is not usually the princess or prince who are their favourite character, but the cheeky sidekick. So, when trying to woo children into eating breakfast cereal, manufacturers adopt these figures. For Green, this exploitation of fairy tale represents the mating of the mythology of those foods with the imperatives of the marketplace.

Fairy tales are therefore another means to refract reality. Through a blend of classical storytelling and archetypal characters, they present ideas in a format that taps into deep rooted cultural conditioning. Through telling such tales it may be possible to influence consumers. Illustrating these approaches are the numerous corporate fables and fairy-tale characters used in marketing.

At their most literal, marketers simply transport fairy-tale imagery directly into their sales pitches. Fairy-tale weddings for example trade on the storybook depictions of princesses, dresses, castles, carriages and happily ever after, making these familiar tropes available for purchase. Likewise, storybook characters crop up with regularity as marketing mascots. These similarly draw upon familiar figures and the associations these bring to mind in the consumer. Aunt Bessie's caring grandmother figure for instance is a familiar protagonist in many fairy stories. Connected with home comforts and safety, associating frozen potatoes with such an archetype is no bad thing.

Commercial case: Comparethemarket.com's adventures of Aleksandr and Sergei

A particularly successful corporate fairy tale is one offered by a British price comparison website. Starting in 2009, Comparethemarket.com began running its anthropomorphic meerkat-based marketing. This is premised on the actual Comparethemarket.com sounding like the fictional Comparethemeerkat.com, a website run by the on-screen CGI meerkats who irritatedly try to explain the difference between the two. From this slightly ropey premise, a long running marketing campaign has built up the fictional meerkat's lives and has made a lasting connection with British consumers.

The campaigns developed by Comparethemarket.com have over the years elaborated a fairy tale that features the four traits of such storytelling. This is in the sense of developing a narrative led by two meerkat protagonists, Aleksandr and Sergei, as well as blending content regarding the real price comparison service and its tangible consumer benefits, with an imaginary meerkat owned business. The meerkats' storylines pick up and respond to their surroundings, covering such things as immigration and digital assistants. Lastly, the lessons learnt from the marketing content are that money can be saved through using the aforementioned price comparison website, but not the aforementioned fictional meerkat one.

Aleksandr Orlov features as the on-going campaign's main protagonist and narrator. A Russian accented wealthy aristocrat and part time businessman, this slightly vain and selfish meerkat is accompanied by his often put-upon servant companion Sergei. Over the years, marketing has looked into the backstory of Alexandr's migrant ancestors. Adverts have visited the ancestral village of Meerkovo, where a number of distant relatives were introduced. Further fleshing out the lives and characteristics of the protagonists, commercials have over the years taken in holidays, hobbies and new business ventures. Recently, the pair have relocated to a Silicon Valley style tech hub.

Holding these disparate ventures together is the dysfunctional but deep relationship between Aleksandr and his servant-companion-partner-enabler Sergei. At one point, Sergei has a date with Nicole Kidman, who we can only presume was between agents at the time. However, he stands her up to take Aleksandr with him to the cinema instead. At another point, Aleksandr and Sergei adopt a baby meerkat, Oleg, left on their doorstep. After raising him together, over the course of various adverts, they later tearfully leave him in his native habitat whilst on safari after recognising that Oleg seemed to want to stay. Later, Oleg returns to join Aleksandr and Sergei in San Francisco, where they have lately been running a digital tech company.

The contents and storyline of Comparethemeerkat over the previous decade are eclectic and bizarre. Why the Russian accents? Is the relationship between Aleksandr and Sergei, which skirts domestic abuse, employee exploitation, co-dependency and homoeroticism, often all at once, healthy? What has Oleg been up to in the intervening years? Why and how is Sergei currently an apparent cyborg? Nonetheless, the adventures of Aleksandr and Sergei have resonated with the British audience. Aleksandr's one-time catchphrase of 'simples' entered national lexicon. The meerkats have an active fandom on social media. Spin off merchandise has included an Aleksandr autobiography and a range of at one point hotly collectible stuffed toys based on the various meerkat protagonists.

Aleksandr and Sergei have become an odd on-going fairy tale and little part of British culture in the process. They illustrate the power of storytelling in marketing as connecting with people, as well as the myth making potential of marketing, to craft a set of ideas and values that might be entirely fabricated, yet have a life well beyond the initial concept being promoted. Comparethemeerkat.com is explicitly not a real site. Comparethemarket.com expressly has nothing to do with small mammals. Yet weaving a fairy tale around these has engaged consumers for over a decade, and turned a basic internet service into a highly memorable brand. Indeed, Patterson, Khogeer and Hodgeson (2013) hold up the campaign as an example of how marketers can be inspired by and write literature themselves, and that leads, in turn, to more compelling brands.

Case questions

1. Are there examples of brand mascots that have failed to connect with or even pushed away consumers?
    Look for any examples of failed mascots and evaluate why these did not work.
2. If a brand relies on fictional characters and fairy tale brand narrative, what does this mean for brand authenticity?
    Authenticity relates to being honest and genuine, transparent and trustworthy. Think about how this may clash with overtly made up brand mascots and narratives.

Refraction extremes: conspiracy theories

Conspiracy theories are an extreme version of refraction through storytelling. Conspiracy theories all attack notions of what is factual and accurate. Knowledge, records of events, personal feelings, and collective experiences, all such ways of knowing reality are dismissed, twisted and countered by conspiracy theories. In so doing, things accepted as real are dismissed as fake, and vice versa. Gradually reality, as it is commonly accepted by individuals and groups, is eroded and replaced.

As with fairy tales, conspiracy theories are old stories found in all cultures. In their playing with reality and fantasy, and development of particular social commentary, conspiracy theories may be akin to contemporary fairy tales. Conspiracy theories similarly tell tall tales that fuse the real and the fantastical in order to put forward a particular version of events.

Conspiracy theories range from big and gradually agglomerating stories, such as those associated with 9/11, to the specific and almost immediate reactions to news events such as the Parkland school shooting. In either format, conspiracy theories are narratives that attempt to do two things. First, they discredit something such as an event, cultural belief or scientific theory. Second, they push forward a perspective that stems from a particular ideological viewpoint.

To illustrate, the Parkland school shooting occurred on 14 February 2018 when a gunman opened fire with a semi-automatic rifle at Marjory Stoneman Douglas High School in Parkland, Florida. Seventeen people were killed and another 17 injured. The perpetrator, a former student, was caught and confessed. Shortly after the tragedy, conspiracy theories began to be shared online. These claimed that the shooting never occurred, that nobody died and that the entire event was in fact staged using actors by the government who wanted to bring in gun control. This attempt to deny and twist the Parkland shooting appears to have been an attempt to discredit survivors who called in the aftermath for gun control. Online and even mainstream right-wing media attacks on the teenage campaigners and their families were vicious and outlandish.

With all conspiracy theories, a pattern is of attempting to discredit the original event, propose wild alternative scenarios and then gradually set these as fact. This is done for purposes of driving forward or at least protecting a particular agenda such as pro-guns. Even if outright denial is an extreme position, various claims tend to be made purposefully, for instance minimising the severity of school shootings or proposing tangential asides, such that these could be reduced if teachers are given guns. Pushing such viewpoints confuses the original event. In addition, extreme conspiracy theories have the effect of making mild-by-comparison, but still calculated, manipulative and dishonest claims, seem normal. They drag our overall perspective in a sought direction.

According to the philosophy professor Quassim Cassam (2019), conspiracy theories subvert received opinion and are based on the idea that things aren't as they seem. Conspiracy theories tend to be highly speculative rather than based on firm evidence. Many are not just based on flimsy or contested evidence, but are pure conjecture, without any basis in reality. Cassam explains that the purpose of conspiracy theories is always propaganda. They promote a political agenda by marketing seductive explanations of major events that are unlikely to be true, but are likely to influence public opinion in the preferred direction.

Conspiracy checks

Conspiracy theories have always existed. Yet conspiracy theories have taken a deep root in contemporary culture, moving from the fringes into the mainstream. Donald Trump's political career was started by peddling the 'birther' conspiracy that his predecessor in office Barack Obama was not born in the United States. That the American president could be elected by drawing on a conspiracy theory, and then continue to spout such theories whilst in office, suggests that these ways of looking at reality have become acceptable for many. Where conspiracy theorists tended to be on the fringe of society, looked down upon as paranoid, devious, dangerous or mentally ill, they have in many cases moved into the highest levels of politics.

This change in the status of conspiracy theorists and theories seems in particular to have been enabled by the internet. Online, people can craft and disseminate alternative facts. As with other aspects of truth and reality, the internet has unleashed a deluge of information, often false. Digital technology has permitted manipulations of facts, images and stories to be performed quickly and convincingly. These can then be distributed far and wide online. Stories can catch on and go viral. These stories are of unclear origins, multi-authored, picked up and distributed through complex networks. The anonymity and scale of online content make it hard to track where theories come from.

To be clear, there are legitimate conspiracies. Actual cover ups exist, and deserve to be exposed via evidence-led work. People are rightly cynical about the sometimes self-serving claims of authorities. During the Covid-19 pandemic for instance, some countries, such as Russia, recorded suspiciously low and statistically all too neat rates of infections and deaths from the virus (Economist, 2020). Doing so might have been motivated by a desire to make political leaders look good.

However, many conspiracies are pure fantasy. The worst of them involve malice, drawing on and seeking to fuel hate. To do this they use manipulation, twisting truth, facts and events to suit own purposes, or if necessary, entirely fabricating these. During Covid-19, various unfounded and easily disprovable conspiracy theories flowered. One that grew in particular was the idea that 5G caused Covid-19. This link was immediately explained by medical experts as entirely false. Linked to China and eventually, inevitably, George Soros, the conspiracy nevertheless proliferated online. The 5G conspiracy is typical of how such theories feed off of people's understandable fear in the moment, by providing them simple (false) answers, and fusing current affairs with age old racism.

The consequences of conspiracy theories are potentially severe. These include fuelling division, leading to violence, feeding flames of racism and helping to get deeply inadequate leaders into positions of power. It is important to review and refute these. Fortunately, there are simple guidelines for checking whether a conspiracy theory is legitimate or otherwise:

> First, check the **source** of a conspiracy theory. Good quality, expert, respected and public sources tend to be more reliable. Comparing a range of quality sources is always a good idea. Second, **scale** relates to how large a purported conspiracy is set out to be. As a rule of thumb, the bigger it is then the less likely. Big complicated conspiracies that require lots of participants to carry off are unfeasible. Humans are bad at keeping secrets. The more of them involved the less likely that they are all keeping schtum. Thirdly, **structure** relates to the contents of the conspiracy theory. Often this contains all too

familiar plot lines, devices and participants. The same groups of people are purported to be running things behind the scenes, using familiar tricks, and with similar goals in mind. Conspiracy theories often peddle the same ideas over and over, just repackaging age old prejudices and paranoia in line with current issues and events.

It is important that such checks are conducted by marketing academics and professionals. Theoretical and market research that underpins conceptual development and business decision making depends on investigating a range of good quality sources, critically evaluating their contents and deciding on the usefulness of these accordingly. Information is not all of equal quality. Data are not free from refractions. In order to delve beneath the distortions and avoid being manipulated by these, it is more important than ever to conduct rigorous background research.

Chapter summary

Refraction of reality has become omnipresent. Veracity of knowledge, events, facts and reality are increasingly contested. Preferred alternatives can be crafted and posted, with the digital realm enabling in particular. This is true in consumer cultures as elsewhere. Augmented and alternative consumer realities, such as those of backpackers, help to make consumption seem more special than it actually is. So too, selective and exaggerated tales can help to mythologise careers, as with dropshipping. Good storytelling meanwhile can help to bring life to even the most mundane of consumer goods, as Comparethemarket. com has done via its meerkat fairy tales. There are troubling undertones to this refraction. As reality becomes malleable, difficult choices and hard truths may become more easily dismissed. Retreating into something of a fantasy might become the case.

References

Canavan, B. (2018). An existentialist exploration of tourism sustainability: Backpackers fleeing and finding themselves. *Journal of Sustainable Tourism*, 26(4), 551–566.

Cassam, Q. (2019). *Conspiracy theories*. Hoboken, NJ: John Wiley & Sons.

Croft, R. (2006). Folklore, families and fear: Exploring the influence of the oral tradition on consumer decision-making. *Journal of Marketing Management*, 22(9–10), 1053–1076.

The Economist. (2020). Anatomy of lies: Russia's covid-19 outbreak is far worse than the Kremlin admits. *The Economist*, 21/05/20. Available at: https://www.economist.com/europe/2020/05/21/russias-covid-19-outbreak-is-far-worse-than-the-kremlin-admits (Accessed 05/06/20).

Kale, S. (2020). 'It's bullshit': Inside the weird, get-rich-quick world of dropshipping. *Wired*, 01/05/20. Available at: https://www.wired.co.uk/article/dropshipping-instagram-ads (accessed 07/05/20)

Madrigal, A. (2018). India's lynching epidemic and the problem with blaming tech. *The Atlantic*. Available at: https://www.theatlantic.com/technology/archive/2018/09/whatsapp/571276/ (accessed 12/03/20).

Maheshwari, S., & Fu, B. (2016). Say no to the dress. *Buzzfeed*, 05/04/16. Available at: https://www.buzzfeednews.com/article/sapna/say-no-to-the-dress (accessed 05/06/20).

Patterson, A., Khogeer, Y., & Hodgson, J. (2013). How to create an influential anthropomorphic mascot: Literary musings on marketing, make-believe, and meerkats. *Journal of Marketing Management*, 29(1–2), 69–85.

Suskind, R. (2004). Faith, certainty and the presidency of George W. Bush. "Faith, certainty and the presidency of George W. Bush". *The New York Times Magazine, 17.* Available at: https://www.nytimes.com/2004/10/17/magazine/faith-certainty-and-the-presidency-of-george-w-bush.html

Ziolkowski, J. M. (2010). *Fairy tales from before fairy tales: The medieval Latin past of wonderful lies.* Ann Arbor: University of Michigan Press.

Žižek, S. (2005). The empty wheelbarrow. *The Guardian, 19,* 23. Available at: https://www.theguardian.com/comment/story/0,3604,1417982,00.html

7
RENOWN

Consumers at the centre of attention – tourists as celebrities and narcissism normalisation

Consumer renown: assuming and asking for attention

Renown refers to fame, notoriety or prominence. It is standing out, being looked at, listened to or a presence felt. This is akin to celebrity in the sense of being well known. The elevation of certain individuals to celebrity status is a relatively new concept. However, it is one which now pervades society and culture and that heavily influences consumers. Celebrities as lifestyle gurus set the ideals that people aspire toward. As endorsers they encourage people to consume things in order to be more like them. Many do want to be. The wealth, beauty and success associated with celebrities are all appealing.

Linking renown and consumption is the idea that in consuming like celebrities it is possible to be more like them. Buying the same underwear as David Beckham triggers the promise of looking a fraction as good as he does in the advertisement. Celebrity endorsement is so successful because people frequently admire, aspire to be closer to and more like renowned individuals. Consumption of endorsed products, services or experiences is positioned as means of doing so. Where Beckham wears H&M boxers, then admirers of his hope to be comparable by buying similarly.

Taking this long established idea of emulating celebrities further, it may now be the case that consumers are internalising these celebrity associations. They do not just look up to renowned individuals, but increasingly feel as if they themselves are renowned. Consumption becomes not just an opportunity to imitate a celebrity, but to some extent actually become one. Buying is often a means of standing out through conspicuous display.

Consumer renown refers to an increasing shift in emphasis towards socially standing out. This is sought by apparently rising numbers of contemporary consumers. Perhaps influenced by celebrities and seeking similar renown, people may use consumption as part of this. Becoming famous, or at least behaving as if so, underlies current consumer attitudes, behaviours and lifestyles. This is an era of consumers not just influenced by or emulating, but actually acting as if celebrities themselves.

Celebritisation

The influence of celebrity on consumer cultures and individuals living within these should not be underestimated. Driessens (2013) distinguishes the terms 'celebritization', for the societal and cultural changes implied by celebrity, and 'celebrification', comprising the changes at the individual level. Taking the first of these, Furedi (2010) argues that the ascendancy of the celebrity is one of the distinctive features of late twentieth and early 21st century Western culture. Hereby, the number, reach and influence of celebrities have all grown in significance.

New technology means that it is easier than ever before to seek and claim renown. The rise of various new media platforms has meant an increase in people able to present themselves through these and use to gain attention. Film stars arose with the growth of Hollywood and the studio system. This groomed and presented select talented and beautiful individuals before the public. Television and social media have meant more opportunities for new types of individuals to gain a profile. Celebrities are now omnipresent in society and culture Furedi suggests. They appear across not just the traditional realm of entertainment related media, such as films and television, but all media. Social media is full of influencers. Marketing communications are saturated with celebrity endorsers.

As a result, societies' attention is incessantly drawn to the performances of celebrities. As people constantly hear their opinions and observe their activities, their behaviour and attitudes are influenced in turn. Celebrities have thus become a recurring reference point for our collective social practices. Marshall (2010) for example observes how celebrity culture articulates a way of thinking about individuality and producing the individual self through the public world. He describes how people's social media profiles imitate the public persona of celebrities. People copy the poses, posts and relationship dynamics of the famous.

Celebrities are pervasive in ways and areas they have never been. Celebrity lifestyle gurus such as Gwyneth Paltrow have built huge brands around selling life hacks. More and more people look to them for guidance on how to live. At the same time as celebrities become more business-like, then business people become more celebrity-like. CEO's such as Elon Musk have built public profiles for themselves and use this to drive their commercial success. Even politicians are increasingly acting akin to and becoming celebrities, as with the savvy social media appearances of Barack Obama whilst US president. Meanwhile, celebrities are becoming politicians, as in the case of Obama's successor, the reality television presenter turned president, Donald Trump.

Celebrification

Although it may be ephemeral, celebrity status has become ever more normalised, aspirational and accessible. Indeed, it has arguably never been easier to become a celebrity. The proliferation of new media, particularly social media, has provided new channels for individuals to build personal profiles and share this before others. Online it is highly unlikely, but also unpredictably possible, for ordinary people to gain massive exposure, gain followers and become famous. There is not even particular need for accomplishments to support this. Social media influencers and other contemporary celebrities are often liked for their relatable ordinariness as much as anything.

The distance between celebrities and ordinary people has shrunk over time. Two media developments have brought us new types and plentiful supply of celebrities like never before. First, reality television has created a phenomenon of people catapulted to fame. The massive popularity of television shows such as Big Brother or X-Factor means participants can go from day-to-day routine to national renown overnight. Second, social media has turned influencers recording videos in their bedrooms into some of the most followed and valuable celebrities in the world. One Direction and Justin Bieber, who have their origins in reality TV and video uploads, respectively, demonstrate the potential of these new media to create huge celebrities.

Celebrification relates to the increased abilities of individuals to enact celebrity. This is facilitated by digital and social media in particular. Considering self-branding online for instance, Khamis, Ang and Welling (2017) contemplate how social media is primed for self-promotion and individualism. Similarly, Marshall evaluates how social media users stage themselves online in ways that are highly conscious of a potential audience. As such, social media users are self-producing themselves online much as celebrities do and as if they are celebrities themselves.

Digital developments mean that it is increasingly possible to become a celebrity. Describing this process of becoming a celebrity, the term celebrification designates the particular way through which celebrity selves are constructed and communicated. This process involves the use of media to create the aura of celebrity. Hereby, an individual is distinguished as special based on some accomplishing feature such as a talent or a look. This distinction is then communicated outwards by using media to let others know this individual is special. As Driessens (2013) explains, being in the media lends a person perceived importance compared with those outside the media.

Consumer case: tourist celebrities taking the Mongol Rally

Looking at one niche group of tourism consumers helps to illustrate the ways in which celebrity is influencing consumption. Those undertaking the Mongol Rally, an extreme tourism consumption experience, are reviewed in this extended case. Highlighted is that the way people consume spaces whilst on vacation may be altered by tendencies towards consumer renown. Wanting to stand out and be noticed becomes more important to such tourism consumers whilst travelling. Briefly speaking, this alters the tourist gaze from outward looking to being looked at.

'Tourist gaze' is a term that articulates the motivations and behaviours of tourists on holiday. Tourists visit destinations. These are spaces where vacation activities take place. Tourists consume spaces primarily visually, by looking at the different sites and scenery of a destination. They travel to see famous landmarks and unfamiliar landscapes. Tourism includes all of the senses. On holiday the smells, sounds, tastes and physical feelings of a space are engaged with as well. It is this sensory stimulation that makes travel rewarding. When on holiday, people engage with spaces through their senses and the thoughts and feelings triggered by these.

The tourist gaze therefore refers to how tourists use their senses to consume a space. This gaze is shaped not just by the individual tourist interacting with their surroundings. It is socially and culturally organized. This means that it reflects the background of the individual. For example, film and television references may create a certain impression of a location before visiting. This might influence how tourists gaze when in the destination. Visiting New York for instance, the things to see, local foods to taste and other sensory experiences considered important to do whilst in the city are shaped by previously established impressions of NYC as shown in media or overheard from peers. Tourist gazing is thus shaped by predetermined expectations. What we expect to see on holiday is anticipated in advance.

In addition to this anticipation, once in a destination, tourist gazing is shaped by immediate surroundings. Local people gaze back at tourists and this can have an effect upon them. They might feel inhibited for example, where they find themselves closely observed by residents. Maoz (2006) describes this two-way interaction as a mutual gaze, explaining that both the tourist and local gazes exist, affecting and feeding each other. Thus, tourism consumption of space is a complex process involving the five senses, in-the-moment experiences and prejudged expectations, and input from others sharing spaces.

From tourist looking … to the tourist looked at

The tourist gaze is furthermore facilitated and shaped by things. Tourists' engagements with spaces are mediated by people, objects and technologies that facilitate the tourism experience. To explain, people such as tour guides can play a role in how tourists interact with a space by promoting certain activities. Similarly, objects such as maps or signposts can provide useful information to help structure a visit. Meanwhile, technology such as cameras may alter how things are looked at, by directing the tourist towards sights that are dramatic or interesting to record.

Recently, new technologies have altered the ways in which travellers interact with holiday spaces. Smartphones with built in cameras and connected via mobile internet to social media have changed the ways that tourists behave. It has been suggested by Lo and McKercher (2015) for example that tourists are highly mindful of their appearances on social media. Accordingly, they are conscious when on holiday of what content is shareable and helps them to portray desirable selves. In this way, travel photography has become less about capturing evidence of visiting a destination, and more about using the destination as a background to support attractive presentations of the self when online.

Dinhopl and Gretzel (2016) label this the 'self-directed' tourist gaze. Hereby, tourists themselves become the tourist sights to be consumed whilst on holiday. Selfies taken on vacation are arguably an example of this. These are photographs focussed on the self rather than surroundings. Dinhopl and Gretzel's insight is that facilitated by new technology tourists are increasingly taking photographs not of the destination, but of themselves in the destination. Sites and landscapes are cropped away as the focus becomes the tourist. They become a flattering backdrop to the travel selfie.

Canavan (2020) develops this idea further to suggest that the sharing of tourist selfies through social media may be sign of tourists assuming that they are interesting to look upon. Rather than the destination, it is the tourist who is of special interest. Internalising this idea, Canavan proposes that tourists have then reversed the traditional gaze. Instead of going on holiday to look at things, the tourist goes to be looked at. People back home are presumed to want to see pictures of the tourist in different settings. So too local people in those settings may be expected to want to look upon the visitor in their midst. This is the tourist as if a celebrity, what Canavan terms the 'tourist celebrity gaze' (Figure 7.1).

| Traditional tourist gaze - tourism sites are looked at, as when taking photographs of | Cropped tourist gaze - tourism sites are a backdrop for looking at the self, as when taking selfies in front of | Tourist celebrity gaze - tourist is looked at whilst at tourism sites, as when photographed by passers by |

FIGURE 7.1 Evolution of the tourist gaze.

The Mongol Rally

To illustrate these new tourists travelling to be looked at, Canavan looks into the social media feeds of those taking part in the Mongol Rally. The Mongol Rally is an annual event organised by the Adventurists, a travel agency who develop and market adventure tourism experiences. First organised in 2004, the rally runs between Europe and Ulan Ude in Russia (no longer ending in Mongolia due to legal issues). The event is premised on three rules. First, participants must undertake in a 'banger' vehicle with an engine less than 1.2 litres in size. Second, teams are entirely on their own in terms of logistics and travel. Third, teams have to raise at least £1000 for charity, including a minimum £500 donation to 'Cool Earth', the charity affiliated with the Adventurists.

This premise and the event's ethos are captured in the introductory description on the organiser's website:

> This is the greatest motoring adventure on the planet. This is 10,000 miles of chaos across mountain, deserts and steppe on roads ranging from bad to not-a-road in a tiny 1000cc car you bought from a scrapyard for £4.60. There's no backup. There's no set route. There's no guarantee you'll make it to the end. It's just you, your rolling turd and planet earth sized bucket of adventure.
> *(TheAdventurists.com, 2019)*

Accordingly, the drama and difficulty of taking part in the event are hyped. Explained is that contestants need to plan their own routes, book all of the visas, accommodation and supplies necessary, and be prepared for various obstacles along the way. The cost of all of these is up to the individual tourists. Fees paid to the Adventurists cover only the right to take part and promotion of contestant's social media. Revealed in this set up is a clever positioning of the Mongol Rally for a new type of celebrity gazing tourist.

Buying a place in the Mongol Rally is a means of setting oneself up as extraordinary. This is an extreme experience that helps to set consumers apart from other types of holiday-makers. A place in the Mongol Rally also links an individual with media. Rally participants get a place on the Adventurists social media pages and can use the event to draw attention to their own. Indeed, many contestants provide press releases as they seek to gain coverage in local news media and aggressively share their online profiles.

Look at us!

Getting attention is clearly important to those taking part in the Mongol Rally. Social media is used before, during and after the event to promote participation. Contestants decorate their vehicles with official rally merchandise, and in some cases produce elaborate designs or paint jobs. Others dress to stand out, wearing only speedos throughout the rally for example. Such efforts mean contestants gain attention everywhere they go. This is especially the case when traversing countries that receive few foreign visitors. Turkmenistan for example, is one of the most unvisited and politically restrictive countries on the planet. Here, the passing through of any outsiders is noteworthy. Rally consumers document and share the attention they receive from bemused onlookers through their social media. Where they are waved at, flagged down and noticed, tourists in the Mongol Rally have their desire to be at the centre of attention apparently rewarded.

Paying for the privilege

The Mongol Rally provides insights into a subset of tourists who seemingly go on holiday in large part to be looked at. Rather than travelling to consume a destination through sensory interactions, they go to be consumed themselves. People in the destinations passed through are encouraged to look upon the visiting tourist show. So too this performance is documented and shared before others online.

What this might mean for the future of tourism consumption, marketing and management is interesting. Clearly, significant opportunity exists to serve such minded tourists with experiences that complement this desire for renown. The Mongol Rally is an innovative tourism product which effectively sells a celebrity experience as much as it does a travel one. By staking out an unconventional and ambitious route, adding a gimmick and encouraging outré behaviour, the rally helps consumers to fulfil a desire to stand out.

This drive to be given attention is so significant that participants will dedicate significant resources to pursuing. The Mongol Rally is an expensive undertaking in terms of the time and money that need to be invested. Visas, fuel, vehicle transport, accommodation and supplies add up. Around a month minimum is required to finish. It is also a challenging consumer event that requires significant physical and emotional effort to complete. As a sophisticated and comprehensive source of consumer renown, these expenses and difficulties are both worthwhile, and even a part of the aura of standing out that participants seek.

The success of the event points towards the business opportunities that might arise from consumer renown. Although only a few hundred tourists take part in the rally each year, this celebrity way of gazing may be more widespread. Technology has allowed all tourists to become more self-centred and has allowed them to behave as if they are mini-celebrities. Other tourism marketers and managers may be inspired to facilitate this desire to be looked at in order to appeal to consumer renown.

> **Case questions**
>
> 1. How might more conventional package tours be modified to include elements that appeal to consumer renown?
>   Not all tourists can go to the extremes of those joining the Mongol Rally, but many may similarly hope to stand out. Think about how packaged holidays might incorporate activities that facilitate standing out. This could be whilst in a destination and also when sharing travel related content on social media.
> 2. How might less well known tourism destinations capitalise on consumer renown?
>   The Mongol Rally brings contestants to some very underdeveloped locations. These are made to be appealing because in such places consumers stand out before local inhabitants. Think about how other locations might encourage tourists to visit by appealing to their desire for renown.
> 3. Other than tourism, what products, services and experiences might be well placed to facilitate consumers acting like mini-celebrities?
>   Consider how less involved or expensive purchases might still be adapted to help consumers feel as if they are standing out and being paid attention to.

Consumption and narcissism

A growing desire amongst consumers, such as Mongol Rally tourists, to think like or act as if celebrities, may be a sign of their increasing narcissism. Where consumers are wanting to be the centre of attention, expecting that others will look at them because are so interesting, or assuming that their actions are unique and likeable, then such behaviours overlap with definitions of narcissism as a personality trait. Renown hints therefore at growing narcissistic tendencies amongst consumers. Indeed, it has been proposed that increased narcissism may be observed within contemporary societies. Suggestion is hereby that people are becoming more self-centred and that this is changing how they interact with others. Although this increase in narcissism is much debated, if it is occurring then it may have significant consequences for marketing.

Narcissism is an aspect of all human personality. This is the part of the inner being that involves a person's sense of self. A degree of narcissism can be healthy, as with a steady sense of self-worth and ability to recover from disappointments. Having too little narcissism may be unhealthy and leave the individual lacking in self-belief. Nevertheless, an overly high level of narcissism can be problematic, both for the individual and for those who they come into contact with. Having too strong a sense of self can translate into antisocial behaviours around being selfish and uncaring towards others.

At the extreme of having an unhealthily high level is what psychologists term 'pathological narcissism'. This is a diagnosable psychological disorder. Pathological narcissism is associated with an abnormal sense of self. This means that pathological narcissists are unusually preoccupied with themselves as the most important thing in any situation. They cannot see things from other people's perspective, only their own. Indeed, they perhaps do not even recognise that other people have perspectives of their own. The only thing in other people that narcissists are interested in is their responses to the narcissist.

Pathological narcissists are also associated with abnormal self-esteem regulation strategies. This means that they have an extreme need for attention and also require constant reassurance. This intense need for admiration and recognition (Pincus & Lukowitsky, 2010) is related to narcissistic egos as simultaneously extremely high and decidedly fragile. Pathological narcissists genuinely believe that they are uniquely special and brilliant in all situations, and hence deserve special attention. At the same time, they are intensely disturbed when their brilliance is not recognised or they are not given attention.

Grandiose and vulnerable

Narcissism is complex and can emerge in different ways. Two distinctive types of narcissism have been identified: grandiose and vulnerable. Grandiose narcissists are described as aggressive and assertive. Meanwhile, vulnerable narcissists are described as defensive, anxious and complaining. Miller *et al.* (2011) explain that whilst both forms of narcissism share a sense of self-significance and entitlement, the rationale for these feelings may differ. Thus, grandiose narcissists believe they are better than others. However, vulnerable narcissists feel that they deserve special consideration because of their fragility.

Narcissistic characteristics

Because of their abnormal sense of self and self-esteem regulation, narcissists can be very difficult to be around. Narcissists may display maladaptive and antisocial traits such as being highly manipulative, coercive, deceitful, cold, uncaring and aggressive towards others. Thus, Golomb (1995) warns that those who come into contact with narcissists can suffer significant negative consequences. The deeply antisocial tendencies of pathological narcissism can be related to the particular characteristics of sufferers. Three broad and overlapping attributes are used to describe narcissists: *self-obsession, entitlement and exploitation,* and *exhibitionism*. These three traits help to explain the pathology and its consequences.

- *Self-obsession* relates to the sense of self, which in the case of the narcissist is over-inflated. Narcissists have heightened feelings of uniqueness and individualism. Indeed, reality as the narcissist sees it revolves around them to the exclusion of all others (Roberts, 2014). As a result, narcissists tend to be unable to maintain intimate long-term relationships, due to an inability to fully recognise or appreciate the individuality of others (Golomb, 1995).
- *Entitlement and exploitation* involve the narcissist believing that they are uniquely special individuals, and therefore better and more deserving than others. As a result, narcissists believe that they are entitled to more than other people. They likewise believe that others are there simply to service their own needs. Lambert and Desmond (2013) summarise how their relationships to people and to brands are more or less the same. Both are treated instrumentally as objects for superficial admiration, enjoyment and self-aggrandisement, until they outlive their usefulness and are discarded.
- *Exhibitionism* relates to the self-promoting strategies of narcissists. These need to be the centre of attention at all times, and will take any opportunity to fulfil this craving. Attention seeking behaviours might include being deliberately shocking, provocative or building grandiose tales around themselves. Exhibitionism is a self-esteem regulatory strategy, employed by narcissists to protect fragile underlying sense of self. Narcissists unconsciously deny an unstated and intolerably poor self-image through inflation, turning themselves into figures of grandeur (Golomb, 1995).

How narcissistic are you?

Narcissism is notoriously difficult to diagnose. Narcissists almost never seek treatment, for they rarely see anything wrong with themselves. Rather the problem always lies elsewhere with other people and situations. Pathological narcissism is also difficult to distinguish from more healthy narcissism. In small doses, confident, articulate and outgoing narcissists can seem healthy and attractive. The severity of self-obsessive, entitled and exploitative, and exhibitionistic traits may only become apparent over prolonged exposure.

The most widely adopted tool for diagnosis of pathological narcissism is the narcissistic personality inventory (NPI). This is an extensive list of binary statements from which the individual must choose which they most closely identify with. Respondents typically score within a mid-range. Pathological narcissists score highly. A short version of the NPI adapted by Schütz, Marcus and Sellin (2004) illustrates this process (Table 7.1). Fill this in to measure your own narcissism score. Tick either the left- or right-hand column for pair of statements depending on which you most closely identify with. Try to answer honestly and without thinking too long over the responses.

According to the NPI-15, the number of narcissistic responses is summed to form a narcissism score between 0 (not at all narcissistic) and 15 (very narcissistic). All choices in the left-hand column earn scores of 0, whilst all scores in the right-hand column earn scores of 1. From adding these up it is possible to gauge a rough narcissism score. Knowing this can be useful, and a number of consumer studies have measured the NPI score of respondents, before going on to explore their consumption habits, in order to test any possible links.

TABLE 7.1 The NPI-15

1	I have a natural talent for influencing people.	I am not good at influencing people.
2	When people compliment me I sometimes get embarrassed.	I know that I am good because everybody keeps telling me so.
3	I prefer to blend in with the crowd.	I like to be the centre of attention.
4	I am no better or worse than most people.	I think I am a special person.
5	I am not sure if I would make a good leader.	I see myself as a good leader.
6	I like to have authority over other people.	I don't mind following orders.
7	I find it easy to manipulate people.	I don't like it when I find myself manipulating people.
8	I just want to be reasonably happy.	I want to amount to something in the eyes of the world.
9	I have a strong will to power.	Power for its own sake doesn't interest me.
10	I really like to be the centre of attention.	It makes me uncomfortable to be the centre of attention.
11	Being an authority doesn't mean that much to me.	People always seem to recognize my authority.
12	I would prefer to be a leader.	It makes little difference to me whether I am a leader or not.
13	I am going to be a great person.	I hope I am going to be successful.
14	I am a born leader.	Leadership is a quality that takes a long time to develop.
15	I am much like everybody else.	I am an extraordinary person.

Schütz, Marcus and Sellin (2004).

The NPI and NPI-15 are nonetheless criticised somewhat. These are blunt instruments, with binary choices perhaps not accurately reflecting the complexity of individuals. Narcissism is moreover flexible and people filling in the NPI at different times may get quite different scores. Finally, narcissists are very adept at hiding that they are narcissistic. Paranoid and hyper-vigilant, they are likely to pick up why the test is being administered and manipulate their answers accordingly. It is quite obvious from the NPI which choices are more narcissistic and hence it is possible to game the test if so desired.

Narcissism normalisation

Although it is an individual personality trait, narcissistic qualities can also be environmentally informed. Because people are shaped by their social and cultural surroundings, if narcissistic individuals and groups are prominent then these may have the effect of making self-obsessive, entitled and exploitative, or exhibitionistic traits more prominent. For example, if celebrity figures seem to display narcissistic attributes, then these may make these attributes seem more normal, acceptable and even desirable. Twenge and Campbell (2009) believe that celebrities have become role models with such negative consequences.

It is not only more possible than ever to follow celebrities thanks to digital technologies, but to emulate them as well. Social media facilitates self-promotion and attention seeking behaviours. At the same time it holds out the promise of letting the users become celebrities themselves. Emphasis is henceforth on using new technologies to become more self-focussed and in the hope that this will get others to similarly focus on oneself.

Gradually, as more people behave in such self-centric ways, this has the effect of making society and culture more narcissistic overall. This process is known as narcissism normalisation. Narcissism normalisation is the idea that narcissistic traits are becoming more widespread and acceptable. To illustrate, research by Twenge and Campbell (2009) has explored this issue amongst students in the United States. Their findings are that increases in narcissistic traits are especially prevalent amongst younger generations. Over time they suggest, undergraduate students are scoring higher averages on narcissism measurement scales.

The result of narcissism normalisation is that although narcissistic personality disorder remains rare, narcissistic characteristics, involving vanity, arrogance, feeling special, lacking empathy and having little regard for others, appear to be increasingly common. In areas such as politics and business, individuals and groups displaying such characteristics seem to be unusually prominent at present. Inevitably influenced by such prominent figures, this narcissism normalisation may be the case amongst consumers as well.

Consumer narcissism

'The customer is always right'. 'Because you're worth it'. Plenty of famous marketing phrases and slogans prioritise and play on the ego of consumers. Serving the needs and desires of customers is an important part of marketing. Yet this attitude risks inflating consumer egos. Anyone who has worked in retail or hospitality will know that the customer often is not right. They make demands that are at times unreasonable, sometimes unsustainable and occasionally harmful. Brand managers meanwhile will be aware that customers are not always worth it. Trying to keep satisfied can exhaust resources, profit margins and brand equity. Nevertheless, the ability to stand up to consumers is often limited. Challenging a narcissist is dangerous. Narcissistic customers who feel they are not treated as they deserve may react aggressively, as parodied in the 'Karen' memes doing the rounds online.

Narcissism has been linked to consumption in a number of ways. Consumption can serve as an outlet for self-obsessive, entitled and exploitative, and exhibitionistic tendencies. For example, buying things and showing these off can be a means of attention seeking. Bellis et al. (2016) find that more narcissistic consumers tend to prefer more unique products, such as brightly coloured options, that help them to stand out and gain attention. Meanwhile, Lambert and Desmond (2013) suggest that narcissists may be more likely to seek out luxury goods and brands for purposes of ostentatious display.

In this way consumption can help to build up a sense of self-importance. Patsiaouras, Fitchett and Davies (2016) suggest the display of luxury brands and material goods is a means to satisfy narcissistic needs for prestige and social status. Zerach (2016) explains that for vulnerable narcissists consumption may be used to distract from negative feelings, whilst for grandiose narcissists it relates to materialistic drive to acquire goods important to self-definition, success and well-being. Such consumption behaviours may be linked with the underlying self-doubt and fear of social rejection that narcissists experience. Acquiring and displaying possessions is a route to feeling better, gaining status, social standing and building self-identity.

If consumption is potentially important to narcissists, then the style of consumption preferred by narcissists is significant. As with everything else narcissists seem to be self-centred in their consumption. They tend to do what they want, when they want, without paying much attention to the needs or wants of others. Accordingly, associations have been noted between narcissism and consumer materialism, impulsiveness, irrationality and compulsive behaviours. These types of consumer behaviours may have significant downsides from a sustainability perspective.

Consumer renown and sustainability

Narcissism and its normalisation have implications for the ways that individuals and groups consume. As noted, a shift towards consumer renown may drive demand for new types of products, services and experiences such as those offered by the Mongol Rally. Yet the sustainability of such consumption may be debateable. Sustainable consumption has become a necessary path towards a greener future, due to the global increase in consumption and its resulting destruction of resources and environmental capacity around the world.

Sustainable consumption involves a number of themes. *Awareness* relates to knowledge of consumer issues. *Empathy* refers to the ability to be open to and connect with others, and with wider issues of social and environmental concern. *Commitment* occurs when consumers do something about an issue. They get involved with tangible actions such as changing consumption habits. *Responsibility* refers to a sense of ownership over behaviours. Where consumers feel responsible, they may be more likely to make choices that are more conscious. Finally, *collaboration* relates to working with other stakeholders. Finding and implementing more sustainable solutions benefits from the creativity stimulated by people working together. Sharing ideas and mutually supporting each other facilitate.

These themes seemingly contrast with narcissistic traits. Characteristics of self-obsession, entitlement and exploitation, and exhibitionism contradict. To illustrate, the self-absorbed narcissist is less likely to be concerned for the well-being of others. Meanwhile, tendencies towards exploitation and entitlement suggest an increased likelihood of irresponsible behaviours. What is more, narcissists tend to be insensitive in terms of a relative lack of concern for impacts of their actions on others. They are unlikely to feel subject to notions of responsibility, due to their tendency to deviate from social norms.

This and their need to be the centre of attention means narcissists are very difficult for others to work with. Narcissists tend for example towards aggressive reactions when their need for attention is not met. Because of their dysfunctional self-esteem regulation, narcissists exhibit excessive emotional volatility following positive and negative feedback, and their responses to this are disproportionate. The abnormal self-esteem regulation of pathological narcissism means that sufferers have a very high opinion of themselves, but need everyone else to share this. Narcissists are hypersensitive regarding the perceptions of others towards themselves. Where these perceptions are not flattering, this distresses the narcissist acutely. Narcissists often react disproportionately towards perceived slights.

Self-sacrifice

Sustainable consumption often implies some form of additional investment or self-sacrifice. Fair Trade goods tend to be slightly more expensive for instance. Meanwhile, public transport may be more climate friendly than private vehicle, but it is not always as convenient. Individuals are not always able or willing to make sustainable consumption choices therefore. The selfish tendencies of narcissism mean that gaining an interest in and commitment to sustainable principles, potentially involving sacrifice, may be especially unlikely. The challenge for marketers is whether a way around this can be found.

Narcissism opportunities for sustainable consumption

Consumer renown may be a trend that contradicts urgent efforts to make consumers more aware, empathetic, committed, responsible and collaborative. Nevertheless, alongside significant challenges for sustainability there may be opportunities to use narcissism to advantageous effect. People buy ethical and sustainable alternatives not purely out of good heartedness. They also get something out of this such as a stronger sense of identity or the ability to affiliate with likeminded ideological groups. It is possible that sustainable consumption could be linked with things valued by narcissists such as self-indulgence, attention or grandiosity.

To illustrate, narcissists spend considerable time and effort trying to get noticed, look good, feel special and surpass others. If sustainable consumption behaviours help them towards these goals, by generating positive status and attention, then narcissists may be inclined to participate. Wielding a reusable straw on a night out for instance may be a contemporary way to solicit positive comments from peers. Amongst millennials who prioritise ideological issues, such actions might generate more peer approval than displaying an expensive watch or pulling up in an opulent vehicle.

In addition, sustainable consumption may be positioned as exclusive. For those looking to show off through the things they buy, unusual purchases are a way to go about this. Rao and Schaefer (2013) explain because niche products are clearly distinguished from other products, they can be used to achieve social visibility, serving the desire for conspicuous consumption and satisfying social needs. It may be that marketers need to further emphasise the conspicuous consumption value of green products. Tesla has done this to great success. Its products are highly desirable as a way to display both wealth and ideological awareness simultaneously.

A final tactic for encouraging more sustainable consumption even amongst self-centred consumers may be to make issues personally relevant. Narcissists do not care about other people or try to understand the things that affect them. However, they are very aware of those which impact themselves. Their heightened sensitivity to perceived external threats may make narcissists more responsive to environmental issues that risk their own well-being. Therefore, if the consequences of issues can be communicated at an individual level, this message may be more powerful persuading the narcissist to change consumption behaviours. To illustrate, letting the narcissist know that it is their health at risk from such things as pollution might be more likely to motivate them to make greener choices.

Chapter summary

Contemporary consumers seem to be asking for attention and assuming they are worthy of it. Influenced by celebrities, enabled by social media, they want and are able to stand out. Consumption may offer useful means of claiming renown. Tourists taking the Mongol Rally travel to obscure parts of the world, wear bizarre outfits, drive elaborately decorated cars and spend significant amounts of money. They do so in large part to stand out before others, feel looked at and celebrated. Consumer renown has significant commercial potential therefore. However, as trends of narcissism normalisation highlight, there may be downsides to facilitating consumer egos and attention seeking. Pathological narcissism is extremely destructive. Rising levels of cultural narcissism may be incompatible with more sustainable consumption. Left unchecked, narcissistic organisations can become narcissistic and collapse. Looking towards the future, marketing needs therefore to be conscious of how it evaluates and responds to consumption trends in more ethical and responsible ways.

References

Canavan, B. (2020). Let's get this show on the road! Introducing the tourist celebrity gaze. *Annals of Tourism Research*, 82, 102898.

De Bellis, E., Sprott, D. E., Herrmann, A., Bierhoff, H. W., & Rohmann, E. (2016). The influence of trait and state narcissism on the uniqueness of mass-customized products. *Journal of Retailing*, 92(2), 162–172.

Dinhopl, A., & Gretzel, U. (2016). GoPro panopticon: Performing in the surveyed leisure experience. In Carnicelli, S.; McGillivray, D.; McPherson, G. (eds.). *Digital Leisure Cultures*. London: Routledge. pp. 78–91.

Driessens, O. (2013). The celebritization of society and culture: Understanding the structural dynamics of celebrity culture. *International Journal of Cultural Studies*, 16(6), 641–657.

Furedi, F. (2010). Celebrity culture. *Society*, 47(6), 493–497.

Golomb, E. (1995). *Trapped in the mirror*. New York: Harper Collins.

Khamis, S., Ang, L., & Welling, R. (2017). Self-branding, 'micro-celebrity' and the rise of social media influencers. *Celebrity Studies*, 8(2), 191–208.

Lambert, A., & Desmond, J. (2013). Loyal now, but not forever! A study of narcissism and male consumer–brand relationships. *Psychology & Marketing*, 30(8), 690–706.

Lo, I. S., & McKercher, B. (2015). Ideal image in process: Online tourist photography and impression management. *Annals of Tourism Research*, *52*, 104–116.

Maoz, D. (2006). The mutual gaze. *Annals of Tourism Research*, *33*(1), 221–239.

Marshall, P. D. (2010). The promotion and presentation of the self: Celebrity as marker of presentational media. *Celebrity Studies*, *1*(1), 35–48.

Miller, J. D., Hoffman, B. J., Gaughan, E. T., Gentile, B., Maples, J., & Keith Campbell, W. (2011). Grandiose and vulnerable narcissism: A nomological network analysis. *Journal of Personality*, *79*(5), 1013–1042.

Patsiaouras, G., Fitchett, J. A., & Davies, A. (2016). Beyond the couch: Psychoanalytic consumer character readings into narcissism and denial. *Marketing Theory*, *16*(1), 57–73.

Pincus, A. L., & Lukowitsky, M. R. (2010). Pathological narcissism and narcissistic personality disorder. *Annual Review of Clinical Psychology*, *6*, 421–446.

Rao, R. S., & Schaefer, R. (2013). Conspicuous consumption and dynamic pricing. *Marketing Science*, *32*(5), 786–804.

Roberts, D. (2014). In defense of defenselessness: Kierkegaard's critique of an accepted narcissism. *The Heythrop Journal*, *55*(5), 827–844.

Schütz, A., Marcus, B., & Sellin, I. (2004). Measuring narcissism as a personality construct: Psychometric properties of a long and a short version of the German Narcissistic Personality Inventory. *Diagnostica*, *50*(4), 202–218.

Twenge, J. M., & Campbell, W. K. (2009). *The narcissism epidemic: Living in the age of entitlement*. New York: Simon and Schuster.

Zerach, G. (2016). The mediating role of emptiness and materialism in the association between pathological narcissism and compulsive buying. *International Journal of Mental Health and Addiction*, *14*(4), 424–437.

8

REBALANCING

Producing as well as consuming – the success of home-made spread versus the failure of Juicero

Consumer society

Marketing as an academic discipline and industry application has its roots in the 19th century. The Industrial Revolution brought disposable incomes to people as they switched to working for wages rather than subsistence. For the first time in human history, large numbers of people had extra money to spend above and beyond the basics. Simultaneously, advances in production meant that goods could be produced on a mass scale, increasing their availability and lowering their costs. People had more money than they needed. Manufacturers had excess production. A perfect match.

Early marketing was tasked with linking this new disposable income and surplus production. Set out in early advertising were detailed rationales for the impetus to buy things. These argued for consumer goods as making improvements to lives. Consumption was explained as a means of gaining efficiencies or experiencing pleasures. This template for consumption has been made more sophisticated and all-encompassing since. Old adverts often seem amusing in their emphasis on health cures, alongside their unsubstantiated claims that everything from alcohol to sugar could cure all manner of ailments.

Nevertheless, the principles underlying consumerism have remained largely the same for the past two centuries. Hereby, human needs and desires are linked to the consumption of products, services and experiences as ways to meet these. Human routines and aspirations are related to consumption as an activity and an end goal. Likewise, human attitudes, behaviours, lifestyles and associated identities are framed around consumption as a means of developing and expressing these.

Thus, many parts of the worlds have experienced a long period where consumption has been prioritised as an important part of the meaning and activity that makes up people's lives. 'Consumer society' is a term that describes how various groups' collective activities, norms and values are framed by the consumption of objects, services and experiences. In a consumer society, all areas of life revolve around consumption. This includes work, which is geared towards earning extra disposable income for consumer goods, as well as leisure, where consumption is an activity to be enjoyed during evenings and weekends.

Society: people, relationships and institutions

Society refers to a grouping of people. A society is anything from two to all humans. Society also relates to the bonds that hold groups together. This includes relationships between members and the institutions that support those relationships. A romantic couple for instance is a relationship that connects two people in a micro society of two. Marriage is an institution that includes religious or state guidelines that may back up such a micro society by providing such things as legal status, financial rewards or cultural obligations.

Relationships of all sizes and types are potentially influenced by consumption. As an activity, consumption facilitates connections between consumers as they consume. As a means of pursuing interests, consumption helps to develop links with others who share similar enthusiasm. Meanwhile, with ideology able to be expressed through consumption, this can bring likeminded individuals together. From partners who bond over their shared love of a certain type of holiday to the billions connected by social media and its attendant advertising, consumption is integral to forming and maintaining social relationships.

Institutions are structures that support group interaction. This might be a physical space, such as a beach, where particular social groups and activities take place. An institution can also be an organisation, such as a university, where again particular social networks and activities may be facilitated. Institutions can vary widely in scope and scale, with everything from national government to a local sports club having the potential to structure social development.

Regardless of their size, institutions that support social bonding often involve consumption. The American shopping mall for example is an important social institution where many societies coalesce and develop. Teenagers hang out with their friends at the weekend. Senior citizens come together in walking clubs during weekday mornings. Retail employees follow set routines together around serving customers and getting paid. These and many others are all groups brought together and influenced by the mall as an institution.

Consumer culture

Culture is concerned with the manifestations of individual and collective identity. This includes things such as dress codes, food, language, festivals and art. Such cultural artefacts transmit particular meanings that may be interpreted differently by different observers. Thus, culture is about how individuals express themselves and how these expressions are used to affirm belonging to particular groups. Listening to a particular type of music for instance aligns with peers who share similar taste. Musical taste expresses to others certain things about the listeners' identity, their personal preferences, references, even their class or politics. These can be used to help decide what groups, values or beliefs they affiliate with.

'Consumer culture' is a term that explores how consumption relates to the ways individuals and groups express themselves. Consumer culture considers the cultural symbolism of consumer goods, trying to understand how these are interpreted by people and then used, in turn, to express themselves. Consumer goods transmit meanings. This includes such things as brands collected, designers worn and vacations taken. All help to tell a story about who the individual consumer is and what social groups they associate with. Feelings, meanings and beliefs are all associated with consumption. Different consumer choices can arrange and display these in alternative ways, conveying different meanings to others as and when required.

With consumption allowing people to choose how they express themselves in myriad ways, as long as they have the resources to do so, culture becomes an activity tied to shopping and spending. In consumer cultures, the ways that people convey their identity are frequently through the items they purchase and the places they make purchases. Hence Wattanasuwan (2005) summarises how people employ consumption symbolically to both locate themselves in society and create the self.

To illustrate, Goths are a subculture with a strong set of identifiers. They listen to certain music, dress in particularly themed clothes and share specific references when interacting on or offline. These cultural expressions clearly signify certain feelings, meanings and beliefs to other Goths and to outsiders. Goth as a lifestyle is heavily supported by the marketplace. Clothing, makeup, jewellery can all be purchased. The spaces where Goths hang out, such as nightclubs, can be paid to access. Thus, the Goth cultural identity is one built and maintained at least partly through consumption. It is an example of a consumer culture.

Blue versus red

How does the colour of liquid being poured onto a sanitary product make you feel? Your reaction is likely a result of your sociocultural surroundings. For decades, adverts for panty-liners and other female menstruation products have used blue liquid to illustrate the absorbency of their wares. Obviously menstrual blood is red not blue, so why use the latter on screen?

The answer lies in the complicated cultural attitudes towards menstruation than many societies have. These take a mundane biological function and cloak in shame. In such surroundings menstruation cannot be openly discussed by marketers or consumers, hence the use of blue liquid as a compromise. This blue is a euphemism that may spare viewers' blushes.

Yet as Elmhirst (2020) reviews, panty-liner adverts are starting to use red liquid for the first time, at least some brands in certain markets. As some cultures have evolved, they have rejected period shame. Now, in some places, it is the blue liquid that is seen as embarrassing, a restrictive throwback to humiliating and controlling women's bodies.

Blue or red, the reaction of individual consumers to menstrual marketing lies in surrounding social and cultural attitudes. Reading these in order to judge correctly is the job of the marketer.

Conspicuous consumption

Consumer societies and cultures suppose that individual and collective status are framed by consumption. Thorstein Veblen was one of the first academics to recognise and define the rise of consumer societies when he wrote 'The Theory of the Leisure Class' in 1899. In this essay Veblen outlined the idea of 'conspicuous consumption' as spending more money on goods than they are worth. He believed that conspicuous consumption serves to demonstrate this ability to spend extra in order to illustrate social stratification. Hereby, conspicuous consumption is undertaken by individuals in order to impress the rest of society by demonstrating their social power and prestige. In short, they show off their ability to spend money.

This new way of demonstrating social success was part of the rise of the importance of consumerism. Hereby, social status becomes earned and displayed by patterns of consumption.

Rather than what the individual produces, people's sense of self-worth has increasingly been linked to the things that they consume. Buying an exotic holiday for example helps to compare favourably with peers in that it demonstrates personal wealth.

Conspicuous consumption involves public displays of wealth through showing off ownership in order to acquire social attention, admiration and status. As part of this self-presentation, consumption style and choices are symbolic. How consumption is conducted symbolises particular characteristics of the consumer. For instance, shopping at a certain store might infer financial status. Likewise, what is bought symbolises certain traits. For example, owning a particular brand of smartphone could indicate disposable income. Grubb and Grathwohl (1967) note how such consumption symbolism helps people to present themselves to others in a desired way. Doing so helps to reinforce and enhance their self-concept.

Going beyond displaying wealth, conspicuous consumption can be used to symbolise an array of personal identifiers. These can include expressing things like personality traits, emotional state, tribal affiliation or ideology. Going to a particular coffee shop for example could symbolise a variety of possible things ranging from subculture belonged to, through to political causes supported. Complex and multifaceted sense of self and feelings of belonging in the world can be developed and expressed through conspicuous consumption.

'Any colour as long as it's black' versus 'A car for every purse and purpose'

Founder of the auto brand that still bears his name, Henry Ford, is best known for developing automobile mass manufacturing methods. Thanks to economies of scale, Ford's Model T was the first car that could be afforded by the middle class, not just the very wealthy. Henry's saying that buyers could get their T in any colour, as long as it was black (Ford & Crowther, 1922), summarised his approach to the consumer. He believed that they wanted the most affordable product possible. Thus, everything about the manufacture of the Model T was designed for efficiency. This included the paint. Black was the colour that dried fastest. Model Ts were painted this colour in order to maximise production speed.

Ford's philosophy was a huge success. Manufactured from 1908 to 1927, millions of Model Ts were sold worldwide. The T is still one of the biggest selling cars of all time. However, Ford's focus on making the T as efficiently as possible meant that the company missed out on ways that consumers actually consume. Consumers bought and buy cars not just based on price, but also for more symbolic reasons. A car is not just an appliance helping to fulfil transportation needs. It is also a means of expressing individual personality, social status and cultural belonging. As the initial novelty of an affordable car wore off, and as more people owned a vehicle and so stood out less through doing so, the symbolic value of cars increased. Ford's resolute focus on the refinement of the product, rather than the whims of the consumer, left the firm increasingly irrelevant.

However, this shift in consumer tastes was picked up by Alfred P. Sloan at Ford's much smaller rival General Motors (GM). Becoming president of GM in 1923, Sloan was a big part of the marketing strategies used by the firm. His team pioneered amongst other things the idea of price differentiation (Blank, 2011). This approach saw multiple brands launched, each with distinctive styling and specific features. Sloan's saying, 'a car for every purse and purpose', captured his vision of providing a wide variety of products targeted at different types of consumers. Using a portfolio approach allowed GM to tailor its goods to the specific means of different sociocultural groups, but also their desire to express themselves in different ways.

Chevrolet for example was the firm's mass market brand, offering simpler products for a lower price. Buying a Chevy marked out as a hard-working American with sensible tastes. Cadillac meanwhile offered extra features and opulent styling important to wealthier conspicuous consumers. Owning a Caddy set apart as financially successful and self-indulgent. Sloan realised that consumers want to express their sociocultural status through their purchases and provided them with the means to do so. These marketing techniques allowed GM to overtake Ford in the 1930s and become the largest car manufacturer in the United States, a position it holds to this day. Eventually, Ford had to follow suit in order to survive. To greater or lesser extent all car brands today offer a portfolio of products designed to reflect not just the utilitarian needs, but also the sociocultural aspirations of consumers.

Consumption consequences: climate crisis and consumer well-being

Consumption can bring many positive individual and collective impacts as it helps consumers to fulfil various needs and desires. Nevertheless, consumption may be associated with various negative impacts. Perhaps the most serious of these, climate change, is in large part driven by consumerism. The manufacture, distribution, use and disposal of consumer goods are an often resource intensive and polluting process.

Moreover, consumption is associated with environmental pollution. Plastic waste for example, much of it linked with moving, wrapping and making up consumer goods, affects all parts of the globe. The Pacific garbage patch may be the most obvious visual representation of how consumption is smothering as well as using up the natural environment. Invisible however is the micro-plastic pollution made up of tiny granules of disposed plastic. This micro-particle pollution, the consequences of which on human and animal health are not yet fully understood, has been found in all human environments, from urban centres to the glaciers of the Antarctic, and even in large quantities on the ocean floor.

Climate crisis is arguably in large part a consumption crisis. This has not gone unnoticed. Consumers are increasingly aware of and concerned about the ecological impacts of consumerism. More willing to question its downsides as well as positives, increasing numbers of people appear to be uncomfortable with consumption being such a dominant part of their lives, societies and cultures. Writers such as Naomi Klein (2005), who captured and informed the early anti-consumerism debate in her influential book 'No Logo', as well as subsequent works, helped promote awareness of the negative consequences of consumption on individuals, societies and the planet as a whole.

This awareness has not only continued to grow but also individuals are increasingly doing something about it. Consumers are waking up to their individual responsibility and collective power. They are revising their consumption. The communal power of consumers is not to be underestimated, as the success of campaigns such as cruelty-free make-up demonstrates. Beauty products that do not involve animal testing in their development have become the industry standard thanks to pressure from consumers. Organic produce, Fair Trade, GMO free, vegan alternatives and shopping local have likewise all become established trends within food consumption. By demanding and supporting more ethical options consumers can help to persuade businesses to respond.

Conscious consumption

There are a number of ways that consumers can be more conscious of their consumption habits and choices. In doing so they can help address concerns over the negative consequences of buying and using things. Reducing consumption by making things last longer, repurposing items, or simply buying less, is an option. The environmental impact of an item is lessened if its lifecycle can be extended, or indeed if it is not created in the first place. So too environmental impacts can be moderated by consuming more carefully. For instance, by sourcing locally in order to reduce the carbon footprint of transporting goods. Substituting certain products for more sustainable alternatives is another option. For example, carrying a reusable coffee cup rather than accepting another disposable one. Consumers can moreover become more involved in making things. This allows for greater control over the type or amount of resources used and how they are used. Making own burgers from scratch for instance, means potential to source local, organic or meat-alternative ingredients that could have environmental advantages. Going beyond changing consumption habits, there are some who resist consumption altogether. This resistance captures a pushback against consumption as an ideology and way of life that prioritises the accumulation of products, services and experiences. Resistance is towards the narratives that consumerism brings things like happiness, meaning, belonging and identity.

Profits over people: empty promises and pressures

Consumption can have negative implications for the wider environment. It may also have negative impacts upon the individual. Some products, such as alcohol or tobacco, are harmful to the user. Nevertheless, they generally remain on sale, and, with restrictions, marketed. Other products, such as highly processed foods, may not in themselves be -harmful. However, if consumed too much they can contribute to serious health problems such as obesity. Although these products may indirectly but cumulatively harm consumers, they continue to be marketed, often aggressively. Sugary cereals for example have long been aimed at children, with marketing featuring cartoon mascots and colourful branding as a way to appeal. Such marketing raises the obvious question as to whether marketers care about consumer well-being or just consumer profitability.

More broadly than these particularly dubious product categories, the promises made by marketers that buying something may resolve a particular need or want might be harmful. Sales pitches often suggest that a buyer will feel better about themselves if they spend their money. Perhaps they will feel more attractive and confident as a result of a purchase. Maybe buying will help to make friends. Making such promises might be irresponsible. In suggesting that consumption can be a source of happiness, attractiveness or popularity, pressure is put on people to pursue these through spending money and obtaining things. People who cannot afford to do so may feel excluded. Even those who can may be disappointed to find that consumption does not live up to the promises made.

In addition, the marketing content and communications can apply pressure to people to live up to certain images or ideals. Often these are unrealistic, as with images of physical perfection prevalent in advertising. Pressuring people to feel bad about themselves can be a sensible marketing strategy. Tell people they are too fat or too thin and they might invest in a diet and exercise spree to lose weight, or protein shakes and gym to bulk up. Make people question their looks, and it is possible they will spend on new clothes, hair and make-up. Making people feel unsure of themselves because they fail to measure up to the images of beauty and success promoted in marketing may be a useful commercial ploy. However, it may likely not be good for individual well-being.

An extreme example of making individuals feel unsure of themselves, and reaping the rewards from, is cosmetic surgery. The cosmetic surgery industry thrives on selling expensive and mostly unnecessary interventions. These promise to make the purchaser more beautiful, when of course there is no such thing, for beauty is infinitely varied, lies in the eye of the beholder, comes from within and ought not to be all that important anyway. Penis enlargement surgery is one of the fastest growing areas of plastic surgery (BBC News, 2018). Methods include injecting saline solution into the shaft of the penis to make it temporarily appear larger. Procedures are medically unnecessary and potentially dangerous. The promise of improving self-esteem influences some men to undertake penis enlargement, despite the risks. Even where physical side effects are avoided, the likelihood that having an expensive and temporary penis enlargement will make a person happier in themselves, long term, is perhaps unlikely. Physical and mental well-being do not come from the tip of a needle. Nevertheless, a profitable industry has been built around exploiting male insecurities at their most superficial level.

Rebalancing of consumption

The previous century witnessed the expansion of consumption as the primary source of individual and collective social status and cultural identity. Consumption displaced other traditional sources of these such as faith, profession or nationality. Yet, although consumption remains important to defining and organising selves individually and socially, it may be less so than before.

Consumers appear to be increasingly aware of the potentially negative consequences of consumption. At the same time, consumers appear to be more cynical as regards the vested interests of marketing messages. Moreover, having lived within consumer societies for many decades, people may be somewhat fatigued with consumerism. People have bought enough expensive items hoping to cheer themselves up, only to find that they do this temporarily at best to become more circumspect. Widespread discovery is that shopping does not necessarily provide deep or long-lasting answers.

The idea of hitting 'peak stuff' is that some people have become saturated with owning too many things and tired of the pressure to keep buying more. Instead, people may be looking to de-clutter, and transition towards other types of consumption that gather less stuff in the first place. Buying more slowly, selectively or choosing a few statement pieces that last are possible reactions. To illustrate, media reports have picked up on the idea that people are buying less stuff (Usher, 2016). Such things as car sales are gradually declining, as is the case in the United States particularly amongst millennials (Kurz, Li & Vine, 2016).

This disenchantment of and fatigue with consumption is contributing to its rebalancing. Hereby, consumption is given less priority as a source of meaning. Instead, involvement in creating and making things is becoming more important as a source of meaning. It seems that what consumers increasingly aspire towards is not so much the ownership of a desired product, as it is the bettering of themselves through the consumption experience itself. This might see consumption more as a way of making memories, connecting with others, or learning new skills, rather than simply accumulating stuff.

Introducing prosumers

Consumer fatigue and concern are being addressed by individuals taking a more active role in consumption. Active consumption implies greater involvement in making purchases. This can mean doing additional research beforehand, so that a carefully judged choice can be made in accordance with environmental or other concerns. It also means participating in making as well as consuming products, services and experiences, such as putting together a tailored design or helping to assemble the final product.

Such involved consumption can be a novel and enjoyable activity. Attending a pottery workshop for instance is fun, sociable and develops new skills. This helps to overcome consumer fatigue by making consumption an engaging and inspiring process once more. Meanwhile, the outputs created can be more special and personal. What you make at the pottery class won't be as good quality as a bowl from the store, but it is more meaningful and memorable. Finally, being involved in the craft of an item is empowering in the sense that moral choices can be made over the resources used.

Veblen associated social status with the things one is able to purchase and put on display. Now, it is demonstrating craft expertise that can be a source of social distinction. Making things is becoming more significant to personal identity and cultural expression. Being able to craft something demonstrates skill and commitment, and accordingly earns social status. Making as well as consuming provides additional opportunities to display personal values and ethical positions. Today, social identity and status come from conspicuous production as well as consumption.

'Prosumer' is a term which combines the words consumer and producer. It reflects the growing involvement of people in their consumption. Taking a more active role, people are taking on aspects of producing the goods, services and experiences that they seek out. As noted, this change may be motivated by increasing dissatisfaction with or concern for the downsides of more passive consumption. Alternatively, it may relate to greater realisation of the rewards that can come from producing as well as consuming. Prosumption can take a number of forms as involvement in both consumption and production, and the balance between the two can vary widely. These include:

- ***Personalisation user***: At the lower end of involvement, consumers can seek out opportunities to personalise their purchases. This means spending some extra time or money to tailor these to suit individual tastes. Several sportswear brands for instance offer customers the chance to pick particular colour combinations, patterns or fabrics when they order in store or online. Such selections are relatively easy, but help to better fit with and express personal preferences.
- ***Product/brand advocate***: An advocate is someone who speaks up for a product or brand. This might be because of their genuine enthusiasm, or as a result of being paid. In either case, advocates are involved in building awareness. Many make-up brands for example work with keen beauty consumers, in order to build positive word of mouth around their products before and immediately after they go on general release.
- ***Craft consumer***: Craft consumers are those who find enjoyment in the production process. They find the tangible aspects of making something rewarding. Making a lump of clay into a finished pot for instance is pleasurable. Craft is about learning new skills, applying these, socialising whilst doing so and then having a finished product to exhibit. Consumption is the overall experience of producing something, not just the final output.

- *Semi-professional producer*: Whereas craft is a hobby, making things for pleasure, semi-professional producers make things for more commercial reasons. In this case, consumer interests are turned into semi-professional goods that can be exchanged for financial or other rewards. For example, a keen jewellery consumer may find that their knowledge of the product lends itself to making and selling it themselves. Semi-professionals are more casual makers than full-time professional producers.

> **Lindt: adding excitement to choosing chocolates**
> Prosumption is about making consumption more interactive. Relatively small changes can facilitate this. Lindt for example, a Swiss chocolate maker, has opened retail stores around the world that follow a pick-n-mix concept. Hereby, shoppers are confronted by vats full of colourfully wrapped chocolate balls. They can take a bag and fill it with as many of the flavours they like. This is a very simple and minimal form of prosumption. Yet by offering, Lindt has made visiting its stores more personalised, interactive and fun. In doing so, they have simultaneously made it easier to give in to temptation and buy more chocolate than perhaps otherwise intended.

Explaining the rise of prosumers

Prosumption is not a new phenomenon. Consumers have always had varying levels of involvement in the production of the goods, services and experiences they seek out. In the 1960s for example, backpackers rejected packaged holiday products and went off the beaten path in order to put together their own unique travel experiences. What is more, each consumer puts their own unique spin on how and what they consume. Even package tourists who pick a standardised product from an agent will still adapt according to personal preferences once in a destination.

Nevertheless, prosumers are currently a significant issue within marketing. Discussed by academics and practitioners alike, there seems to be a trend towards an increasing involvement of more people in their consumption. Underpinned by new technologies that have empowered and motivated, a number of underlying causes are suggested as behind the rise of prosumption:

- *Availability of information:* Thanks to new technology people can access large amounts of information quickly and easily. Such things as tutorials, reviews, product comparisons or marketplace data are all readily available online. Online influencers help to raise awareness of prosumption and encourage more people to do similar things. Food bloggers for instance have been an important part of increasing the number of home bakers and smoothie makers, by advocating for the benefits of doing it yourself. This plethora of information provides consumers with confidence and inspiration. It has enabled consumers to go beyond what they were used to, and get more demanding of their purchases, involved in their hobbies and pursuits and more skilled at making things themselves.
- *Online retailing:* Interested consumers and producers can find each other relatively easily online. The ability to identify and serve consumers online has made it easier for semi-professional producers to set up exchange relationships. This has meant more opportunities for people to become part- or full-time entrepreneurs. In turn, others are inspired to emulate online success stories.

- *Social media:* The rise of social media has facilitated conspicuous prosumption. Through platforms such as Pinterest, it is easy to display prosumption experiences, skills and activities. Attending an art class can be recorded and shared online for example. Social media has enhanced the ability to show off and acquire social status from prosumption.
- *Customisation:* Technology has made it easier to customise products, services and experiences, meaning that more personalised consumer offerings are becoming the norm. For example, 3D printing has meant that unique designs can be custom made on a one-off basis.

The result of these various influences is that consumers are shifting to become prosumers. This means that they expect to have some level of input into and control over their consumption. It is no longer enough to simply make consumers aware of a particular product, service or experience. Now, consumers need to be brought into the design, delivery and use of these from the outset. In doing so, consumers may develop an increased sense of connection with and ownership over their purchases. This has advantages of fostering a deeper connection between customers and brands, but also disadvantages of these being potentially more demanding.

Responding to prosumers can be challenging in the sense that this requires creative thinking about ways to facilitate their involvement. Letting customers into the design process may require advanced IT systems to enable their participation. Personalising footwear for instance, requires a website agile and interactive enough to host customer's creativity. Prosumers additionally need more active management if they are to be kept satisfied. This may include such things as providing learning materials for and feedback on their inputs. Lastly, prosumers may appreciate opportunities to display their production inputs before others. If conspicuous production is a source of status, then facilitating displays of this, through such things as social media, may be valuable. Making such efforts may be necessary to remain relevant as consumers evolve.

Consumer case: craft and hazelnut spread

Rebalancing of consumption as something that is more involved might be witnessed in the area of craft consumption. This is the activity of making objects. With craft consumption, getting involved in researching, designing and making something is an enjoyable and rewarding experience. Indeed, Elliot (2016) describes craft consumption as an activity than can provide a deep sense of meaning and satisfaction. Learning new skills and applying these can be a challenging and rewarding individual process. People often learn crafts from each other and work together on the making, meaning this is also a highly sociable activity.

The ethos of craft consumption has become big business. This is in the sense of smaller scale manufacturing where the art of production as well as the end product is emphasised to the customer. Craft beer for example involves typically small breweries taking pleasure in their sourcing and assembling of ingredients into niche products. Although craft beer drinkers are unlikely to have been actively involved in brewing their pint, they can feel more involved through the sharing of information and building of background knowledge around their interest. Mutual relationships are built for invested prosumers around developing their knowledge of craft beer as well as purchasing preferred products. It is such interaction which provides a more stimulating consumer experience.

Craft consumption is increasingly significant. Somewhat unlikely, chocolate spread illustrates this. The hazelnut-based Nutella brand spread is a wildly successful product throughout Continental Europe, where it has long been positioned as a children's snack. Developed by the Italian confectioner Ferrero after the Second World War, when rationing meant cocoa was in short supply, hazelnuts were used to bulk out the recipe. Launched as Supercrema in 1951, and then rebranded as Nutella in 1964, the black and red brand has become omnipresent in European kitchen cupboards, supermarkets and food vendors. Yet, as Cova and D'Antone (2016) note, even this powerful brand is not immune to rebalancing of consumption and production.

Hazelnut spread is simple and cheap to make. Nonetheless, for decades consumers have been willing to pay for the convenience of it readily prepared and jarred. This is beginning to change. A quick online search reveals a plenitude of posts depicting home-made hazelnut spread. Thanks to the connectivity of the internet, people have discovered how easy it is to produce their own. What is more, they have cottoned on to the idea that home-made spread can be adjusted according to personal taste, dietary requirements or ideological concerns. Whipped up in a blender, home-made spread does not have to contain palm oil for instance, if the sustainability of this commodity is a concern. Not only is Nutella easy to substitute and personalise, but doing so can be fun. Crafting in the kitchen can be an activity to share with children. Chocolate spread is enjoyably messy and playful. Even more than this, making your own spread can be a status symbol. Creativity, concern for the environment, good parenting and other such status symbols can all be communicated via a jar of home-made hazelnut put up on Pinterest. The same can't be said of the original.

Co-creation and co-production

Co-creation and co-involvement are overlapping terms, which recognise that consumers do not just passively consume goods, services and experiences. Rather, they get actively involved in making, shaping, adapting and reinventing these. Such involvement is a rewarding way to explore and develop identities. Wearing a logo T-shirt is one thing. But custom designing and then wearing a unique T-shirt, allows for deeper self-expression. This creative involvement can also be more fun and intellectually stimulating than just picking something off the shelf. For these reasons, co-creation and co-involvement are seen as possible ways to reengage with consumers who have become dissatisfied with more traditional forms of consumption.

Case questions

1. How might Nutella and similar brands respond to the rise of at home variations?
   Think about ways that Nutella could make their product more interactive for prosumers. It may be easier to deal with some types of prosumers more than others.
2. What non-food brands might be similarly at risk from a switch to prosumption?
   Think about products, services and experiences that are easy and enjoyable to produce oneself. Likewise, think about ideological and well-being issues that might nudge consumers to become more actively involved.
3. What are the underlying drivers of home-made hazelnut spread?
   Consider how suggested factors in the rise of prosumers may apply in the case of home-made spread. Some may be more influential than others.

Commercial case: the cautionary tale of Juicero

Working with prosumers can be a recipe for success. Interest in making things can be responded to with new products, services or experiences that can facilitate. A number of food retailers for instance have branched out into providing cooking classes during evenings or weekends. Not only is this an additional revenue stream, but it helps to build brand equity by linking with customers' interests. A high street bakery becomes more than just a place to buy bread. It additionally provides the raw materials, inspiration, professional skills and shared community to support an amateur bakers' enthusiasm. Working with prosumers needs to be done well however. As with other areas of marketing, this means understanding these and other stakeholders, as well as sincerity and commitment to exchange relationships.

An example of how not to work with prosumers is Juicero. Founded in 2013, Juicero sold expensive juicer machines. These would only work with pre-packed pouches of crushed fruits and vegetables, also retailed by the company and available via subscription. Juicero sold itself on the premise that users could easily make their own healthy juice at home. At first glance, this was a topical business model, linking with trends of healthier eating and consumers growing interest in production. The brand was briefly trendy, attracting significant investment from amongst others like Alphabet, Google's parent company.

Juicero's success was short lived however. The company attracted ridicule when media reported that the packets of juice sold could be just as easily squeezed by hand without the expensive machine. Juicero was criticised as offering a pointless solution to a non-problem (Hern, 2017). Meanwhile, analysis of the juicer itself criticised it as unnecessarily complex and hence expensive to buy. Inside sources suggested that even at $699 per juice press (the initial retail price that was quickly lowered to $399 in a bid to grow sales), Juicero was losing money on each unit sold (Zaleski, Huet & Stone, 2017).

Unable to attract enough customers, or to convince further investors, Juicero shut down in September 2017. The business' demise seems to illustrate how prosumers cannot be treated without due care and respect. Attempts to sell under-necessary or over-expensive (and in this case both at the same time) goods will not work. Prosumers are involved, informed, skilled and interested. Consequently, they rapidly see through empty marketing claims. Businesses which do not share and support prosumers' enthusiasm will not succeed.

Exchange relationships

If marketing facilitates exchange relationships between stakeholders, then prosumption complicates these somewhat. It does this by blurring the boundaries between stakeholders as consumers or producers. The style or direction of exchanges may shift. How to manage these more fuzzy roles and swaps can require creative thinking. Nonetheless, if it can be done right, then more mutually rewarding relationships can result. Through working with them more closely, marketing managers can benefit from the ideas and insights of customers. Customers meanwhile, gain from improved service and an increased sense of being taken seriously. Allowing customers to get more involved in production as well as consumption can result in stronger relationships.

> **Case questions**
>
> 1 What can be taken from the experience of Juicero as regards what not to do when dealing with prosumers?
>   *Think about how and why prosumers like to be more involved in production as well as consumption. In addition, how this affects product and brand expectations.*
> 2 Why would a product mocked in the media not complement the accrual of social status through conspicuous prosumption?
>   *Consider how social status is acquired and displayed through symbols, and how the meaning of symbols can be changed by surrounding conversations.*
> 3 Which brand, unlike Juicero, works successfully with prosumers?
>   *Identity and explain your selection in terms of how prosumers are interacted with by this particular brand. Think about what the benefits are for both prosumers and brand from this.*

Working with prosumers

The threat to Nutella from home-made spread, and the failure of Juicero to convince homemakers of its relevance to them, points towards the importance of working carefully with prosumers. These have a number of distinctive needs above and beyond more casual consumers, which need to be taken into account. Prosumers are perhaps even more cynical than less active consumers, and so will quickly spot exploitative marketing. Moreover, prosumers are likely more invested in their personal interest than general consumers. This means that they will be more sensitive to and critical of businesses that do not meet expectations. Detailed market research to better understand these interests and expectations is therefore a must when working with prosumers. Beyond this underlying research, a simple 4S checklist is a helpful way of considering how to work well with prosumers:

1 **Space:** Prosumers need to be given space where they can try out and develop their own skills. This means allowing room for them to put together own combinations, play around with recipes or try out different designs. Providing components and then the space to assemble these may be more important than providing a finished product.
2 **Stretch:** Because prosumers get a sense of reward from learning and doing, it is important that an element of challenge is built into their offering. Allowing for intellectual, physical or emotional stretch around a consumer purchase increases chances of developing more enduring exchange relationships. Things like new combinations may contain an element of surprise that keeps interesting. Involving in product development or brand management meanwhile gives prosumers outlet for their creativity.
3 **Support:** Although they like a challenge, most prosumers, most of the time, make a fairly minimal commitment to learning and doing. Making hazelnut spread is popular for example, because it is quick and easy. Making home-made jam is less so because it is more complicated, messy and harder to get right. Prosumers need to be given support if their activities are to stay enjoyable rather than become arduous. This means such things as simple recipes, easily shared techniques and communities who can encourage each other.

4   **Status:** Prosumption is popular where it can be used to display social status. If learning and making are accorded prestige amongst peers, then it is more likely that people will pursue such products. Thanks to negative media reports, Juicero went from being an aspirational product associated with Silicon Valley tech status to one that seemed overpriced, useless and embarrassing to display ownership of.

Chapter summary

Consumer societies and cultures seem to be shifting somewhat. Emphasis is edging away from consumption and towards production of items. To some extent this increased involvement may reflect fresh enthusiasm for craft. It might also be a result of changes in sources of social status, with making skills now more widely appreciated and easier to show off via things like social media. Opportunities are to develop and present products, services and experiences in more involving ways. Such things as personalisation can help to engage more active consumers. Nevertheless, rising interest in production may be accompanied by waning enthusiasm for consumption. Consumers are potentially reaching peak stuff. They are perhaps becoming more aware of the limitations and downsides of consumerism. Similarly, they are more cynical towards marketing content and communications. As demonstrated by things as innocuous and simple as home-made spread or juice, rebalancing raises major challenges for marketers to accommodate. If consumption is losing some of its lustre, then time is for re-evaluation of this and accompanying marketing.

References

BBC News. (2018). The men having penis fillers to boost their self-esteem. Available at: https://www.bbc.co.uk/news/health-45735061 (Accessed 30/09/20).

Blank, S. (2011). Apple's marketing playbook was written in the 1920s. *The Atlantic*, 26/10/11. Available at: https://www.theatlantic.com/business/archive/2011/10/apples-marketing-playbook-was-written-in-the-1920s/247417/ (Accessed 25/05/20).

Cova, B., & D'Antone, S. (2016). Brand iconicity vs. anti-consumption well-being concerns: The Nutella palm oil conflict. *Journal of Consumer Affairs*, 50(1), 166–192.

Elliot, E. A. (2016). Craft consumption and consumer transformation in a transmodern era. *Journal of Business Research*, 69(1), 18–24.

Elmhirst, S. (2020). Tampon wars: the battle to overthrow the Tampax empire. *The Guardian*, 11/02/20. Available at: https://www.theguardian.com/society/2020/feb/11/tampon-wars-the-battle-to-overthrow-the-tampax-empire (Accessed 30/09/20).

Ford, H., & Crowther, S. (1922). *My life and work*. Scotts Valley, CA: CreateSpace Independent Publishing Platform.

Grubb, E. L., & Grathwohl, H. L. (1967). Consumer self-concept, symbolism and market behavior: A theoretical approach. *Journal of Marketing*, 31(4), 22–27.

Hern, A. (2017). The five most pointless tech solutions to non-problems. *The Guardian*, 24/04/17. Available at: https://www.theguardian.com/commentisfree/2017/apr/24/the-five-most-pointless-tech-solutions-to-non-problems (Accessed 03/05/20).

Klein, N. (2005). *No logo*. London: Harper Perennial.

Kurz, C., Li, G., & Vine, D. (2016). The young and the carless? The demographics of new vehicle purchases. *FEDS Notes*, 24/06/16. Available at: https://www.federalreserve.gov/econresdata/notes/feds-notes/2016/the-young-and-the-carless-the-demographics-of-new-vehicle-purchases-20160624.html (Accessed 16/06/20).

Usher, T. (2016). We asked a removal guy if people really have less stuff. *Vice*, 02/03/16. Available at: https://www.vice.com/en_uk/article/xd79n3/we-asked-a-removal-guy-if-people-really-have-less-stuff (Accessed 16/06/20).

Veblen, T. (1899). *The theory of the leisure Class*. In Banta, Martha (eds.). *Oxford world's classics*. Oxford: Oxford University Press, 2007.

Wattanasuwan, K. (2005). The self and symbolic consumption. *Journal of American Academy of Business*, 6(1), 179–184.

Zaleski, O., Huet, E., & Stone, B. (2017). Inside Juicero's demise, from prized start-up to fire sale. *Bloomberg*. Available at: https://www.bloomberg.com/news/features/2017-09-08/inside-juicero-s-demise-from-prized-startup-to-fire-sale (Accessed 03/05/20).

9

RE-EVALUATING

Marketing amidst shit life syndrome – Oxycontin and iron challenges

Shit life syndrome

Rebalancing of consumption may be a positive choice. As explored previously, the rise of prosumers is testament to the willingness and ability of many consumers to get more involved in their purchases. Consumers may be motivated to do so by such things as environmental concerns. Wanting to do their bit in making a difference to help the planet, they might become more involved in and careful with their purchasing. However, reorientation of consumption may also be a decision forced on consumers by circumstances. Consumerism supposes that people have disposable income. This means spare money left over after essential bills are paid, which they can spend on themselves. The expansion of marketing in the 20th century paralleled the rising wages of workers in developed countries.

Yet over more recent decades, wages have in many locations stagnated. According to the Pew Research Center (2018), for most US workers wages have barely increased for the past 40 years when adjusted for inflation (the rising cost of goods). Indeed, the cost of living has in many places dramatically increased, with housing particularly expensive in various global cities. Moreover, job security has frequently been eroded, meaning people's incomes are less predictable. In such circumstances it may be necessary to consume differently or less.

Economic uncertainty and inequality play a part in what has been informally termed 'Shit Life Syndrome' (Hutton, 2018), abbreviated to SLS. This refers to the growing numbers of people who are trapped in low level poverty, poor quality housing, with restricted access to goods and services, and whose quality of life suffers as a result. Food deserts for example refer to places where inhabitants have little access to good quality or affordable nutrition. In certain US suburbs it can be difficult to find anything other than fast food within a reasonable transport distance. Poor public transportation, lack of variety of businesses or unaffordability of options means that many people struggle to eat healthily. SLS involves various interrelated factors therefore, which cumulatively make life difficult.

The negative consequences of SLS are readily apparent. In particular, SLS is linked with poor health. In parts of the developed world average life expectancy is falling for the first time in a century. Mortality in midlife in the United States has increased in recent years.

This has been linked to increasing rates of drug overdoses, obesity, alcohol and suicide (Woolf et al., 2018). Such health issues are moreover not distributed equally, but rather affect the most deprived areas disproportionately. In the United Kingdom for instance, healthy life expectancy, meaning the number of years an individual can expect to live a physically and mentally fit life, differs by around 20 years for women across local areas (ONS, 2018).

Clearly some places and people are struggling. In areas where SLS is an issue, these socioeconomic issues have made it harder to be a consumer. Consequences of SLS such as ill health mean that people are less able to work and earn money to spend. Simultaneously, healthcare costs increase to manage illness, reducing disposable incomes that are already more likely to be reduced or unstable in deprived areas, which tend to have fewer and less good quality overall employment. Spending on frivolous purchases or saving up for big ones becomes a challenge when less money is available. If a larger portion of income has to go on covering essentials such as rent, then less money is left over for everything else. When people are uncertain about what next month's pay packet will be, then consumerism loses its lustre.

Too much avocado toast?
In May 2017, the millionaire Australian property developer Tim Gurner gained brief media notoriety for stating that millennials would be able to save up a deposit on a home if they stop eating so much expensive avocado toast (Levin, 2017). His comments went down badly. Australia is a country with high house prices and where many young people cannot afford to get on the property ladder. The little pick-ups provided by small luxuries, such as mashed avocado on sourdough, can't really make up for lost decades being exploited by landlords in substandard and overpriced rentals, but they may help distract for a morning. Nevertheless, young people often face such dismissive comments that further undermine their uphill struggle to gain access to many of the things, such as housing, that are integral to a good life.

Commercial case: OxyContin

Prescription drug addiction is an especially stark example of the causes and consequences of SLS. Addiction, rates of which tend to be higher in socio-economically stressed areas, destroys lives and communities. Where people are addicted to substances they are often not able to be economically productive. They also frequently become a burden on formal and informal care systems. Addiction therefore brings a dual negative impact for local economies. Tax revenues decrease at the same time as resources are diverted towards coping with and managing addiction.

A growing problem in many parts of the world, the United States is considered to have a particular issue with prescription drug addiction. In certain states large numbers of people are dependent on synthetic opioid painkilling drugs. These have been overly prescribed and become too easily available. The result has been many people hooked on medications they were only meant to take temporarily or perhaps never even needed. Nicknamed the 'opioid crisis', this is in reference to the high strength pain killers derived from opium that drive the addiction problem. Illustrating how dangerous they are, Heroin and Morphine are classified in the same category of drug as synthetic opioids. These synthetics are cheap to make, powerful and highly addictive.

Originally, synthetic opioids were developed to relieve extreme pain in patients such as those facing late stage and terminal cancer. In such medical situations the problem of rapid addiction would not be a problem, given that patients would not be expected to live for much longer. Here, the powerful pain relief of synthetic opioids is important to maintaining quality end of life. However, this particular malignant pain market is relatively minor. In order to increase sales, synthetic opioid manufacturers had to look elsewhere. During the late 1990s and into the 2000s there was a push to make these drugs available to the wider American population, as pain relief for more chronic medical conditions. The chronic pain relief market, which refers to long-term issues of such things as sports or workplace injuries and managing associated on-going pain, is much larger than the malignant pain one.

One of the biggest businesses pushing this change in pain relief consumers' attitudes and behaviours was Purdue Pharma. Their OxyContin brand of synthetic opioid pain relief is one of the most successful. Van Zee (2009) reviews the marketing that made OxyContin. When Purdue Pharma was introduced in 1996, the pain relief brand was aggressively marketed. From 1996 to 2001, this included Purdue Pharma holding more than 40 national 'pain management symposia'. These events hosted thousands of American doctors, nurses and pharmacists, often in attractive surroundings, and then promoted OxyContin to them. Moreover, from 1996 to 2002, Purdue more than doubled its sales force. A lucrative bonus system for sales representatives encouraged them to increase sales, with income from sales bonuses often much larger than annual salary. Sales staff liaised with medical professionals and promoted OxyContin to them. According to Van Zee, they distributed coupons so doctors could let patients try a 30-day free supply of these highly addictive drugs.

Thus, medical practitioners were made aware of and encouraged to prescribe the OxyContin brand. They became sales people for the brand themselves. Because synthetic opioids were seen as medical drugs, rather than illicit ones, and came recommended by medical practitioners, they were trusted as appropriate by patients.

Commercial triumph, public health tragedy

From a purely commercial perspective, OxyContin is one of the most successful new product launches of the past quarter century. If annual brand rankings were more imaginative, they might have included OxyContin amongst their top tens alongside perennial favourites from the tech and FMCG sectors. Indeed, few consumer goods are as fast moving as prescription opioids. Brand loyalty meanwhile is to be envied. Customers just cannot help but come back for more.

Only introduced in 1996, the OxyContin brand has generated a fortune for its parent company. As reviewed by Van Zee, prescriptions for this type of pain medication increased from about 670,000 in 1997 to about 6.2 million in 2002. Sales grew from $48 million in 1996 to almost $1.1 billion in 2000. Exponential prescriptions and sales growth since these dated statistics appear to be the case. OxyContin, as a leading brand, has played a major part in developing and profiting from this market.

The huge success of OxyContin comes from the brand's relevance to many contemporary consumers. In the context of SLS, the temporary relief from higher levels of ill health provided by prescription opioids is especially pertinent. Taking an OxyContin tablet can provide brief relief from physical and mental pain. This may enable workers without access to sick days to keep going and keep their jobs. More broadly, substances such as opioids are a means of escaping immediate self and wider surroundings. This escapism is particularly tempting where SLS has brought various anxieties relating to external circumstances.

Consequently, Van Zee describes the marketing of OxyContin a commercial triumph. This is a brand that helped redefine the market for pain medication. Nevertheless, they go on to confirm this as simultaneously a public health tragedy. The brief escape from pain provided by an OxyContin comes with potentially terrible long-term consequences. According to the Centers for Disease Control and Prevention (2011), growing sales of OxyContin correlated with increases in prescription opioid abuse and overdose deaths.

Prescription opioids can be dangerous in themselves. However, their further threat to public health is the link that they may have with increasing use of Heroin, as well as strong synthetic forms of Heroin such as Fentanyl. Prescription drugs like OxyContin may for some be a gateway to stronger opioid drugs. When prescriptions run out or are no longer affordable, the addiction remains and some may turn to alternatives. In 2014, among 47,055 drug overdose deaths in the United States, 61% involved an opioid (Rudd et al., 2016). By 2016, there were more than 63,600 drug overdose deaths in the United States (Hedegaard, Warner & Miniño, 2017).

Ethics and responsibilities of marketing

The over-prescription of powerful and addictive painkillers has undoubtedly played a role in the US opioid epidemic. The only doubts are over how extensive or deliberate were businesses such as Purdue Pharma in encouraging this over-prescription. The responsibility for the terrible addiction situation has been pushed between pharmaceutical companies, regulators and politicians. In 2019, Purdue Pharma declared bankruptcy as part of a legal settlement of claims against it, which had argued the company had aggressively and misleadingly marketed OxyContin. The legal situation remains on-going, and the health crisis, addiction and mortality consequences remain likewise.

For marketers, the case of OxyContin raises difficult questions over the ethics of our discipline. Historically, marketing owes much to the development of harmful products such as tobacco. A highly damaging and addictive substance, marketing nonetheless helped build the tobacco industry into a global powerhouse. It continues to do so. According to the multinational British American Tobacco, in 2018 estimates for the legal global tobacco market were sales worth approximately US$814 billion, to over one billion users worldwide (BAT, 2018).

The aggressive marketing of tobacco is now notorious. Player's cigarette cards were a collector's item with appeal to children that recruited new generations of customers. It can be easy to assume that the worlds of business and marketing have moved on. The misleading claims of early 20th-century adverts that cigarettes were actually good for health are now laughed at. Nevertheless, what seems to have been learned from the shame of looking back on last century's tobacco marketing is not that marketing must do better to protect consumers, for example not promoting damaging products on behalf of paying clients. Rather, learned are techniques for doing marketing better. This means getting around regulations and displacing shame, so that damaging products can continue to be sold on behalf of paying clients.

Illustrating this, big tobacco firms continue to aggressively push their products on people, particularly in places which are less well regulated such as developing economies in full knowledge of how harmful what they sell actually is. The marketing of pain medication has followed a similarly cynical prescription to that of big tobacco, for instance manipulation of public, corruption of healthcare professionals, buying off politicians and intimidation of opponents. These tactics that could come from a classic 20th-century marketing textbook have earned a number of businesses a lot of money at the expense of the long-term health of their consumers.

With such a historical and on-going track record of putting profit before people, it is apparent that marketers have not always acted in the best interests of consumers. Consumers know this and they increasingly do not trust marketers as a result. Our discipline has not and still is not always conducted ethically or responsibly. Commercial priorities have repeatedly been prioritised over consumer welfare. This needs to change if consumer trust is to be restored and consumer well-being respected. When facilitating exchange relationships marketers must be responsible arbitrators with a duty of care to all stakeholders involved. Whether marketing can kick its bad habit of shilling dangerous goods remains to be seen.

Case questions

1. What does the opioid crisis tell us about the state of consumer society and culture in the contemporary United States?
    Consider the state of the American dream where increasing polarisation between and exclusion of individuals and groups may be observed.
2. Why are some of the most successful brands those that sell addictive substances?
    Prescription medicines, tobacco, alcohol, marijuana are large global industries with billions of consumers. Evaluating the underlying causes of their success may help to understand how to address these.
3. What are you addicted to?
    Think about the products, services or experiences that you might find very difficult to give up. Consider why you might need these and how these perhaps help you to cope with personal issues or surroundings.

Inverting Maslow's pyramid

Beyond the uncomfortable success story of Oxycontin, SLS has implications for the reconfiguration of consumer society and culture more extensively. The long influential American dream associated a successful life with earning money in order to buy progressively better things. Consumer goods and services could facilitate a more comfortable existence. A washing machine could reduce chore time, a car bring freedom, a bigger house more space to raise a family in. Abraham Maslow's (1943, 1954) hierarchy of needs is a well-known model that captures this emphasis on quality of life as involving various needs from more essential to more aspirational (Figure 9.1). Within classic consumer culture, consumption plays an important role in fulfilling these needs. This is often done progressively. First, lifestyle fundamentals are purchased such as a place to live. Then over time, lifestyle enhancements might be acquired such as a place to vacation.

To greater or lesser extent the American dream has influenced consumers worldwide, thanks to the immense cultural influence of the United States. Yet this dream, which placed

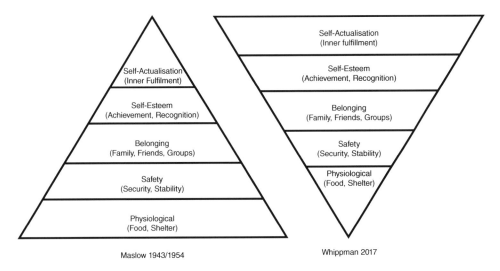

FIGURE 9.1 Inverting Maslow.

consumerism at its heart, has been fading. Fewer and fewer Americans are upwardly mobile in this established consumerist sense. Indeed, fewer Americans are able to afford basics such as healthcare. Illustrating this point, Dickman, Himmelstein and Woolhandler (2017) provide a detailed overview of the inequality of healthcare access in the United States. They report how for individuals with private insurance, rising premiums and cost sharing have undermined wage gains and driven many households into debt and even bankruptcy. With millions of poorer Americans unable to receive adequate care, the life expectancy of the wealthiest Americans now exceeds that of the poorest by 10–15 years.

Looking back to Maslow's hierarchy therefore, it can be seen that lower order needs are increasingly difficult for millions of Americans to obtain. Safety needs relating to a sense of stability and security that comes from things like reliable world and functioning communities are not met in many cases. Even physiological needs, those at the base of the pyramid relating to health, shelter and food, are difficult to guarantee when things like adequate housing, affordable healthcare and access to quality nutrition are uncertain, and then compounded by such things as the opioid crisis.

Maslow's pyramid was elaborated in his works of 1943 and 1954. This placed human needs in order from the base to the tip, with lower order needs needing to be fulfilled, before progressing onto higher levels of human advancement. Since Maslow's popular theory was developed, consumer surroundings have shifted markedly. What is more or less obtainable for mainstream consumers, as well as their priorities, have evolved. Whippman (2017) proposes that Maslow's hierarchy of needs has been inverted. She describes how the costs of the fundamentals that form the base of Maslow's pyramid have skyrocketed. At the same time, those needs at the top of the pyramid have become more accessible. Self-actualisation-related consumption, in terms of things like foreign travel, has never been more affordable. Meanwhile, opportunities to consume self-actualisation-related experiences, such as yoga classes, have never been more readily available.

Whippman characterises the last couple of decades in the United States as the age of self-actualisation. She describes how a new and pervasive cultural narrative around human well-being has seeped through virtually all sections of society. "This narrative inverts Maslow's pyramid, positing self-realization not just as something to pursue when the basic fundamentals are in place, but as a viable alternative to those fundamentals" (p. 527). Accordingly, Maslow's hierarchy has turned on its head. Hereby, self-actualisation is not just something to pursue when the basic fundamentals are in place, but is considered a more urgent priority. Rather than good housing or employment being considered as essentials to quality of life, sense of self-discovery, identity development and group belonging may be. In addition, such esteem and actualisation type needs may be far more accessible than safety or physiological ones. Thus consumption is inverted. Things like housing may no longer be within reach of or considered important by many young people, but juice cleanses and Ayurvedic retreats are. Young consumers may typically face differently accessible lifestyle opportunities and challenges from older generations and also have distinct priorities regarding these.

> **Pyramid collapse**
> The inversion of Maslow's pyramid challenges marketers to rethink consumer needs and aspirations. Self-actualisation may now be a basic requirement, not a far-flung future ambition. Consumers may expect intellectually and emotionally stimulating and stretching experiences with even quite minor and mundane purchases. Coffee for instance, is a cheap commodity product. Yet independent coffee producers and retailers have managed to market as an entire lifestyle. Coffee shops are a place to learn about the science of coffee, train taste buds, and become a more sophisticated connoisseur. This is coffee as a self-actualisation experience rather than simply consumption. Yet Whippman points out that although self-actualization is important to human flourishing, without the fundamentals of affordable shelter, healthcare, and a living wage, it means little. Hollowing out the base of Maslow's pyramid risks its collapse.

Consumer case: iron challenges

The ambitious pursuit of actualisation by contemporary consumers may be observed in the case of iron challenges. These are extreme physical endurance events structured around lengthy and difficult races and obstacle courses. Iron challenges present participants with a range of physical and mental trials. Their current popularity is testament to the willingness of many current consumers to take on such trials as part of building their sense of self-esteem and actualisation. Indeed, such endurance experiences have rapidly grown into a major leisure activity and commercial opportunity in a short space of time. Iron challenges include the Tough Mudder and Spartan Race endurance obstacle courses. Both were founded in 2010. The older established Ironman extended triathlon series, marathons and various ultra-runs are other examples. These events attract large numbers of competitors worldwide.

The emphasis of iron challenges is less on winning, and more on overcoming the difficulties of taking part in order to successfully finish. Making it to the end of an event is more important than beating others. Managing to do so is emphasised as a source of prestige. Completion demonstrates toughness and resilience in the face of difficulty. As such, iron challenges represent a form of prosumption that heavily involves consumers in producing the experience itself. It is their sweat and occasional blood which gets them over the finish line, as much as it is their credit cards which allow them to sign up.

Lamb and Hillman (2015) examine Tough Mudder and conclude that this is a form of conspicuous consumption that is perfect for online displays and social status building: "It became clear from our observations that a primary motivation of Tough Mudder participants was documenting the event by taking photos of themselves and posting them immediately to one's several online profiles" (p. 94). Through displaying their participation, participants are able to brand themselves as physically and mentally fit.

This branding is useful in contemporary environments, such as workplaces, where there may be a need to project such an image. Lamb and Hillman summarise:

> Tough Mudder is an accurate metaphor for corporate success that explains its popularity, where corporate types can test themselves in order to provide additional rhetorical proof of being able to navigate the cutthroat, hostile, and insecure world of corporate capitalism
>
> *(p. 97)*

Iron challenges appeal because of their relevance to contemporary consumers need to demonstrate certain attributes in order to navigate their surroundings. Lamb and Hillman suggest that Tough Mudder is an event which reinforces values of masculinity, survival, competitiveness and risk for participants. These may appeal in contemporary societies characterised by precarity, where people feel that their working and social lives are unstable. Extreme sports events are a way to channel this uncertainty into something focused. Rather than a brief Oxycontin fuelled escape from such issues, Tough Mudder offers a chance to face up to a survival of the fittest event, and triumph by making it to the end of a course. This gives a sense of competitive success that might not be felt elsewhere.

CrossFitting in

Iron challenges can result in feelings of personal growth from overcoming a difficult challenge. This ties in with Whippman's age of self-actualisation. Consumers looking to stretch themselves physically and mentally, can readily sign up and work towards. In a similar way, CrossFit, a global fitness phenomenon, sells more than just the development of a fit body and physical skill, but is a continual project of self-actualization. This is noted by Nash (2018), who analyses how CrossFit, repurposes military discipline and hypermasculinity in order to shape processes of self-transformation. Nash argues that CrossFit may help to compensate for the loss of other sources of identity. As with other iron challenges, this focus on survival, competitiveness, and self-actualisation, may be very relevant in contemporary surroundings. Indeed, CrossFit has built a multibillion-dollar brand present in over 140 countries.

Consumer confidence

With Maslow's pyramid inverted, traditional sources of consumer identity, meaning and overall confidence have become harder to acquire. Iron challenges are an example of successfully repositioning consumption to meet the needs of contemporary consumers in these respects. At a time when resource constraints exclude many from longstanding consumer goals, iron challenges are accessible. Rather than financial commitment (although they do cost), they ask for physical and mental dedication. Once undertaken meanwhile, iron challenges provide a focus and a social support system leading up to, during and following on from individual events. At a time of consumer uncertainty and anxiety, the sense of identity, meaning and confidence that comes from iron challenges is an attractive sales pitch.

These endurance events sell self-esteem and actualisation. Through participation consumers are reputedly able to better themselves bodily and emotionally. If they make it to the finish line then they have endured and beaten a difficult obstacle course. This is an achievement that is recognised by the event organisers and that can be shared amongst peers. If not, then they still tried and there is always next time for self-improvement is ever a work in progress. Around 80% of contestants in such events do make the finish line. Nevertheless, iron challenges tend to play down the idea of 'winning'. Instead, they emphasise the camaraderie of the experience and value of just taking part. Personal bests are more important than overall placing.

This ethos is a refreshing one. Ironically it is less competitive perhaps than the day-to-day life for many people who feel pressured to compete at school, work or via social media. Whether triumphant at the finish line or not, displayed to the self and to others through taking part in an endurance event, is a willingness to take on adversity. Where SLS has eroded such things as reliable employment, it has likewise undermined accompanying sense of direction, identity, community or achievement, which may come from. Iron challenges offer an alternative source of such human desires.

What is more, unlike such things as education, employment or Instagram, where the individual has relatively little control over their achievements and must rely on the feedback of others, iron challenges are singular. By focussing on individual physicality-mentality participants can take control of something that does not have to involve others. How they manage their bodies, diets and training can be entirely solo. Measuring progress is likewise in the control of the individual. Personal bests can be set and recorded individually. Goals and the fulfilment of these likewise. Iron challenges facilitate and profit off of this singular focus by offering training and measurement goods, services and experiences. They package and sell a sense of identity, meaning and confidence through endurance.

Consequently, iron challenges offer an experience that is relevant to contemporary consumers living in strained circumstances. Consumption may be undergoing a re-evaluation thanks to wider environmental issues. Established models such as Maslow's, and the accompanying consumption assumptions and marketing practices that derive from these, may be changing quite markedly. In the process, certain styles of consumption or types of goods may fall from favour or become inaccessible. However, consumption itself clearly remains relevant in these changing circumstances, if and where it adapts accordingly.

Dissipation versus actualisation

Consumers appear to be prioritising forms of consumption that fit in with contemporary surroundings. Demand is for consumption that distracts from frequently uncertain circumstances. OxyContin may be an extreme and form of this. Dissipation refers to abandonment of structures and systems and instead indulgence in immediate pleasures. Focus is on instant gratification. Such an approach can be destructive, because difficulties are not dealt with and may only be worse when eventually they have to be. At the same time, rising demand is for consumption that confronts challenging circumstances and provides new sources of identity, meaning and confidence, as with iron challenges. Actualisation is about fulfilling potential. An actualised state is a place of self-realisation, acceptance and contentment. Reaching such a place involves things like confronting challenges, taking responsibility for own actions, and connecting with others. It is through navigating difficult events or decisions, learning from these, and in taking ownership of successes and mistakes, that actualisation is worked towards.

> **Case questions**
>
> 1. What do consumers get out of consumption experiences that are mentally and physically challenging?
>   *Think about the outcomes that come from participating in and perhaps completing such endurance activities.*
> 2. Which consumers display particular demand for iron challenges?
>   *Consider the profile of participants in endurance events or activities, and evaluate why these might be particularly drawn towards consuming these.*
> 3. Are dissipation and self-actualisation mutually exclusive?
>   *Think about how these two consumer states may overlap or interact. It may be possible for consumer goods to provide either, neither or both.*

Re-evaluation: marketing moving forward

As consumers are shaped by their changing surroundings marketing has to re-evaluate its concepts and practices. Traditional approaches to such things as market positioning may need to be modified. With consumers pushed towards extremes, centrism is less of an option than it was. Middle market brands have struggled to accommodate newly polarised consumer attitudes and behaviours. Henceforth, marketers need to re-evaluate what and how products, services and experiences remain relevant to contemporary consumers. This included understanding their circumstances and adapting offerings to remain relevant.

Opportunities may lie in emphasising dissipation or actualisation. Escapism through such things as focus on niche interests may provide welcome respite for consumers. The fandoms explored throughout this book are examples of consumers acting individually and together to find new sources of pleasure, status and identity around shared enthusiasms. Embracing challenges meanwhile, more mentally or physically committed prosumption may bring rewarding outcomes for consumers. Getting involved in the craft or challenge of more active consumption and accompanying production has various advantages for consumers. These include taking greater control over consumption and its consequences and finding more rewarding outcomes.

In such ways consumers are rising to the challenges, difficulties and uncertainties of 21st-century consumerism. They are finding creative ways to engage with forms of consumption that continue to meet their changing needs, desires and means of pursuing these goals. This consumer inventiveness is taking place even as many people face exclusion from marketplaces due to resource inequalities. Clearly consumers are re-evaluating consumerism and finding new ways of engaging with marketplaces, products, services and experiences.

Are marketers rising to this challenge as proactively? All too often it can seem as if marketing remains disengaged from the consumer cultures it is rooted in and helps to create. As these consumer cultures are changing, there is a need to adapt as well. Yet more than this, consumer cultures are in many cases not working. Too many consumers are being excluded from having their needs or desires fulfilled. This is especially the case for certain types of consumers such as younger people. In addition, too many consumers are being manipulated and mistreated by the marketplace. They are sold on partial, misleading or even harmful promises.

This is not sustainable. Marketing needs to re-evaluate its role, impacts and principles. Tweaking consumer goods and associated brands to remain relevant in altered surroundings is one thing, but pre-emptively challenging and changing surroundings is more ambitious and necessary. Consumer cultures are worth fighting for. Marketplaces are vibrant sources of exchange between stakeholders. Diverse ideas, goods, skills, services and experiences can be shared. Borders and divides are bridged in the process. Human needs and desires can be fulfilled as well, thus improving quality of life. Nevertheless, this positive potential is in danger of ebbing away unless marketers do something.

Facilitating stakeholders, exchanges and relationships

Re-evaluating marketing means going back to the fundamentals of what the discipline and profession focuses upon, and reflecting upon these. Marketers' role is to facilitate exchange relationships between stakeholders. Each of these key words implies certain responsibilities (see Figure 9.2). Re-evaluation of these four fundamentals is made necessary because of the changing nature of contemporary consumption. This is altering what is facilitated through consumption, for who, how exchange negotiations take place and why relationships fail or succeed. In addition, the fundamentals of marketing need to be re-evaluated because of the sometimes poor track record of past marketing in terms of ethical or responsible conduct.

Inspired by ecosystems

A way forward for marketing may come from an ecosystems approach. Taking a holistic perspective, this considers the complexity, balance and overall health of stakeholder exchange relationships as they take place in intricate overall structures. The ecosystems way of thinking supposes that a complex web is made up of and around stakeholders. Ecosystems comprise the resources distributed within extensive networks of directly and indirectly connected stakeholders. Taking an ecosystems approach has the advantage of appreciating the complexity of webs in which organisations find themselves. This helps to understand that the significance of any one actor in a network is limited. Instead, appreciation can better be that all members of a network are dependent on multiple others.

It can be convenient to draw a line around a particular ecosystem such as a geographic region or particular industry. However, ecosystems are also extensive, intertwined and messily demarcated. For example, the fast food ecosystem comprises potentially wide ranging stakeholders. This obviously includes restaurants, their customers, suppliers and employees. In addition, delivery services are now an important part of the fast food ecosystem. These may complement and compete with restaurants. So too technology providers that support those delivery services are part of the overall fast food habitat. The boundary of the fast food ecosystem potentially expands extensively.

Marketing amidst shit life syndrome **139**

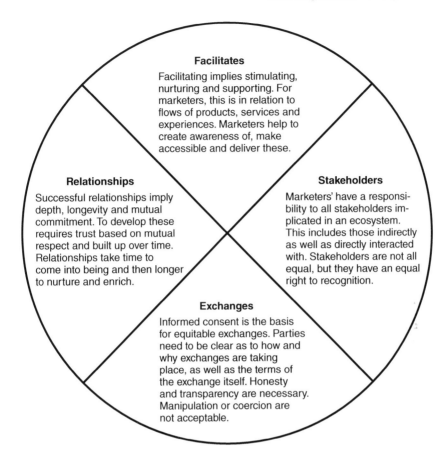

FIGURE 9.2 The four fundamentals of marketing.

Henceforth, mapping ecosystems is an important activity. Doing so helps organisations to appreciate the complex web of their surroundings, including various competitors and enabling services. Appreciating the extent and nuances of an ecosystem is important towards identifying opportunities for collaboration. Iansiti and Levien (2004) for example looked at Wal-Mart's surrounding ecosystem and found that a large part of the retailer's cost advantage came from identifying and managing partners within this. By sharing information with suppliers and distributors for instance, Wal-Mart increased productivity and reduced costs. A significant percentage of the firm's cost advantage comes from this ecosystem mapping and management.

As with individual species in a biological ecosystem, each member of a business ecosystem ultimately shares the fate of the network as a whole. Every individual business depends on surrounding stakeholders. This includes direct and indirect, complementary and even competing stakeholders. Briefly speaking, more diverse ecosystems that feature higher numbers of stakeholders and greater numbers of interactions between them tend to be more vibrant and productive for all members. This is because diversity stimulates ideas, innovation and solutions. Although stakeholders within ecosystems may at times compete, this competition can push them to be more creative. Within ecosystems, stakeholders also collaborate. They work together to find mutually beneficial solutions. Collaboration allows for pooling resources and capitalising on complementary capabilities.

Consumer cultures are complex ecosystems made up of a wide range of stakeholders such as brands, customers, sales associates and the marketers who often introduce and hold these together. As with any ecosystem, these consumer cultures can be damaged over time if they are not appreciated. Such things as over emphasis on individual stakeholders, exploitative interactions or too narrow a focus on immediate surroundings can undermine consumer cultures. Iansiti and Levien (2004) believe that a firm which takes an action without understanding the impact on the ecosystem as a whole is ignoring the reality and the possibilities of the networked environment in which it operates. It is important for marketers to realise their role in, responsibility for and the rewards from nurturing consumer ecosystems.

Chapter summary

Consumer society and culture is going through a difficult time. Growing numbers of consumers face exclusion from marketplaces. They may turn to dissipation to distract from this. Alternately, self-actualisation can be prioritised. OxyContin and Iron Challenges illustrate commercially successful responses to these trends, albeit clearly the first of these comes with devastating individual and community consequences. With consumption changing in such challenging circumstances, marketers need to be conscious not just of the opportunities and threats associated with, but also the ethics of consumption. Re-evaluating marketing's roles and responsibilities is essential if stakeholders' well-being is to be respected and consumer cultures are to survive. The next chapter will further develop this theme. Looked at is the need to more than re-evaluate marketing, to revive it.

References

British American Tobacco. (2018). *The global market: Trends affecting our industry*. Retrieved from https://www.bat.com/group/sites/UK__9D9KCY.nsf/vwPagesWebLive/DO9DCKFM# (accessed 24/06/20).
Centers for Disease Control and Prevention. (2011). *Vital signs report*. Available at: https://www.cdc.gov/mmwr/preview/mmwrhtml/mm6043a4.htm?s_cid=mm6043a4_w.
Dickman, S. L., Himmelstein, D. U., & Woolhandler, S. (2017). Inequality and the health-care system in the USA. *The Lancet*, *389*(10077), 1431–1441.
Hedegaard, H., Warner, M., & Miniño, A. M. (2017). *Drug overdose deaths in the United States, 1999–2015. NCHS data brief, no 273*. Hyattsville, MD: National Center for Health Statistics.
Hutton, W. (2018). The bad news is we're dying early in Britain – and it's all down to 'shit-life syndrome'. *The Guardian*, 19/08/18. Available at: https://www.theguardian.com/commentisfree/2018/aug/19/bad-news-is-were-dying-earlier-in-britain-down-to-shit-life-syndrome.
Iansiti, M., & Levien, R. (2004). Strategy as ecology. *Harvard Business Review*, *82*(3), 68–81.
Lamb, M. D., & Hillman, C. (2015). Whiners go home: Tough Mudder, conspicuous consumption, and the rhetorical proof of "fitness". *Communication & Sport*, *3*(1), 81–99.
Levin, S. (2017). Millionaire tells millennials: If you want a house, stop buying avocado toast. *The Guardian*. https://www.theguardian.com/lifeandstyle/2017/may/15/australian-millionaire-millennials-avocado-toast-house (accessed 06/02/20).
Maslow, A. H. (1943). A theory of human motivation. *Psychological Review*, *50*(4), 370–396.

Maslow, A. H. (1954). *Motivation and personality.* New York: Harper.

Nash, M. (2018). Let's work on your weaknesses': Australian CrossFit coaching, masculinity and neoliberal framings of 'health' and 'fitness. *Sport in Society, 21*(9), 1432–1453.

Office for National Statistics. (2018). Health state life expectancies, UK: 2016 to 2018. Report available at: https://www.ons.gov.uk/peoplepopulationandcommunity/healthandsocialcare/healthandlifeexpectancies/bulletins/healthstatelifeexpectanciesuk/2016to2018 (accessed 24/06/20).

Pew Research Centre. (2018). *For most U.S. workers, real wages have barely budged in decades.* https://www.pewresearch.org/fact-tank/2018/08/07/for-most-us-workers-real-wages-have-barely-budged-for-decades/ (accessed 06/02/20).

Rudd, R. A., Seth, P., David, F., & Scholl, L. (2016). *Increases in drug and opioid-involved overdose deaths — United States, 2010–2015.* MMWR Morbidity and Mortality Weekly Report 65, pp. 1445–1452.

Van Zee, A. (2009). The promotion and marketing of oxycontin: Commercial triumph, public health tragedy. *American Journal of Public Health, 99*(2), 221–227.

Whippman, R. (2017). Where were we while the pyramid was collapsing? At a yoga class. *Society, 54*(6), 527–529.

Woolf, S. H., Chapman, D. A., Buchanich, J. M., Bobby, K. J., Zimmerman, E. B., & Blackburn, S. M. (2018). Changes in midlife death rates across racial and ethnic groups in the United States: Systematic analysis of vital statistics. *BMJ Clinical Research, 362,* k3096.

10
REVIVING

Bringing marketing back – inspired by sex toys, slave-free sugar and Marks & Spencer

Time for a marketing revival

What does marketing do? Ask that question of a random sample and the reply might not be that positive. 'Manipulate people' is a common answer. People are often cynical towards and wary of marketing. They arguably have good reason to be. Marketing has a mixed track record in terms of its application. Indeed, introducing people to addictive and harmful substances, including prescription medications, has been one of marketing's biggest success stories.

Therefore, marketing has something of an image problem. This is deservedly so to some extent, but also unfair given its potential to bring about positive change. Exchanges nurtured by marketing can challenge, subvert and change cultural attitudes, and do so in ways that extend equality. This has been the case around perceptions of sex-sexuality for example. Exchanges can additionally inspire new solutions to address challenges, for instance finding more sustainable solutions to the global climate emergency.

Indeed, marketing is a uniquely insightful and comprehensive approach to facilitating exchanges, and through these formulating and implementing change. Marketers are experts at collecting data. They are trained to seek out a variety of sources of potentially interesting information, and then to draw out, record, store, analyse and utilise that info. Marketing is an activity that includes data collection and analysis tools, but also a wider set of theoretical and practitioner frameworks that help to make sense of and give purpose to this data. Marketing concepts are there to help understand individual and collective consumers, in order to support those marketing functions that assist in the exchanges within consumption ecosystems. Marketing not only delivers data but also develops knowledge.

Marketing needs reviving if this positive potential is to be realised, and if individuals and communities are to benefit. Climate crisis, socioeconomic inequality and culture clashes are urgent issues that need immediate solutions. Through its role in developing understanding, proposing solutions and facilitating stakeholder exchanges, marketing can help to address the major issues of the contemporary world.

Looking to marketing's historical ability to do so may be source of inspiration. Learning from such examples as those reviewed in this chapter, marketers can rediscover their radical side and reaffirm their place in shaping current conversations. Marketing is due a revival. This chapter explores how this might be inspired and achieved.

Culture and marketing

This book began by looking at the idea of cultural relevance and the importance to marketing of being up to date with contemporary cultural trends and issues. This is especially so if connections are to be made with younger consumers. Their unique experiences and surroundings shape distinctive attitudes and behaviours. Because culture is always changing, marketing has to be engaged in monitoring and responding to change.

Good marketing is reactive. This means that it responds rapidly to changes in consumer culture. If a new type of youth consumer emerges, with distinctive values and forms of self-expression, then marketers ought to adapt their offerings and messages to suit. In this way connections are fostered as early as possible. In marketing, delays will be exploited by competitors. Consumers do not wait for organisations to respond to them. Rather, marketers need to keep focus on the evolution of consumers in order to react accordingly.

Beyond reactive however, proactive marketing suggests more than just following shifts in consumer culture. Instead, aspiration can be to lead those cultural changes. Marketers have potentially significant influence over individuals and groups. They can set the tone and topic of public conversations, highlight different lifestyles, share alternative ideas and shape behaviours. Marketing can challenge existing social and cultural norms and it can also propose alternatives.

Indeed, marketing can be a vehicle for dramatic cultural change. The dominance of retail spaces in the 20th century for example altered the leisure habits of generations of consumers. Department stores, superstores, high streets and shopping malls have transformed the physical geography of communities worldwide, at the same time as they have set the template for the weekend activities and group socialising setting for generations. More recently this centrepiece of consumer culture has been upended by the expansion of online shopping and digital leisure. Marketing is once more driving shifts in the ways individuals and groups interact.

Marketing is both influenced by and influences culture. This influence implies responsibility. Changes driven by marketing can have varied consequences. At times positive, for some. At times, less so. Consequences are often apparent only years or decades later. The impact of social media imagery on young men's physical self-esteem for example is only slowly becoming a concern. Consequences also take time to be understood. What the shift to virtual shopping means for natural and social environments for instance remains to be seen. Understanding the basics of culture and how marketing interacts with culture is therefore necessary.

Heteronormativity

Heteronormativity is the word used to describe how attitudes, behaviours and lifestyles are often influenced by a heterosexual perspective. This particular outlook takes the idea that being heterosexual is normal; an assumption which permeates many contemporary societies. Thus, things like romantic relationships are assumed as being between a man and a woman. By extension, queer perspectives and experiences may not normally be represented. Their lack of visibility can make these initially seem strange on those rarer occasions they do appear. However, queer people are not abnormal. They exist everywhere and always. Marketing is about looking beyond what is taken for granted culturally, challenging cultural assumptions, and conducting research without prejudices. It is through these that more detailed, nuanced and representative understanding of consumers and the variety of their attitudes, behaviours and lifestyles is developed.

Defining culture

According to Rothman (2014), culture has three divergent meanings:

1. There is culture as a process of individual enrichment, as when we say that someone is cultured.
2. There is culture as an activity, as when we pursue by means of museums, concerts, books and movies.
3. There is also culture as a group's particular way of life, as when we talk about French culture, company culture or multiculturalism.

Marketing and consumption are implicated in all three dimensions of culture. Purchasing experiences, such as holidays, can add to individual cultural enrichment. Cultural activities, including such things as theatre trips, can be consumed. Culture as a way of life can be expressed through purchases, as with fashion.

Looking further at the third of Rothman's meanings, culture relates to the ways in which groups of people identify and express themselves. Culture as a concept relates to how the individual acts in these social contexts. Here, cultural standards define acceptable and unacceptable expressions when amongst certain people or in particular places. In this way culture shapes how individuals think and act in group situations.

These influences are known as 'cultural norms'. Norms set the template for desirable public conduct. To illustrate, in a more liberal culture, women may be considered equal to men and able to behave accordingly. In more conservative cultures however, women may be required to act in a more deferential manner to their male counterparts.

What are known as 'cultural institutions' propagate these norms. Institutions are larger structures and influencers that set specific criteria for desirable behaviours. For example, large organisations have influence over their employees in terms of telling them how they should act whilst at work. Employers that have equal pay for male and female employees propagate a norm of gender equality.

Gender norms and institutions

The influence of culture can be observed in relation to gender. The feminist philosopher Judith Butler (1988) has written about how gender is both biological and cultural. Hereby, gender in a biological sense is inherited, as people are born with physical differences. Simultaneously, gender in a cultural sense is learned. People interpret and perform gender according to surrounding cultural expectations. Men and women dress according to established cultural norms. Not following these norms can be risky, as when women wearing short skirts during the 1960s were considered sexually explicit. Hence, people tend to conform to cultural norms, and consequently keep them going. Institutions, such as religion, tell men and women how they should behave, dress, and the roles they might take up. Because of their established influence institutions are powerful, and again going against them can be difficult. Cultural changes tend to happen slowly, particularly where they are markedly different from prevailing norms and institutions.

Marketing and culture

Marketing is a part of cultures and has its own culture. Marketing sets its own norms in terms of communicating desirable cultural expressions. Advertising for example establishes a particular template for what is considered physically attractive. This is reinforced through an on-going stream of adverts depicting certain types of bodies, faces, smiles and skin tones. Consumers are persuaded by this and will often buy into. In doing so they propagate the beauty norms of advertising.

Marketing is additionally an institution. Marketing structures how people think and behave. Shopping routines for instance frame daily lifestyles. Marketing influence meanwhile is pervasive. Desirable ways to be, both individually and socially, are constantly depicted in marketing. Consciously and unconsciously they help to shape consumer's attitudes and behaviours.

In addition to setting its own norms as a powerful institution, marketing can challenge existing cultural norms and institutions. Consumption can be a means for people to express themselves. Products, services and experiences are sources of self-exploration. This can be in unconventional ways as consumers try out new options.

Culture is constantly evolving as what is considered normal or desirable in one time period may not be so in another. People's attitudes and behaviours shift over time in line with their surroundings. So too are the norms and institutions that guide. Rimal and Lapinski (2015) summarize how "social norms are not static phenomena, lurking in the background, ready to pounce on individuals contemplating action; they both affect and are affected by human action" (p. 393). People can challenge norms and institutions and assert alternative criteria for acceptable and desirable cultural expressions.

Explaining this further, Bouchet (2018) defines normalisation as changes in the relationship between norms and values involving diverse active participants in society. As an influential institution, marketing has had a role in the evolution of cultural norms and what is considered normal or desirable within consumer societies. This cultural influence of marketing can be observed in relation to taboos, and how these are broken and made over time by representations in marketing communications.

Taboo breaking

Taboos are topics or actions considered shameful. These are things that cannot be said or performed publicly, for fear of being criticised. Thus, Sabri, Manceau and Pras (2010) describe a taboo as a verbal or behavioural act that provokes emotional ambivalence, is prohibited by societal norms and generally considered to be publicly unmentionable. Culturally determined, taboos are set by the people, influencers and institutions that make up a particular society. Different cultures have different things that they consider to be taboo. Typically however, taboos are especially associated with sex, money and death.

Taboos affect the ways in which people think and act. Certain subjects or behaviours may not be publicly expressed for example, because these are deemed unacceptable. This inhibition is true in relation to consumption. Muhamad and Mizerski (2013) find for example that religious motivation moderates consumers' decision to purchase products proscribed by their faith. In other words, consumers who are religious may avoid purchasing things, such as alcohol, that are considered taboo by their religion.

Ironically, because they are buried taboos are tantalising. The French philosopher Georges Bataille (1986) described taboos as being forbidden yet alluring at the same time. Bataille realised that when something is culturally not allowed, it becomes associated with shame. This shame keeps it hidden from view. However, this secrecy is also intriguing, bringing the taboo into the realm of danger, naughtiness and desire. According to Larsen and Patterson (2018), in the realm of consumption, taboos operate simultaneously to prohibit consumption objects and experiences, and to make those objects and activities the focus of desire. What this means is that though some forms of consumption might be forbidden by surrounding culture, this ban is simultaneously tempting.

If something is not allowed, it becomes an object of curiosity. Where people try not to think of something taboo, they end up thinking all the more about it. In this highly strung context, if a taboo is broken then it will often trigger a strong reaction. Nudity in an advert for instance may shock because it transgresses taboos and all of their shame, secrecy and curiosity. Indeed, in relation to advertising, research by Vézina and Paul (1997) concluded that provocation based on the transgression of taboos is an effective creative strategy for gaining audience attention. It is tempting for marketers to break taboos as a means of gaining audience attention and triggering emotional responses.

By bringing taboos forward in things such as advertising, where nudity and sex are frequently referenced, marketing lessens these. Taboos only have power if they are hidden. Once brought forward and made normal, they lose their secret appeal. A consequence of marketing therefore is that taboos are broken. This can be seen in the case of sex toys, which as the following case study reviews have gone from being shameful and hidden to more acceptable and openly consumed. A number of researchers have explored how marketing, in drawing attention towards sex toys, has gradually eroded the sense of secrecy and embarrassment surrounding these items specifically, and towards sex-sexuality more broadly.

Commercial case: sex toy story

Marketing's effect on culture and its influence on cultural change should not be underestimated. One area where marketing has had a particularly profound cultural impact is sex. Marketing has long been associated with sex, because marketers have realised its commercial potential. An early pioneer of sexual imagery in advertising was the Springmaid fabric brand. Starting in 1948, pretty female protagonists and subtle double-entendres were used in adverts that shocked industry, distinguished from competitors and amused customers. Sales turned around from a post-war slump and then rose dramatically over the next decade (Taylor, 1982). The old adage that 'sex sells' has deep roots.

One reason the Springmaid adverts were so successful is that sex is an attention getter. In advertising, research suggests that sexual signals, such as nudity, can trigger responses amongst audiences (Harrison, 2001). With nudity and sex tending to grab people's attention, these are readily used by marketers hoping to get their messages across in crowded media landscapes. Consumers are very good at filtering out and ignoring marketing messages. Anything that helps to hook them is useful.

In addition, marketers have long realised the power of sex, sexuality and desire as strong motivators of human behaviour. As summarised by Harrison (2001), sex motivates many of our wants and actions, including our desire to impress and attract others. As with other areas of human hope and desire, consumption can promise to fulfil these motivations. Diverse, products, services and experiences are sold making explicit or implicit references to sex. Perfume and aftershave adverts are particularly obvious in their association of smelling nice with arousing the desire of potential sexual partners for example.

What is more, marketers can try to link positive associations of sex with brands and products. To illustrate, Gould (1992) discusses how if an advertisement causes sexual arousal, then that which is being advertised is likely to be marked by these aroused feelings. Sex has many positive associations such as pleasure, togetherness and happiness. Linking a product with sex means that consumers may think of these positives when they are shopping and be encouraged to purchase.

In pursuing such commercial objectives, marketing can challenge and break down taboos. The increased acceptability of sex toys, reviewed in the following, helps to illustrate how marketing can get involved with and shape cultural conversations. Over more than a century, sex toys have gone from an unmentionable taboo to a normal consumer purchase. Illustrated by this process is how marketing has helped to influence attitudes towards sex at the individual and collective level. From this sex toy story, it can be seen that marketing has considerable influence to shape contemporary discussions around important issues, including on-going conversations regarding sexuality and broader issues such as sustainability.

The evolution of sex toy consumption

Sex toys is the term given to a product category containing various devices that can be used during solo or partnered sex in order to increase sexual arousal, pleasure and connection. These range greatly in terms of their purpose, complexity and expense. The product category has been around for a long time. Indeed, archaeologists have uncovered ancient sex toys across diverse cultures and time periods. The contemporary sex toy category has evolved over the past century or so however, and has only become a mainstream product niche, in certain markets, since the turn of the 21st century.

Worth many billions of dollars, the global sex toy market holds plentiful opportunities, but has and continues to face restrictions on its development. These are largely related to culture. With sex a taboo subject in many cultures, the ability to sell sex toys can be heavily restricted. Nevertheless, cultural attitudes are not fixed. Market research suggests that the sector is fastest growing in China, India and other marketplaces where attitudes towards sex have until recently been more conservative (Technavio, 2020).

Gradually, in some parts of the world and for some consumer groups at least, sex toys have moved from being a taboo item, restricted to niche and semi-legal consumer channels, towards being legitimate and big business. Piha et al. (2018) for example discuss how in Finland it has become relatively normal to consume sex toys openly.

Although sex toys remain a somewhat controversial and niche market, their growing mainstream demonstrates the power of marketing to engage with and alter cultural norms. Many of the themes picked up or pioneered by the sex toy sector, such as female empowerment, self-actualisation or sex as part of personal health and overall well-being, have become large scale consumer trends. Looking towards less well accepted and subsequently hidden cultural groups and practices can therefore be a source of wider inspiration.

The trajectory of increasingly acceptable sex toy consumption is interesting in that it demonstrates the power of marketing to change cultural attitudes and behaviours over time. The evolution of sex toys, from hidden consumer purchases masquerading as something else to legitimate and even desirable items, highlights the power of marketing to shape cultural conversations. Pioneering sex toy designers, manufacturers, promoters and sellers contributed to this shift. The sex toy timeline describes how this progressively came about.

1890s: medical instruments

- In the late 1800s sex was generally seen as shameful and something to be repressed. It could not be openly discussed. Sexual pleasure was a taboo subject and female sexual pleasure even more so. Even during this repressed period there was demand for sex toys, albeit they were not termed as such. Focus was on tools for treating female 'hysteria'. A catch-all term for various women's ailments, one treatment for hysteria was to be masturbated by a medical professional. Different implements and machines were developed by pioneering companies to serve this quasi medical market.

Early 20th century: discreet marketing

- During the early 20th century society became increasingly liberal as various major changes took place. Social mixing of sexes became more acceptable. Nevertheless, sex itself remained largely taboo and not something for public discussion. Sex toys began to be promoted more widely, often in catalogues and magazines, but using euphemisms or through indirect references. They were for instance sold as stress relievers, exercise aids or massagers, with the consumer left to join up the dots.

1960s: sexual revolution

- During the 1960s, counter culture movements took off. Led by young people, and often clashing with older generations, these celebrated individual freedom and collective diversity. As part of this, sex became seen as something to be enjoyed and celebrated. Female sexual satisfaction was fought for and championed. Early LGBTQ movements formed and began campaigning for gay visibility and equality. Although such changing attitudes towards sex were much contested, sex was becoming more public, more about pleasure and more inclusive. Marketing could likewise start to be more overtly and positively sexual. Subtle hints and careful innuendo were replaced with more provocative and overt sex references in marketing.

1970s and 1980s: product development

- The 1970s and 1980s were decades of innovation, experimentation and creativity in terms of developing sex toys. The pioneering sex toy designer and manufacturer Doc Johnson was founded in 1976. This and many other small companies innovated in terms of new product development, with many small, informal and experimental companies in operation. Similarly, sex toy retail went through a period of new ideas and ways of doing things. After being humiliated by a department-store clerk when she tried to buy a vibrator, Dell Williams founded Eve's Garden in 1974. The sex toy shop and catalogue retailer was the first catering specifically to women. It inspired many imitators in its approach to sex toy selling as normal, friendly and frank.

1990s and 2000s: going mainstream
- In 1999 the Rampant Rabbit vibrator became a brand in its own right and a pop cultural reference. For the first time a sex toy was a high profile, even desirable consumer object. Vibrator ownership began to be discussed openly, with these, and other sex toys, becoming seen as a legitimate, empowering and fun consumer purchase. Attwood (2005), who attributes much of this breakthrough into cultural consciousness to the television show Sex and the City, describes the increased commercialisation and accompanying visibility of sex toys during the early 2000s, especially for women.

2020s: sexual empowerment
- Reaching the present time period, people in many parts of the world are increasingly open to discussions around concepts of sexuality and gender. These discussions are moreover often ideological. From South Korea, through Mexico, to Russia, public debates around gender and sexual violence have been pushed forward. The #MeToo movement originating in the United States has stimulated such conversations. It appears to be the case that people are willing to talk about sex in terms of sexual pleasure, but also in the context of wider power dynamics. The imbalances between men and women, political and cultural stigmas associated with sex, and issues of sexual violence, are all being debated and challenged. In this context, sex toys are not just a pleasure product, but a symbol of sexual self-assertion. Gender neutral and LGBTQ friendly sex toys are some of the fastest growing product categories.

2030s: sexual automation
- What does the future of sex toy marketing hold? Experiments with virtual reality and sex robots hint at new avenues. Although voyeuristic documentaries on these subjects are currently played for laughs, this was the case for vibrators just a decade ago. As VR and robotics become more sophisticated, will these become commercially viable and even mainstream in the sex toy sector? Marketers need to consider the things that need to happen in terms of product development and public attitudes change. These are significant, but not insurmountable. Marketers should also consider the ethics and implications of such developments were they to happen.

Case questions
1. What pattern does the evolution of consumer attitudes towards sex toys take?
   Consider whether this liberalisation is a linear or more disjointed process. Also, whether attitudes have evolved at the same pace or in the same direction for all consumers.
2. What needs to happen if sex robots are to become a commercial success?
   Think about social taboos that shape current consumer attitudes and behaviours regarding sex robots. Think about where these taboos come from, why they arise and how they might evolve in future. Consider what role marketing might have in shaping such taboos.
3. What are the ethical implications, both positive and negative, of sex robots?
   Think about the social advantages and disadvantages of these products. Consider how marketing might accentuate the positives or ameliorate the negatives as part of shaping the evolution of this debate.

Consumer case study: slave-free sugar and the abolition movement

Increasing ideological consumption might be a current theme. However, there is a long history of cause-related marketing and consumer activism. What can be seen as the original ideological marketing is 250 years old. Associated with the abolition movement that campaigned against slavery, marketing was used by the abolitionists to get their points concerning the evils of slavery across, raise awareness amongst the general public and eventually to outlaw the slave trade. Many of the marketing techniques used by the abolitionists remain familiar and offer insights into the force for good that marketing has been and can be.

Slavery has existed in various forms across diverse cultures, but the 17–18th-century slave triangle was dominated by European colonial empires, particularly Britain. The slave trade saw an estimated 12 million black Africans transported to the Americas where they were forced to work. Approximately a quarter of slaves died on the sea crossing, and another quarter within the first months of arrival. A slave had no rights and was entirely dependent on their owner. Abuse of slaves where they were forced to work, usually until death, was rife.

This brutal trade was hugely profitable and vast fortunes were built on the back of slaves. This meant that there were powerful vested interests in slavery's continuation. People tried to defend the inhumanity of the slave trade. Racism was used to undermine the humanity of black people in order to make more acceptable their exploitation. Religious justifications were provided by church leaders that had invested heavily in the slave trade and reaped the financial rewards. These tried to justify the destruction of non-Christian African communities as part of civilising projects. Many politicians did likewise. Aggressive discrediting of opponents of slavery helped to quieten opposition. Perhaps most effectively, euphemisms and silence kept the slave trade out of sight and out of mind. Such actions enabled the prioritisation of money over morality.

Even faced with this strong opposition and encouraged apathy, people nonetheless campaigned against the slave trade. The abolition movement began in the late 1700s to campaign against slavery within the British Empire and beyond. People of various backgrounds came together to campaign for humanity. Abolition campaigns included efforts to highlight the diversity and sophistication of African cultures. The humanisation of black Africans came through the prominence of black public figures such as the former slave Olaudah Equiano. Descriptions of and revelations about the crimes and inhumanity of the slave trade challenged the public. Marketing content and communications available at the time were used to share these messages. This included public lectures, religious sermons, autobiographies of former slaves and newspaper articles. Three short examples are outlined below.

Thomas Clarkson's Chest
- Thomas Clarkson's Chest embodies the imaginative marketing of the abolitionists. Clarkson's chest was a compact trunk. This he took with him as he toured the country giving anti-slavery lectures. To illustrate his message, Clarkson's chest had three layers (Devenish, 1994). The first of these displayed handicrafts from Africa in order to illustrate the sophistication of local cultures. This helped to combat stereotypes of Africans as uncivilised. The second layer comprised goods from the continent such as grains. These were brought out to show that trade in alternatives to slaves existed. The final layer was made up of the implements used by slavers such as shackles. The purpose of this was to shock the audience with the ugliness of slavery. Carefully researched,

including many interviews with former slave trade employees (Webster, 2017), and thoughtfully put together, Clarkson's chest was a powerful marketing artefact used effectively to generate public awareness and influence opinion.

The Wedgwood medallion
- The 1787 Wedgwood Medallion was designed, produced and freely distributed by Josiah Wedgwood. Best known for the pottery that bore his name, Wedgwood was an influential inventor, entrepreneur and abolition campaigner. The ceramic medals depicted a kneeling slave in chains with the inscription 'am I not a man and a brother' above. Worn by supporters of the abolition movement, the Wedgwood medallion is one of the earliest examples of a fashion item that was used to support a cause. Wearing it was an opportunity to display ideological values for all to see.

Slave-free sugar
- Alongside cotton, sugar was the main industry that relied on slaves. Slaves were used in all aspects of the sugar cane industry, from planting, through harvesting to processing. Sugar was a valuable commodity highly prized by European consumers who had acquired a sweet tooth and penchant for sugary foods. Using slaves to provide free labour, sugar could be mass-produced and exported cheaply, reaching new mass markets in the process. In the late 1700s, abolitionists started up slave-free produce campaigns. These were boycotts of products made using slaves (Holcomb, 2016). Sugar was a particular target. Free produce stores were also set up selling only slave-free alternatives (Glickman, 2004). People could display their opposition to slavery by using branded products such as sugar dispensers that prominently promoted their slave-free status. An early example of consumer activism, the free produce movement helped to push businesses to change.

The abolitionists helped to inform, change and motivate public opinion against the slave trade. In turn, they pressured religious, business and political figures. Slavery was made into a moral issue, the evils of which could not be easily ignored. The abolition movement played a significant part in influencing the political process that gradually led to the end of slavery. Progress was painfully slow. Improved conditions for transported slaves were passed by the British parliament in 1788. Transportation of slaves was abolished in 1807. Finally, slave ownership was abolished throughout the British Empire in 1833. Economic factors, particularly the declining profitability of the slave trade, did much to influence the turn against slavery. Nevertheless, the abolitionists, and their skilful use of marketing to get their message across and change opinions, had an important role to play.

Sustainability and marketing

The abolition movement illustrates the challenge of getting an important, evidence-based message across to consumers. Demonstrated are the potential impacts that educating for change can bring. Individually and collectively consumers have a lot of power. If this can be harnessed and directed, then not only consumption can be changed for the better but also wider culture. The abolition campaign was a grassroots movement made up of lots of small individuals, who by coming together pressured the general public, powerful organisations and influential leaders to change.

In the contemporary marketplace there is a continued need for similar campaigns to harness the power of concerned consumers, and to use their motivated attitudes and behaviours to drive wider transformation. Perhaps the most pressing changes that need to be made are around issues of environmental protection and combatting climate change. Encouraging more sustainable consumption is a necessity if habitats, species and climates are to be preserved, and the livelihoods of humans depending on these are to survive likewise.

Sustainability is about balancing economic development with resource conservation so that both of these last long term. This means that resources are protected for future generations, rather than being over-exploited and thus damaged or destroyed. Sustainability recognises that economic development is needed in order to meet human needs. However, a greener and more equitable model is necessary if those needs are to be met fairly and long term. Without a sustainable approach there are risks of short-term developments that over-exploit resources in order to get rich quick.

With the tourism industry for instance, so called hit-and-run developments highlight the problems of exploiting resources in the short term. Set up in previously overlooked locations, these are rapidly built up to host an influx of tourists. Short-term profits can be made. Yet quickly these types of destinations tend to fall out of favour. This is because their hastily planned and often poor-quality development spoils the very things visitors wanted to come and see. Once the tourists have moved on, local inhabitants are left behind in a damaged landscape.

Sustainability not only looks long term but also tries to develop mutually beneficial relationships. If resources are protected, then they continue to provide economic benefits into the future. They are also able to support a greater range of economic and social activities. Maintaining forest cover for example not only has ecological benefits but also helps to sustain everything from soil quality to local microclimates. This helps local farmers to improve outputs, at the same time as it brings health advantages to local communities that can benefit from experiencing nature on their doorstep, and may additionally support the local tourism industry as visitors are attracted by unspoilt landscapes.

Nauru: paradise lost

The case of the tiny pacific island of Nauru serves as a reminder that places are vulnerable to short term overexploitation, by any industry. Extremely isolated, Nauru is an important seabird breeding ground. In the 1970s, phosphate mining set up on the island. This extracted the layers of bird shit that had built up metres thick over thousands of years. Briefly, this industry generated significant wealth for the mostly foreign owned businesses involved, and some local residents. Exotic Italian sports cars were reputedly imported to the nation with one short strip of tarmac road and then left to rot in the humidity. Phosphate mining destroyed the interior of the island. Nauru now looks like a wasteland. Nazzal-Batayneh (2005) summarises how a narrow coastal band hosts the increasingly overcrowded population. Loss of arable land means residents are dependent on food imports. Often fatty and sugary preserved goods, these imports have been linked with the high local obesity rate. Loss of natural forest cover meanwhile, has led to a disastrous and total disruption of island ecosystems. Reduced rainfall and increased occurrences of drought typify Nauru today. The short-lived phosphate boom on Nauru came at the expense of the island's long-term ecological, economic and social survival.

Normalising green demand

In order to initiate sustainable change there needs to be an awareness of the problems of unsustainable actions. To illustrate, many people have become conscious of the destructive potential of palm oil, thanks to awareness-raising campaigns by charities such as WWF. An ingredient in many household products, unregulated palm oil plantations are often located in former rainforest cut down to make way for the crop. Because palm oil is farmed in tropical regions, far from major consumer marketplaces, it is easy to be ignorant of the issue. Once focus is put on palm oil however, consumers will often want to do something.

Following on from awareness, building knowledge about an issue means that people can better understand a situation. WWF for example provides information about palm oil, its possible problems and solutions (WWF, 2020). Such info helps to empower individuals as better knowing what can be done in certain situations. Knowledge encourages sense of individual responsibility and allows for alternatives to be evaluated. From this, it is then possible to take actions to address issues. In the case of palm oil, various actions can be taken to do something about this. These could include cutting out certain products, switching to alternatives or looking out for certified palm oil labels. Actions are when knowledge is put into practice. They are conscious and tangible acts that take effort and that are done deliberately with an outcome in mind.

Marketing has a role to play in fostering sustainability awareness, knowledge and action. Indeed, many organisations, such as WWF, use marketing to get their messages across to the public. As with the abolitionists, consumer awareness, knowledge and action can bring about significant change. An increasing number of businesses, such as Unilever, have made pledges to source sustainable palm oil in their products. For 2019, WWF scored the company as a 14.8 out of 22 on its palm oil buyers score card, and described it as well on the path to being a responsible user of palm oil.

Such environmental issues are increasingly important to consumers. With high awareness of and ready access to knowledge about such things as climate crisis, plastic pollution, resource degradation and ecosystem loss, it is becoming harder to just buy things and then throw them away uncaringly. Correspondingly, it has become easier for consumers to take action, connected to each other as they are. As a result, many consumers and brands are now making sustainably minded changes. More ethical consumption is becoming the norm. Marketing has to adjust to and facilitate these consumer changes. Not only is this the moral thing to do, but it is good commercial practice. Connections can be made or deepened with consumers concerned about climate change. Opportunities lie in helping to facilitate their desire to take action and make changes for the better.

Research by Nielsen (2018) highlights the global scale of consumer concern for the natural environment. This is the case across all age groups, and not just in developed economies, but also developing ones such as India, Mexico or the Philippines. These nations are places where local issues mean that it is especially important that companies implement programs to improve the environment. Air pollution in India for instance is some of the world's worst and the public there is dissatisfied. Businesses that can demonstrate they share this concern and are doing something to address it stand to benefit. Nielsen's global survey found that significant numbers of consumers are willing to pay higher-than-average prices for products associated with strong sustainability practices. This is because these products are seen as better for the planet. In addition, they are often seen as healthier, safer and of better quality.

Thus, Nielsen argues that brands can gain relevance for consumers, stand out from competitors and build enduring customer relationships if they focus on sustainability.

Commercial case study: Marks & Spencer Plan A

Founded in 1884, Marks & Spencer (M&S) is a British clothing, food and home-ware retailing giant. The company's stores are a feature of high streets across Britain, as well as intermittently in various international markets where the brand has appeared, disappeared and reappeared over the years. M&S is firmly middle class. It stocks a product range that is of good quality, but on the slightly expensive side. As with many mid-market brands, the business's non-food side has struggled somewhat over the past 20 years. The retailer has suffered from an ageing core customer base and conservative brand image associated with serving this demographic. As with many high street retailers, M&S has also faced pressure from the rise of online shopping. Recent strategy updates have seen the firm closing underperforming stores, concentrating resources on its trendier food halls and revamping its online business.

Despite some on-going difficulties and a brand profile that is firmly orientated towards older customers, M&S is a pioneer of sustainable business strategy. In 2007 the company launched 'Plan A' (Marks and Spencer, 2020). This strategy map involved 100 commitments to tackle five big issues: climate change, waste, resources, fair partnerships and health. Measures taken included the sourcing of more sustainable products, investing in low energy lighting and introducing charges for plastic carrier bags (ahead of this becoming UK law). The programme is summarised on the M&S website:

> Plan A is Marks & Spencer's eco and ethical programme that tackles both today's and tomorrow's sustainable retail challenges. Plan A was launched in 2007 and given its name because we think there is no Plan B for our one planet. We're committed to helping to build a sustainable future by being a business that enables our customers to have a positive impact on wellbeing, communities and the planet through all we do
>
> *(MarksandSpencer.com)*

After ten years, an updated Plan A was launched to extend the success of the original (Marks and Spencer, 2017). Company stakeholders were consulted in drafting the revised plan, which is formed around three pillars of well-being, communities and the planet. Targets include increasing the amount of recyclable packaging, combating modern day slavery in supply chains and making food sold in stores healthier. Through its updated Plan A, M&S demonstrates how it tries to think about the various stakeholders in the business and how these can mutually benefit from working together.

The benefits to M&S of the sustainable actions taken since 2007 are significant. Initially the initiative was expected to cost a significant amount of money. This investment was nevertheless seen to be worthwhile as morally doing the right thing. However, within the first three years sustainability measures were saving M&S more money than they cost to implement. Things like switching to low energy lighting cut related bills. Over its first ten years Plan A was estimated to have saved the business around £750 million in reduced costs (according to Plan A 2025 review). These savings could then be reinvested in continuing to improve the business, proving the case that money and morality are positively intertwined.

More than this, Plan A initiatives have generated significant brand equity. Visiting an M&S food hall the sustainable emphasis of the business is clear to see. Such things as dispensing stations for dried and frozen goods are available. Not only are these services ethical, in that they reduce packaging, but they are enjoyable, in that they are interactive, and they facilitate personalisation. The best M&S food halls are vibrant and engaging retail spaces. If the brand is to survive its current trials and connect with generation Y and Z consumers, then doing so through ideological commitment and mutual involvement is an excellent attempt.

Case questions

1. Why is Plan A an example of good contemporary marketing practice?
   Think about how the Plan A initiative and its component actions link with the themes of chapter in this book.
2. Looking forward, what actions might a third iteration of Plan A encompass?
   Think about emerging issues relating to sustainability and well-being, as well as trends within retail. Consider how these might be incorporated into and addressed via a future strategy plan.

Chapter summary

We can and should be cynical about marketing. It is important to always analyse the motives behind a marketing campaign, and likewise consider alternative meanings or interpretations of marketing contents and communications and finally critically evaluate the impacts of marketing. As covered throughout this book, marketing and the interests it serves are not always honest, caring or sustainable. Nevertheless, there is significant potential with marketing to have an independent opinion, represent diverse voices, highlight issues and spread awareness. Through these, cmarketing can make a positive difference to the world. Opening up conversations around such things as sexuality, slavery and sustainability, marketing has helped to make space for needed conversations and changes around these. Many more such conversations are urgently required in the contemporary world. As touched upon in this text, culture clashes, climate crisis and inequality are pressing issues affecting many consumers and their consumption. Marketing has a proud history to draw upon when engaging with these conversations and shaping how they unfold.

References

Attwood, F. (2005). Fashion and passion: Marketing sex to women. *Sexualities*, *8*(4), 392–406.
Bataille, G. (1986). *Erotism: Death and sensuality*, trans. Mary Dalwood. San Francisco, CA: City Lights, p. 273.
Bouchet, D. (2018). Marketing, violence and social cohesion: First steps to a conceptual approach to the understanding of the normalising role of marketing. *Journal of Marketing Management*, *34*(11–12), 1048–1062.

Butler, J. (1988). Performative acts and gender constitution: An essay in phenomenology and feminist theory. *Theatre Journal*, 40(4), 519–531.

Devenish, D. C. (1994). The slave trade and Thomas Clarkson's chest. *Journal of Museum Ethnography*, 6, 84–90.

Glickman, L. B. (2004). "Buy for the sake of the slave": Abolitionism and the origins of American consumer activism. *American Quarterly*, 56(4), 889–912.

Gould, S. J. (1992). A model of the scripting of consumer lovemaps: The consumer sexual behaviour sequence. In Sherry, Jr., J. F.; Sternthal, B. (eds.). *NA – Advances in Consumer Research*, Vol. 19, Provo, UT: Association for Consumer Research, pp. 304–310.

Harrison, N. E. (2001). All consuming desire: Advertisers prey on our sexual insecurities to mass-market products and services. *Alternatives Journal*, 27(3), 24.

Holcomb, J. L. (2016). *Moral commerce: Quakers and the transatlantic boycott of the slave labor economy*. Ithaca, NY: Cornell University Press.

Larsen, G., & Patterson, M. (2018). Consumption, marketing and taboo. *Journal of Marketing Management*, 34, 13–14.

Marks and Spencer. (2017). *Plan A 2025*. https://corporate.marksandspencer.com/documents/plan-a/plan-a-2025-commitments.pdf (accessed 20/05/20).

Marks and Spencer. (2020). https://global.marksandspencer.com/plan-a/ (accessed 20/05/2020).

Nazzal-Batayneh, M. (2005). Nauru: An environment destroyed and international law. *Law and Development*. Available at: http://www.lawanddevelopment.org/docs/nauru.pdf (accessed 05/03/2020).

Nielsen. (2018). *The evolution of the sustainability mindset*. https://www.nielsen.com/us/en/insights/report/2018/the-education-of-the-sustainable-mindset/ (accessed 25/02/20).

Piha, S., Hurmerinta, L., Sandberg, B., & Järvinen, E. (2018). From filthy to healthy and beyond: Finding the boundaries of taboo destruction in sex toy buying. *Journal of Marketing Management*, 34(13–14), 1078–1104.

Rimal, R. N., & Lapinski, M. K. (2015). A re-explication of social norms, ten years later. *Communication Theory*, 25(4), 393–409.

Rothman, J. (2014). The meaning of "Culture". *The New Yorker*, 26 December 2014. Available at: https://www.newyorker.com/books/joshua-rothman/meaning-culture (accessed 26/06/20).

Sabri, O., Manceau, D., & Pras, B. (2010). Taboo: An underexplored concept in marketing. *Recherche et Applications en Marketing (English Edition)*, 25(1), 59–85.

Taylor, J. D. (1982). Elliott White Springs-Maverick AD leader. *Journal of Advertising*, 11(2), 40–46.

Technavio. (2020). *Online sex toys market by product and geography – Forecast and analysis 2020–2024*. Available at: https://www.technavio.com/report/online-sex-toys-market-industry-analysis (accessed 30/03/20).

Vézina, R., & Paul, O. (1997). Provocation in advertising: A conceptualization and an empirical assessment. *International Journal of Research in Marketing*, 14(2), 177–192.

Webster, J. (2017). Collecting for the cabinet of freedom: The parliamentary history of Thomas Clarkson's chest. *Slavery & Abolition*, 38(1), 135–154.

WWF. (2020). *8 things to know about palm oil*. Available at: https://www.wwf.org.uk/updates/8-things-know-about-palm-oil (accessed 05/03/2020).

INDEX

Note: **Bold** page numbers refer to tables and *italic* page numbers refer to figures.

Aaker, D. A. 4
abnormal self-esteem regulation 106, 110
abolition campaigns 150, 151
abolition movement 150–151
actualisation 134, 136–137
age-based generations 8
age of anxiety 43; consumption in 36–38
American Marketing Association 3
Angelababy 74–76
Angela Yeung Wing 74
Ang, L. 101
Antorini, Y. M. 48
apathetic brands 32
Askildsen, T. 48
asserting reality 86
attitudes, consumer actions 56
Attwood, F. 149
authenticity 75
awareness 14, 30, 71, 72, 109, 111, 117, 120, 121, 150, 153; consumer 77; positive and negative 73

baby boomers 10
Bainbridge, J. 43
Bataille, Georges 146
Beckham, David 99
behaviours, consumer actions 56
'The best men can be' campaign 26
Bieber, Justin 101
big tobacco firms 131
black Africans, humanisation of 150
Blackberry 4
Black cultures 63

Black Lives Matter movement 16, 25
Bottom of the pyramid (BoP) 54, 55, 57
Bouchet, D. 145
brand ageing 4, 6
brand authenticity 75
brand birth 5
brand lifecycle 4–7, *6*
brand longevity 7
brand maturing 5–6
brand narrative 72–73, 75, 81
brand rejuvenation 6
brand reputation 68, *69,* 70–71, 75, 81
brand specialisation 6
BrewDog's revolutionary rise 33–34
BS reality of dropshipping 89–91
Bush, George W. 84
Butler, Judith 144

Campbell, W. K. 108
Canavan, B. 63, 66, 88, 102
'cancel culture' 40
careful management 6, 7
Cassam, Quassim 95
celebration, culture checklist 64
celebrification 100–101
celebritisation 100
celebrity 74, 77, 99, 101, 102, 104, 108; on consumer cultures 100; endorsement 99; lifestyle 100
centrist brands 33
Clarkson, Thomas 150–151
climate crisis 12, 14, 22, 117–119, 142, 153
collaboration 109, 140

Index

combative consumers 15–16
commercial case: Angelababy 74–75; BrewDog's revolutionary rise 33–34; Comparethemarket.com 93–94; Fan BingBing 77–79; Halo Top 71–73; hikikomori 50–52; Lego 47–49; OxyContin 129–132; Pokémon 42–43; sex toy story 146–149; study 154–155
commercial triumph 130–131
commitment, culture checklist 64
commonality, culture checklist 64
community brands 33
company stakeholders 154
Comparethemarket.com 93–94
confidence, culture checklist 64
conscious consumption 118
conspicuous consumption 79, 110, 111, 115–117, 135
conspiracy theories 22, 36, 84, 86, 95–97
consumer actions 56, 57
consumer case 87–91; craft and hazelnut spread 122–123; Drag Race 61–62; iron challenges 134–137; K-pop phenomenon 16–19; Mongol Rally 101–104; study 38–41, 150–151; Taylor Swift's lyrical reinventions 65–66; vegan extremism 27–28
consumer complexity 15
consumer confidence 14, 135–137
consumer culture 18, 110, 138, 140, 143; celebrity on 100; classic 132; contemporary 48; rebalancing 114–115
consumer empowerment 14, 80–81
consumer goods 113, 117, 130, 138; cultural symbolism of 114; and services 132
consumer habit 49; and loyalty 60, *61*
consumer identities 135; reinvention and 57–61
consumer introversion 51
consumerism 10, 11, 56, 79, 113, 115, 117–119, 128, 129, 133, 137
consumer narcissism 108–109
consumer outcomes 55–57
consumer perceptions 32; mapping 31
consumer plurality 16
consumer renown and sustainability 109–111
consumers: combative 15–16; contemporary 23–24, 28, 36, 41, 48–50, 71, 81, 99, 111, 130, 134–137; contradictory 14–15; generations Z 14, 49, 155; new and distinctive 13–16; reassurance 37, *37*, 51; reinvention 54–57; using marketing, breaking through to 3–4; value-driven 26
consumer societies 113–115, 119, 126, 132, 140, 145
consumer temperature-brand exposure index 30, *30*
consumer well-being 117–119, 132

consumption 1–2; in age of anxiety 36–38; behaviours 109–111; conscious 118; consequences 117–119; craft 122; habitual 59, 60; loyal 60; and narcissism 105–109; reassurance and 51–52; self-actualisation-related 133; self-indulgent 38; under surveillance 79–81; sustainable 109–111
contemporary consumers 23–24, 28, 36, 41, 48–50, 71, 81, 99, 111, 130, 134–137
contemporary culture 16, 73, 79, 96
contemporary marketplace 152
contradictory consumers 14–15
Conway, Kellyanne 85
'cool' teenage archetypes 42
cosmetic surgery industry 119
Cova, B. 123
'craftale' movement 33
craft beer 122
craft consumer 120
craft consumption 122
Croft, R. 92
cultural activities 17, 144
cultural appreciation 64
cultural appropriation 63–65
cultural breakthrough 5
cultural changes 100, 143, 145
cultural establishment 5
'cultural institutions' 144
culturally appropriate *versus* cultural appropriation 63–64
'cultural norms' 23, 57, 143–145, 147
cultural standards 144
cultural subversion 63–64
culture: benefit 63; and marketing 143–146
customisation 15, 122
cyber bullying 19, 86

D'Antone, S. 123
Davies, A. 109
De Bellis, E. 109
declining market 5
deepfakes 83–84
defying ageing 7
Desmond, J. 106, 109
Dholakia, N. 80
Dickie, Martin 33
Dickman, S. L. 133
digital communications 4
digital developments 101
digital media 86
digital technologies 50, 70, 79–81, 84, 88, 96, 108
Dinhopl, A. 102
discreet marketing 148
dissipation 136–137
distant nostalgia 45

diversity 16, 139, 148, 150
Dorson, Richard 92
Drag Race 61–64
Driessens, O. 100, 101
dropshipping hubs 90
dysfunctional self-esteem regulation 110

East Asian markets 23
economic recovery 22
ecosystems approach 138–140
elite brands 33
Elliot, E. A. 122
Elmhirst, S. 115
emotional value 24
entitlement and exploitation 106, 109
environmental analysis 57
ethics: and beliefs 24, 32; and responsibilities of marketing 131–132
exhibitionism 106, 109
experienced nostalgia 45
extended adolescence 12, 37–38, 41, 45, 51
Extinction Rebellion 16
extremism 28

fairy tales and marketing 92–93
fairy-tale weddings 93
fakelore 92
fake nostalgia 45–46
Fan BingBing 77–79
fancier customer service 5
fast food ecosystem 138
Fitchett, J. A. 109
folklure 92, 93
folk nostalgia 45–46
Ford, Henry 116
Foucault, Michel 42
Fuentes, C. 28
Fuentes, M. 28
Furedi, F. 100

'geek dollar' 41–42
gender norms and institutions 144–145
generational behaviour 8
generational cohorts 8–13, 37
generational theory 8–9
generation X 11
generation Y 9, 11–14, 18, 27, 37, 38, 43, 49, 65, 66, 78, 155; childhood references of 48; contradictory consumers 14–15; cultural activities of 17; enthusiasm of 45
generation Z 12–14, 18, 37, 65; combative consumers 15–16; consumers 14, 49, 155; cultural activities of 17
Gillette 26, 27
Golomb, E. 106
Goth cultural identity 115
Gould, S. J. 147

Grathwohl, H. L. 116
greatest generation 9
green demand, normalising 153–154
Gretzel, U. 102
growing market 5
Grubb, E. L. 116
Gurner, Tim 129

habitual consumption 59, 60
habitual customers 59
habitual loyalty 60–61
habit versus loyalty 59–61
Halo Top 71–73
Harris, M. A. 59
Harrison, N. E. 147
Haytko, D. L. 63
heritage, brand narrative 72
heteronormativity 143–144
hikikomori 50–52
Hillman, C. 135
Himmelstein, D. U. 133
Hodgson, J. 94
Holt, D. 4

Iansiti, M. 139, 140
identity blurring 62
identity bonding 62
identity breaking 62
identity reinventions 65–66
ideological consumer 24
ideological marketing 28–30; consumer temperature-brand exposure index 30, *30*; ideological perceptual mapping 31–33, *32*; segmentation, targeting and positioning (STP) 31
ideological market positioning 33
ideological perceptual mapping 31–33, *32*
ideological value 24, 58, 151
ideology 16, 28–32, 40, 43, 57, 58, 114, 116, 118; CCP 79; conservative 66; into consumption and marketing 23–27
'i-generation' label 9
inclusive-exclusive continuum 32
innovative tourism product 104

Jenner, Kendall 25–26
Jeong, M. 78
Jones, D. B. 3

Kaepernick, Colin 24, 25
Kale, S. 90
Kanba, S. 50
Kapferer, J.-N. 7
Kato, T. A. 50
Key Opinion Leaders (KOLs) 74–75
Khamis, S. 101
Khogeer, Y. 94

kidult brands 47
Klein, Naomi 117
Kolar, T. 7
Kolbl, Z. 7
KOLs *see* Key Opinion Leaders (KOLs)
Konecnik Ruzzier, M. 7
Korean dream 17–18
K-pop phenomenon 16–19

Lambert, A. 106, 109
Lamb, M. D. 135
Lapinski, M. K. 145
Larsen, G. 146
La Sape 63–64
Lego 47–49
Lehu, J. M. 7
Leone, M. 44
Levien, R. 139
lifestyles, consumer actions 56
Lo, I. S. 102
loyal consumption 60
loyal customers 6, 59–60

Manceau, D. 145
manipulating reality 86, 88
Mannheim, Karl: 'The Problem of Generations' 8
Maoz, D. 102
Marcus, B. 107
marketing 2–3, 153; breaking through to consumers using 3–4; and culture 145; culture and 143–146; discreet 148; ethics and responsibilities of 131–132; fairy tales and 92–93; four fundamentals of 138, *139*; ideological (*see* ideological marketing); Nostalgia and 45–46; re-evaluating 138; relevance 2–3; reviving 142–143; social media 73–74; sustainability and 151–154; tourism 51
Marks & Spencer (M&S) Plan A 154–155
Marshall, P. D. 100, 101
Maslow, Abraham 132
Maslow's pyramid, inverting 132–134
McCamley, C. 66
McKercher, B. 102
medical instruments 148
#MeToo movement 149
metrosexual identity 57
'millennials' 9, 38, 40–42, 48, 110, 119
Miller, J. D. 106
Mizerski, Dick 146
Mongol Rally 101–104
Moutinho, L. 71
Mudder, Tough 135
Muhamad, Nizlida 146
Muñiz, A. M., Jr. 48
Musk, Elon 100

Nakamori, Akio 39
narcissism: consumption and 105–109; normalisation 108; opportunities for sustainable consumption 110–111
narcissistic characteristics 106–108
narcissistic customers 109
narcissistic personality inventory (NPI) 107, 108
Nash, M. 135
Nazzal-Batayneh, M. 152
Nielsen (2018) 153, 154
non-Christian African communities 150
nostalgia 44, 48, 49, 51; brands 46–47; and marketing 45–46
NPI *see* narcissistic personality inventory (NPI)
NPI-15 107, **107,** 108
Nuttall, P. 63

Obama, Barack 85, 96, 100
online retailing 121
otaku 38–41, 44, 50–52
overheard nostalgia 45
OxyContin 129–132

'pain management symposia' 130
pain medication 132
Paltrow, Gwyneth 100
Parish, Jane 36
Patsiaouras, G. 109
Patterson, A. 94
Patterson, M. 146
Paul, O. 146
penis enlargement surgery 119
perceptual mapping 31–33, *32*
personalisation user 120
Piha, S. 147
Pokémon 42–43
Ponzi schemes 90–91
poor public transportation 128
positive reputations 71, 76, 79, 81
Pras, B. 145
prescription drugs 129, 131
prescription opioids 130, 131
'The Problem of Generations' (Mannheim) 8
product/brand advocate 120
product development 17, 72, 125, 148, 149
prosumers/prosumption 120, 121–122, 124–126, 128, 134, 137
provenance, brand narrative 72
public brands 33
public health tragedy 130–131
Purdue Pharma 130, 131
Putin, Vladimir 86

racism 25, 96, 150
Rao, R. S. 110

reality refraction 89, *89*
reassurance: commercial case 42–43, 47–52; consumer case study 38–41; consumption in age of anxiety 36–38; geek dollar 41–42; Nostalgia 44–47
rebalancing: commercial case 124; conspicuous consumption 115–117; consumer case 122–123; consumer culture 114–115; consumer society 113–114; consumption consequences 117–119; rebalancing of consumption 119–122; working with prosumers 125–126
recent nostalgia 45
reconstruction: bringing ideology into consumption and marketing 23–27; commercial case 33–34; consumer case 27–28; ideological marketing 28–33; 21st century 22–23
rediscovered brands 47
re-evaluating: commercial case 129–132; consumer case 134–137; inverting Maslow's pyramid 132–134; marketing moving forward 137–140; shit life syndrome 128–129
re-evaluating marketing 138
refraction: commercial case 93–94; conspiracy theories 95–97; consumer case 87–91; manipulating reality 88–89; marketing myth 91–93; reality as complicated and malleable 83–87
reinvention: consumer case 61–62, 65–66; and consumer identities 57–61; consumers 54–57; culturally appropriate *versus* cultural appropriation 63–64
relevance: brand lifecycle 4–7; brand longevity 7; breaking through to consumers using marketing 3; consumption 1–2; gaining and loosing 4; generational cohorts 8–13; generations Y and Z 13–16; K-pop phenomenon 16–19; marketing 2–3
religious justifications 150
renown: consumer 99–101; consumer case 101–104; consumer renown and sustainability 109–111; consumption and narcissism 105–109
reputation: brand aura and appeal 68–71; commercial case 71–75, 77–79; consumption under surveillance 79–81; social media exchange relationships 76–77; social media marketing 73–74
reputation management 70
responsibility 37, 109, 110, 117, 131, 137, 140, 143, 153
reviving: commercial case 146–149; commercial case study 154–155; consumer case study 150–151; culture and marketing 143–146; marketing 142–143; sustainability and marketing 151–154

Rimal, R. N. 145
romantic brands 47
Rothman, J. 144
Rumpelstiltskin 92
Rumsfeld, Donald 83, 84

Sabri, O. 145
Saitō, Tamaki 50
Schaefer, R. 110
Schütz, A. 107
segmentation, targeting and positioning (STP) 31
selective reporting 84, 89
self-actualisation 134
self-actualisation-related consumption 133
self-belief 25, 105
self-esteem influences 119
self-indulgent consumption 38
self-obsession 106, 109
self-sacrifice 110
Sellin, I. 107
semi-professional producer 121
sex toy consumption, evolution of 147–149
sex toy story 146; evolution of sex toy consumption 147–149
sexual automation 149
sexual empowerment 149
sexual revolution 148
Shaw, E. H. 3
Shibata, M. 39
Shin, H. 17
shit life syndrome (SLS) 128–129, 136
shūkatsu 39–40
silent generation 9–10, 47
slave-free sugar 150–151
Sloan, Alfred P. 116
SLS *see* shit life syndrome (SLS)
'snake oil salesperson' 90–91
snake oil scams 90–91
social media 14, 15, 71, 78–81, 88–91, 94, 100–102, 108, 114, 122, 136, 143; exchange relationships 76–77; marketing 73–74
social ranking 78–79
social reputation 79
social value 24
society, definition of 114
stakeholders 2–5, 70, 71, 109, 124, 132, 139, 140, 142; company 154; facilitating 138
steampunk brands 46
STP *see* segmentation, targeting and positioning (STP)
stratified brands 33
sugary cereals 118
Sullenberger, Tom 93
supressing reality 86
Suskind, Ron 84, 85
sustainability 123, 147; consumer renown and 109–111; and marketing 151–154; planetary 27

sustainable consumption 109, 152; narcissism opportunities for 110–111
Swift, Taylor 65–66
symbolism 58, 61; consumption 116; cultural 114
synthetic opioids 129, 130

taboo breaking 145–146
Teo, Alan 50
'The Theory of the Leisure Class' (Veblen) 115
Thompson, C. J. 63
Tinson, J. 63
tourism marketing 51
'tourist celebrity gaze' 102
'tourist gaze' 101–102, *103*
tribalism, reputation *versus* 71
Trump, Donald 71, 85, 96, 100
Twenge, J. M. 108

utilitarian value 24

value-driven consumers 26
values-laden marketing strategy 29
Van Zee, A. 130, 131
Veblen, Thorstein: 'The Theory of the Leisure Class' 115
Vegan extremism 27–28
veganism 27, 28

vegan movement 27
Veloutsou, C. 71
Vézina, R. 146
vibrator ownership 149
virtual connectivity 11–12
virtual realities 86–87, 149
vranyo 85–86, 88

Walder, D. 44
Wal-Mart, surrounding ecosystem 139
Watson, Donald 27
Wattanasuwan, K. 115
Watt, James 33
Wedgwood medallion 151
Welling, R. 101
Whippman, R. 133
Williams, Dell 148
Wong, J. 19
Woolhandler, S. 133

youth culture 10, 63

Zerach, G. 109
Žižek, Slavoj 83
Zimmerman, M. A. 80
Ziolkowski, J. M. 92
Zoflora 77
Zwick, D. 80